Ten Thousand Things

Ten Thousand Things

Nurturing Life in Contemporary Beijing

Judith Farquhar and Qicheng Zhang

ZONE BOOKS · NEW YORK

2012

ZONE BOOKS
1226 Prospect Avenue
Brooklyn, NY 11218

Printed in the United States of America.

Distributed by The MIT Press,
Cambridge, Massachusetts, and London, England

Library of Congress Cataloging-in-Publication Data

Farquhar, Judith.
    Ten thousand things : nurturing life in contemporary
Beijing / Judith Farquhar and Qicheng Zhang.
        p.   cm.
    Includes bibliographical references and index.
    ISBN 978-1-935408-18-5 (alk. paper)
        1. Ethnology—China—Beijing. 2. Socialization—
China—Beijing. 3. Community life—China—Beijing.
4. Philosophy, Chinese. 5. Medicine, Chinese—China—
Beijing. 6. Beijing (China)—Social life and customs.
I. Zhang, Qicheng. II. Title.

    GN635.C5F37 2012
    306.0951'156—dc23

                        2011037199

Contents

Acknowledgments

Ten Thousand Things originated in collaboration, built its form and content through collaboration, and was made possible only through collective labors, most of which are not adequately noted in its pages. Here we would like to acknowledge the participation of many others, some of them no longer living, some of them institutions, rather than individuals, in the life of this project.

This research has had a life of its own, enjoyed by both of its authors. Together we have drawn from a number of vibrant, vivid resources made available by many friends and associates. We two were first brought together in 1999 through the good offices of Eric Karchmer, then a student at the Beijing University of Chinese Medicine, and Lai Lili, a staff member at BJUCM and graduate of their medical school. They organized a workshop there about anthropology and Chinese medicine and arranged for Judith Farquhar to be invited. At the workshop, with the notable support of senior scholars Yan Jianhua, Wang Hongtu, and Lu Guangxin (something we're sure all of them have since forgotten), we discovered our shared interest in life nurturance, embodiment, and ethnography. It was then that we first began to plan collaborative research, with the approval of the Inner Canon, Classical Medical Chinese, and Cultural Studies Programs at the university.

The most intense period of broad collaboration was several months each year between 2002 and 2004 (though we were delayed and interrupted by outbreak of SARS—severe acute respiratory syndrome—in 2003), when a group of graduate students and others helped the two of us to conduct interviews in Beijing's West City District and to join in life-nurturing activities there. The attentive and sensitive field research of Qiu Hao, Lai Lili, Luo Hao, Wang Minghao, Yu Hong, Guo Hua, and Shen Yi extended the reach of this project in many ways. At one point Assistant Professor Qu Limin joined our group for a couple of interviews, increasing the fun; she later added a number of popular works on life nurturance to her significant scholarly publications, and a discussion of some of her writing appears in Chapter 2. One of the most productive elements of this group fieldwork was the lively conversations we had during, after, and between interviews. We were able both to extend the power of our preliminary analyses and to check each other's interpretive enthusiasms as we talked, transcribed, and talked some more.

The process of writing was long and often interrupted. One of the challenges and pleasures of this long process had to do with the fact that each of this book's two authors was writing various other things in his or her own language while this book was coming into existence; producing the elements gathered into *Ten Thousand Things* was an asymmetrical process stretching over more than five years. Everything Farquhar wrote needed to be translated into Chinese, at least roughly, for Zhang's editing and supplementation; much that Zhang wrote had to be carefully translated into English as it was incorporated into the English draft. In practice, we found ourselves spending scattered long afternoons together going through drafts sentence by sentence and paragraph by paragraph. Lai Lili often provided stalwart translation support, and Shen Yi filled in wonderfully some of the time. Together, our little group obsessed over the right word, the right degree of verbosity, presence or absence of modifiers, and many other delights and frustrations of translation. This was as rewarding a process as any work among comrades in "the field." We hope that the effort we all expended resulted in both symmetrical and shared authorial voices, and we remain grateful for Lai Lili's and Shen Yi's full partnership in this project and others far beyond *Ten Thousand Things*.

This research project was funded in part with a generous grant for collaborative research from the Wenner-Gren Foundation for Anthropological Research. Judith Farquhar also received significant support from the Horace W. Goldsmith Foundation of New York, which allowed a year-long writing fellowship at the National Humanities Center in North Carolina. She also benefited from research funds provided at the University of Chicago by the Adolph and Marian Lichtstern Anthropology Research Endowment and by the Division of the Social Sciences. Zhang Qicheng received institutional support from the Beijing University of Chinese Medicine, especially the Library and the Graduate School. We are both immensely grateful for these irreplaceable gifts.

Judith Farquhar wishes to thank many friends and colleagues whose insights about at least ten thousand things have inspired various gestures made in *Ten Thousand Things*. Scattered conversations and readings shared with Lily Hope Chumley, Nicholas Harkness, Larisa Jasarevic, Kiho Kim, Tong Lam, Li Chengwei, Margaret Lock, Luo Hongguang, George Marcus, Meng Yue, Vinh-kim Nguyen, Mariella Pandolfi, David B. Sutton, Tatiana Chudakova, Wang Jun, Wang Min'an, Wu Yiching, Yue Gang, Zhao Chengguang, and Zhao Dingxin have been more influential than any of them realize. Marisol de la Cadena pushed for more thorough, more ethical collaboration in ethnography and in this project; this was a most welcome pressure. Stephan Feuchtwang continued to hear the political resonances in life nurturing, which reassured at times when it seemed that no one understood that part. Jim Hevia read a number of drafts and helped to keep things logical and exciting. Comrades at the National Humanities Center, especially Maud Ellman, Geoffrey Harpham, Elizabeth Helsinger, Louise Meintjes, Amelie Rorty, Terry Smith, and John Wilkinson welcomed life-nurturing China into wholesome circulation with other wonderful research projects in a way that markedly increased the robustness of our topic and our approach. We are especially grateful as well to those who provided research assistance and logistical support at the University of Chicago: Betsey Brada, Anne Ch'ien, Kathryn Goldfarb, Sandra Hagen, and Britta Ingebretson.

Judith Farquhar has two writing groups to thank for whatever felicities the English prose achieved. In North Carolina, the advice of Kathryn Burns, Jane Danielewicz, Mary Floyd-Wilson, Joy Kasson, Megan Matchinske, and Laurie Langbauer was crucial at early stages; and in Chicago the demanding readings of Jessica Cattelino, Jennifer Cole, Kesha Fikes, Danilyn Rutherford, and Shawn Michelle Smith solved many problems of structure, argument, and phrasing. Ramona Naddaff of Zone Books had very useful suggestions after reading the first full English draft, and Bud Bynack in the course of copyediting provided a sophisticated critical reading that led to a number of important refinements in the book. It is generous collaborations such as these, more than any others, that give us the confidence to release this mixed bag of a book to the Anglophone reading public.

Zhang Qicheng, beyond sharing some of the Beijing debts noted above, wishes to acknowledge several teachers and thinkers who have made his understanding of life nurturance possible. We have benefited from Zhang's Ph.D. advisor Zhu Bogun's refinement of a philosophical approach to the *Book of Changes* tradition; in a way, it is he who should be credited with our viewpoint on life as a process of unceasing genesis and transformation upon transformation (*shengsheng huahua* 生生化化, see Chapter 4). Professor Zhu studied with and assisted modern China's most prominent historian of Chinese philosophy, Fung Yulan, whose commitment to using philosophy in the service of a higher human life we share. Finally, the well-known scholar of National Studies (see the Conclusion) Chen Yinke has been an inspiration in our efforts to overcome a chronic subject-object divide in modern scholarship. We would like to think we have lived up to his call for a truly engaged process of writing in fellow feeling (*tongqing de liaojie* 同情的了解), one that achieves moments of shared understanding between authors ancient and modern, readers of many literatures including this book, and the life-nurturing experts who kindly spoke with us—some of them again and again—in Beijing. Both of us extend our special thanks to these warm-hearted city dwellers living well-gathered lives.

Life Well Nurtured

Life is a process of unceasing genesis. The Chinese ancients considered that life is an evolutionary process of becoming, uninterrupted birth and more birth, continuous without cessation. The natural world is vast and unbounded, infinite and without horizon, always in the midst of limitless activity and change. The natural world's unceasing birthing and growing, producing and ripening is called "giving life to life" or "birthing birth." With regard to the myriad ["ten thousand," *wanwu* 万物] things, this is called "the power and virtue of life giving rise to more life." . . . Among the myriad things of nature, humans are not only the product of the power and virtue of giving life to life, they also are most suited to embodying and making use of the power and virtue of giving life to life.
—Zhang Qicheng, "Life"

Life: the word escapes all attempts—scientific, philosophical, religious, linguistic—to pin it down in definitions or summaries. In a secular age, life is constantly invoked as the criterion of all value, the unquestioned positive term toward which the action of living beings orients itself, the matrix within which any orientation at all becomes possible. Under the banner of life, modern governments legislate everything from school milk programs to end-of-life technologies; in the name of the quality of life, disciplinary institutions control births, police the uses of urban space, regulate the purity of food and drugs, and fund (or not) our processes of dying.[1] But efforts to fix the meaning of life constantly fail. Neither the existentialist argument that life takes on meaning through the human encounter with death nor the technical notions of "life itself" or "bare life" that have developed in bioscience and political theory can deliver a universally useful sense of what life is. People are not simply living organisms adapted to ecological niches; our strategies for getting by are not entirely explainable with biology or reducible to rational calculation. Everywhere we insist on the specificity, complexity, and quality of our lives. We humans are located in places, and we all have particular vantage points and blind spots; our living experience is inseparable from remembered and inscribed pasts, even as it is open to and promising uncertain futures. We are always engaged in "giving life to life" in a "myriad" of forms.[2]

The quote above, drawn from a review essay Zhang Qicheng wrote especially for this book, draws on and reaches out to a very diverse literature, but it is not a scholarly summary.[3] Rather, it is a characterization of the way things are. The phrasing—relying much more on verbs than nouns in the original Chinese—insists on life as a process, an emergence both manifold in its diversity and rooted in a nature that is dynamic. Zhang's definition emphasizes at the same time the generativity, constant change, and irreducible multiplicity of "the myriad things." The very excessiveness of these words, with so many exuberant redundancies—life is both "uninterrupted" and "continuous," the natural world is "vast," "unbounded," "limitless," "without horizon" and "infinite" all in the same sentence—indexes a linguistic productivity and an authorial participation in "myriad" living processes. At the same time, it expresses both awe in the face of the vastness of life and a focused ethical commitment: "humans...are most suited to embodying and making use of [this] power and virtue."[4] If, however, humans are but one of these ten thousand things, or even if each human is only one of a myriad of always emergent objects, or things, there are new limits and possibilities to what we can hope to be and do. Chinese ways of nurturing life, the subject of this book, live within and explore these limits and possibilities, the power and virtue of life.

But we do not aim to understand "life itself." It is difficult to

12

turn a scientific or scholarly gaze on life. No distance from living that would allow us to stand back and contemplate life as an object is available. John Dewey saw this when he spoke of efforts to study vision by abstracting "the eye itself": "There is no such thing as 'the eye'; there is only the seeing."[5] In this remark, Dewey rejects an anatomical tradition of analyzing "the human body" as an object, knowable as an object of contemplation. In a similar vein, Chinese medical writers and teachers,[6] as they engage in the comparisons between "Chinese medicine" and "Western medicine" that global communication and health-care regulation seem to make necessary, argue that their tradition is a medicine of the living body, not the dissected corpse.[7] As Michel Foucault argued in *The Birth of the Clinic*, it was the modern objectification of bodily space in the medical study of death that allowed biology to conceive of something as abstract and pure as "life itself." But for our philosophical and anthropological purposes, one could paraphrase Dewey: There is no such thing as "life itself"; there is only the living.

"The Chinese ancients" invoked by Zhang Qicheng in this chapter's epigraph saw their lives as nothing if not susceptible to active forming and crafting.[8] A long tradition of self-cultivation (*zixiu* 自修), quite prominent in the earliest Daoist and Confucian works and much invoked in scholarly movements over the last two thousand years throughout Chinese and East Asian history, forms a historical setting for the contemporary emphasis on nurturing life that we consider here. In hoary analogies and ancient language that are often quoted in the twenty-first century, not least as proverbs or catch phrases, Mencius's (fourth-century B.C.E.) insistence that the "first teacher," Confucius, saw human nature as essentially benign still lives.[9] His contemporary Xunzi's stronger emphasis on the need for correct training to guarantee propriety and rectitude in flawed human beings is just as influential, and neo-Confucians such as Wang Yangming (1472–1529) more than a thousand years later further elaborated the natural relationship of human goodness and active cultivation. The whole Confucian tradition, so deeply embedded in everyday language, even today, maintained an expectation that people will actively strive to attain the goodness proper to humans. (Very few Chinese philosophers held that humans could be good or responsible naturally, if "naturally" means by default.)

So, too, the many residents of contemporary Beijing of whom we will speak in this book actively seek to form and craft—to nurture (*yang* 养)—their lives.[10] Many of them agree with Zhang Qicheng that humans, and perhaps especially modern or contemporary humans, are most suited to "nurturing life" (*yangsheng* 养生) in cultured, deliberate, and creative ways. Though few of them are theorists or philosophers, they tacitly presume that *yangsheng* activity participates in the natural power and virtue of giving life to life. We cannot delimit or objectify life, but we can generate it, feed it, train it, make it flourish.

This book explores the myriad forms of life, or, in ancient Chinese parlance, "the ten thousand things" that life is and is becoming, through an ethnographic and philosophical study of everyday life activism in contemporary Beijing. "Ten thousand things" is a term that, in modern Chinese, names everything and nothing, the sheer miscellany of manifest reality, just one thing after another, the overwhelming noise of the material world against which the signals of important matters can appear as discrete and meaningful. Ancient cosmogony had it that the Way (*dao* 道) gave rise to the two aspects, kinds, or forces of *yin* and *yang qi*, that the interaction of *yin* and *yang qi* generated space in the form of heaven and earth, and then time emerged in the form of the four seasons. From these even-numbered formations arose, just as spontaneously and without divine intention, the ten thousand things, the *wanwu*.[11] There is no great commitment to the quantity of ten thousand in this philosophy, of course; rather, "ten thousand" comes to mean "manifold," "myriad," "particular," "manifest," "emergent," and even a bit "miscellaneous." (Nowhere in Chinese cosmogony do we find the Great Chain of Being hierarchy prefigured in Genesis.)[12] Perhaps it is precisely because the ten thousand things were relatively unstructured at their mythic beginnings—certainly subject to a *yinyang* dynamic (generative oscillations of dark and light, warm and cool, senior and junior, and so forth), but not neatly sorted into ontological kinds or essences and (mere) manifestations—that people with desires and intentions must be active in cultivating, crafting, and nurturing the forms of life that are good, for themselves, their families, their communities. Perhaps the myriad things *are* just one thing after another, all active in "giving life to life," but none in their very nature more or less generative. Productivity, in a metaphysics of the Way and its manifestations, its *wanwu*, must be seized and made human, made good. This book, then, is a study of social and sociable craftwork, cultural practices that produce articulate forms of life in an environment of at least imaginable plenty: the myriad things are generative in ten thousand ways; we can "embody and make use of" this power and virtue.

Life nurturing in Beijing is instructive beyond China—this study of it is, therefore, both more and less than ethnography or history. We began this study with a common interest in urban ethnography, with the thought that in talking with those who nurtured their lives in the present, we might find embodiment especially well articulated, and with the hope that the historicity of Beijing's urban life—including its connection to both ancient and recent sources of significance, from ancient metaphysics to Maoist values and terms, could be appreciated. Undertaking ethnographic research centering on participant observation in parks and a series of interviews with *yangsheng* enthusiasts, we found a great deal of common ground with our own "life" experience. Gentle exercise and simple eating, fresh air and regular habits, became topics that we—a Chinese and an American academic, neither of us a "native" of the city—joined in exploring with many who were more than willing to advise us on the nurturing of our own lives. In what these Beijingers said, we heard echoes of questions we had already developed as researchers;[13] but as we worked, we were more engaged by everyday matters than by anthropological theory or living history. We all—*yangsheng* practitioners and researchers alike—naturalized, as it were, the contingencies of body and discourse. Everything began to look like obvious common sense.

Nevertheless, we have sustained a sense of urban Beijing's social and historical distinctiveness, and we devote much of this book to conveying a sense of the place and the time. Chinese people all over the world are turning up in urban parks to practice *taiji* and *qigong*, to jog and do calisthenics. But Beijing, and especially its old downtown neighborhoods, recommended itself to us as an especially good site for *yangsheng* research. We felt we knew the city well (though we discovered otherwise), and we had witnessed there a growing popular enthusiasm for "self-health" (*ziwo baojian* 自我保健) activities that everyone classified under the heading of *yangsheng*. The neighborhood in which we did most of our fieldwork included both large and small parks, around which much of the housing was low-rise, overcrowded, and occupied by retirees. These older residents had lived there for a long time, at the heart of several cultural revolutions, one of the most dramatic having been a radical turn toward global capitalist participation in the early 1990s. Their enthusiasm for a little-commodified, constitutively local, pleasurable way (Way?) of crafting lives impressed us as both responsive to historical experience and a way of making history, crafting an urban culture for a present and future Beijing.[14] This study is not about China or Chinese people, exactly, though surely, Beijing urban life much resembles that of other Chinese cities and Chinatowns around the world. It is, rather, searching in one place for those specificities that can nuance our sense of the common ground we all must try to occupy.

To this end, though we eschew direct practical advice, we have found in sharing our drafts with colleagues that this study is more likely to be read for its insights on how to live than for its character as ethnography or history. We hope it can also propose—drawing on local resources both ancient and recent in Beijing—some productive terms for philosophical and historical thought not yet imagined by Anglophone social theory. Further, our reflections and those of the Beijingers we talked with might be a way to bring the taken-for-granted habitus—that of readers, that of *yangsheng* enthusiasts—into awareness in a way that encourages a better, but not necessarily Chinese craft of living. We hope that a book, too, can contribute to the nurturance of life.

Yangsheng *and Ten Thousand Things*

In the late twentieth and early twenty-first centuries, a culture of nurturing life has become a widely recognized feature of Chinese public life and "local color."[15] Parks are full of exercisers and hobbyists who speak of their activities as life nurturance, and media outlets provide much advice on how most effectively and enjoyably to nurture life. *Yangsheng* discourses and practices are forms of modern self-help (or self-health), but the term itself is ancient. The nurturance of life is locally spoken of and globally recognized as peculiarly Chinese and particularly traditional.[16] A recent study by François Jullien has reminded those who work in Chinese Studies that the second chapter of the influential Daoist writings attributed to Zhuangzi is all about the nurturance of life,[17] and a globalizing traditional Chinese medicine claims the term *yangsheng* as rubric for its classical orientation toward preventive medicine, or "treating the not yet ill."[18] Some in the Chinese intellectual movement known as National Studies (*guoxue* 国学), to which we return below, would place a great deal of the national heritage under the heading of *yangsheng*, as well. This impression of Chinese traditionalism in a popular health movement holds even though the techniques drawn on in the literature of modern *yangsheng* are often indebted to global science, medicine, and psychology and are propagated through a modern state's public-health apparatus. (There are echoes of this scientific modernity in Zhang's epigraph, in his evocation of evolutionary process and nature.) They are propagated so successfully, in fact, that it is methodologically difficult to separate discourses from practices, thoughts and intentions from embodied activities. As we will see, health information is an immensely popular arena of media consumption, and the people we met in parks and community centers often assiduously tried to develop their lives along recommended lines.

The prototypical life-nurturing citizen, in the highly mediated images that circulate especially through photojournalism, is an elderly person who practices *taiji quan* (t'ai chi) or *qigong* among friends in a public park. But there are many other activities that fall under the heading of *yangsheng*, including exercises such as calisthenics, jogging, swimming, and walking backward; hobbies such as water calligraphy (performed outdoors with large sponge brushes on pavement), dancing, singing, and keeping birds (which must be exercised outdoors in their cages); forms of connoisseurship such as the appreciation of tea, wine, and medicinal cuisine; and many forms of "spiritual" self-cultivation ranging from meditation to learning a foreign language.[19]

A popular ditty explains what sort of culture *yangsheng* is:

The Way (*dao*) of *yangsheng* is eating and sleeping, talking and singing,
playing ball and taking pictures, writing and painting,
writing poetry line by line, playing chess to banish the blues,
chatting of heaven, speaking of earth.[20]

This bit of lore suggests considerable variety within the category of life nurturance. The proverb mentions the most necessary and obvious elements of everyday life, "eating and sleeping," alongside physical exercises such as playing ball and cosmopolitan hobbies such as taking pictures. This Way is pleasant, good for "banishing the blues." Some things are even philosophical: "chatting of heaven, speaking of earth." This list of activities, short as it is, belies any resort to oversimplification that the term "nurturing life" might suggest. Instead, we glimpse a manifold culture of the everyday, one that is global and local, embodied and discursive, even ecological and cosmic.[21]

Readers for whom the foregoing comments raise no theoretical or critical questions are encouraged to skip what remains of this introduction and plunge right into "City Life" (Chapter 1). Our *yangsheng* interlocutors in Beijing do not share our concern to position our writing in relation to the shared dilemmas that have arisen in our own fields, and it is arguably more important to begin to hear from them than to split more academic hairs in this introduction. But some readers may be curious about how we have conceived, for this project, the responsibilities and challenges of anthropology, Chinese Studies, and cultural studies in the contemporary world. These curious

companions are encouraged to read on as we dwell a bit further on
the political nature of *yangsheng*, on methodological problems that
have arisen in translation, on the particular character of time(s) in
today's Beijing, and on ways of being inventive about tradition.

Chronic Concerns: The (Bio)political
When China is mentioned, politics is never far behind. We have
noted above that *yangsheng* takes on some of its significance (for us,
at least) in the context of state-driven biopolitical reorganizations
of the social. The power/knowledge formations of institutionalized medicine and public health are also fundamental influences
in the emergence of a *yangsheng* movement. But power is generated, sustained, and challenged through everyday practices; ordinary
life—especially in China—is full of political concerns. The carnal life
that flourishes in Beijing's parks, vacant lots, and back alleys, aided
by the arts of life nurturance, is both a case of and a challenge to the
biopolitical projects of state and transnational apparatuses. Where
life itself is felt to be at stake, and the civil and deliberate lives of
ordinary people are under construction, sovereign power merges
into personal effectiveness, and the resources that can be mobilized
in the service of the good life yield both pleasure and strength.

It is common to remark, along with the Aristotelian tradition of
political thought, that the aim of politics is the good (collective) life.
By this reasoning, modern Chinese practices of life nurturance are
political by definition. But the politics of modern nation-states and
the institutions they authorize have seized upon life in particular
ways; to some extent, modern biopower has traveled with the nation-
state form wherever it has been established. Thus, China is no exception in the field of modern biopolitics, despite its indigenous political
philosophies, its long history of imperial bureaucracy, and its more
recent revolutionary history of Maoist socialism. At the same time,
the particular convergence of power and life that we study here is
deeply historical, which is to say nonmodern, in instructive ways.[22]

Obviously, we draw not only on Foucault's well-known explo-
rations of biopower and the care of the self, but also on Giorgio

Agamben's extension of these ideas into a broad theory of modern nation-state sovereignty. In an earlier paper, we found Agamben's grounding of modern sovereignty in a distinction between "bare life" (*zoë*) and "the form or way of living of an individual or group" (*bios*)[23] rather eerily useful, and since the constitutive violence of the founding of the Chinese party-state still lives in modern memory, we have had to acknowledge the pertinence of his analysis of states of exception to the history of the People's Republic of China. Similarly, it is tempting to adopt Foucault's translations of Hellenistic and Roman concerns such as "the arts of existence" and "practices of the self" to talk about the activities we have observed, discussed, and read about in Beijing.[24] We will suggest, however, that resemblances between the broad topics and special terminologies taken up by Foucault and Agamben and the forms of life and techniques of cultivation employed by contemporary Beijingers are more superficial than they might seem. While some forms of life and arts of existence appear to be encouraged by modern nation-states anywhere, we argue that classical Chinese theories of sovereignty and modern practices of life in China offer inspiration to theory and resources for anthropological understanding that have not been properly appreciated in the Anglophone human sciences.

As anthropologists of everyday life in the peaceful and well-managed neighborhoods of the Chinese capital, we have wondered to what extent the violent history of the state still lives in the experience and tactics of citizens. Following the literature of everyday life, there seems little doubt that sometimes subtle, but deeply felt political agendas can inhabit the practices of space, time, and embodiment.[25] As Chairman Mao said, via a *Red Flag* editorial writer a long time ago, "class struggle exists even at the tips of your chopsticks."[26] Though the literature of everyday life has often focused on intimate dominations such as those of race, class, and gender, in modern situations where the history and development of the nation-state forms part of the daily consciousness of the people, questions of state sovereignty and legitimacy are far from absent in daily practice. Some studies of modern China have seen the burgeoning consumerist and business-centered life of the coastal cities, which appears so thoroughly depoliticized and "naturalized," as still haunted by the deprivations, idealisms, and anxieties of the Maoist past.[27] Similarly, the simple common sense about bodies and health reported by Beijingers, when it is placed in historical perspective, can be seen to harbor a sense of the political that has everything to do with life and death. But this everyday lore also draws on another theoretical world concerned with power and life: classical Chinese philosophies of lordship in which the power of the exemplar generates social form through enlightened and exemplary self-cultivation. Many of the materials we cite herein relate more to that model of power than to neoliberal governmentality or biopolitics.

We have elsewhere discussed the political and social contradictions experienced by Beijingers before the present Reform Era truly got underway and have considered the influence these lived histories might have had on the emergence of a *yangsheng* movement.[28] It could be argued that nowadays, the state and its Communist Party politics is more benign and that its violent sovereignty has become the generative and cajoling voice of a classically Foucauldian power/knowledge apparatus. Power most often appears as the voice of the state-supported expert, pushing good nutrition or "quality births," explaining why a cancellation of state social supports amounts to a greater freedom to thrive.

Indeed, most important for the topic of *yangsheng* is the withdrawal of the state from the provision of health care. In the 1980s, a great deal of national government support was withdrawn from hospitals, medical schools, and clinics, and there was a rapid shift to fee-for-service models of payment. In the 1990s, there was a massive growth in health-insurance schemes, bringing in train many of the same problems we see in North America. Health insurance is too expensive for many, the premiums and copay amounts are too high, and the costs of medical care are rising fast. In this anxious climate, an aging population is bombarded with state-sponsored public-health information and free disease-screening programs, even while they complain ever more vociferously that it is almost impossible to "find a doctor,"[29] much less pay for medical services. Where their health is concerned, most people realize that they are on their own.

So when people say that they swim in frozen lakes or walk backward up mountains in the early morning "for their health," we take them at their word. Some of these *yangsheng* regimes are very good for physical health, and if the Beijingers of today don't take care of their health, who will? But within this sensible instrumental reasoning lies a historically nuanced formation of the passions. Utilizing all manner of socialist apparatuses of power, the Maoist state determined what proper life would be—collective, productive, egalitarian, and so on—while openly and violently expelling bare life from its polity. For a long time, the particular Maoist relationship between *bios* (the life of the citizen) and *zoë* (bare life) engaged the emotional commitment of many Chinese people. Now, however, the strong collectivist state has transformed itself into a rather conventional neoliberal regime whose relation to life is—or appears to be—simply to "let [citizens] live." At this point in this history, then, when we see a pointed assertion of deliberate forms of life on the part of ordinary citizens, however humble they may be, we can presume that there is some deeply felt strategy at work. In a context of modern biopower, life in myriad forms is a focus of the political passions of the people.[30]

Yangsheng is not about freedom or overt political power. One is reminded of de Certeau's discussion of the tactics of everyday life, actions that involve "a logic articulated on situations and the will of others." *Yangsheng* allows people to "escape without leaving" a sometimes uncertain social and political order that is both experienced and remembered as hand built, but fragile, always threatened by "chaos" (*luan* 乱). The politics of everyday tactics developed by de Certeau can accommodate the classical Chinese notion of nonaction with respect to sovereignty (*wuwei* 无为), even as it emphasizes an almost resistant agency: "Such a politics should also inquire into...the microscopic, multiform, and innumerable connections between manipulating and enjoying, the fleeting and massive reality of a social activity at play with the order that contains it."

The politics proposed by de Certeau and framed by the theorists of biopower allows us to think more clearly about the possible and actual relations between the pleasures involved in creative life—*bios*—and the power of the state, which reserves its rights over bare life, *zoë*.

These reflections on pleasure and power lead us back to an even fuller appreciation of the literature and daily practice of *yangsheng*. The vision of health and pleasure these materials offer can ground civil, rich, and enjoyable lives in the activity of an individual, but one who is inseparable from an unbounded collective while demanding little from others. No wonder so many in Beijing are practicing the arts of *yangsheng*.

Chronic Concerns: Translation

The only language we two authors have in common is Chinese. Planning, researching, and writing *Ten Thousand Things* has been a long process of translating between manuscript drafts, intellectual projects, and the textual materials in two languages that have inspired these projects. Each of us knows enough about the other's literary world to guess well the significance of texts and the agenda of the schools of thought that have produced them. But we both also worry about how much is lost in translation. The historical significance of contemporary writings—how they are read, in effect—and the context of citations from "old" texts are the first things to go. We have done what we could here to provide historical context for *yangsheng* in Beijing, but we have found no way to preserve the Chinese-language-specific heteroglossia of many of our materials. In rendering classical Chinese medical writing for an Anglophone audience, for example, one must often choose between the technical English of biomedicine and the poetics of folklore and cosmology, even though the original Chinese language manages to be medical, philosophical, and commonsensical all at once. Rendering a term for "heart depot" (*xinzang* 心脏) as "cardiac visceral system" transforms a localizing storage and processing function that is as concerned with thoughts as with blood into an anatomical structure, that is, a discrete organ

23

that can ground a known physiology or be the site of a lesion.[31] The management problem, the relationship between local accumulation and wide circulation, presented by a depot, storehouse, or granary is in such a translation decentered or even forgotten. But "cardiac visceral system" has other virtues; it renders a Chinese medical entity as rationally materialistic, grounded in a known body. It sounds altogether less symbolic than "heart depot."

Another example: translating *jingshen* 精神 as "spirit" captures the modern importance of this Christian and Cartesian notion—invoked, for example, in the "antispiritual pollution campaigns" of the early reform period. But it loses any sense of the Chinese medical entities *jing*-essence and *shen*-vitality, not to mention the physiological relationship between them, which has a *yinyang* character. Quite often, the better translation for *jingshen* involves translating them as two substances, "essence" and "vitality," and making some reference to their dynamic relationship. Readers of medical and philosophical works in Chinese can easily see the commonsense metaphors and images that enrich and enchant an ancient language and that combine practical healing concerns and massy bodily entities with aesthetic and cosmological insights. This rich reading is much harder to achieve in English translation.

These translation tactics are consistent with our title, *Ten Thousand Things*, a phrase that invokes both multiplicity and materiality, as we have said. The term is a very ancient one, *wanwu* (万物), and as noted, the number "ten thousand" is not literal; *wanwu* refers rather to an unthinkable vastness, an infinity of forms, all manifest reality. And the *wu* of the term truly is "things"—the materiality is clear. As such, the word could just as well evoke a sense of burdensomeness, rather than the exuberance evident in this chapter's epigraph. Because it doesn't seem to do so for speakers of modern Chinese, we have at times adopted a Dante-esque word like "myriad" to preserve a certain teeming enjoyment in sheer quantity. But once heard as awe-inspiring, "ten thousand," too, rolls off the tongue with pleasure. *Wanwu* may be just one thing after another; but this is life, and life can be enjoyed. As the argument that follows will gradually

24

show, Chinese philosophy and (even) modern commonsense Chinese language presume a natural scatter, a kind of entropic diffusion of many, many things: human activity involves gathering and holding a few things together, assembling contingency into form in the service of local and temporary human ends.

Chronic Concerns: History and Temporality

Our title also invokes the contemporary.[32] It might have been more modest to refer to a "modern," "reform," or "postsocialist" moment, as so many other studies have done. But all of these terms have a way of distancing us and our readers from our contemporaries in Beijing. Rapid globalization and the emergence of Beijing as a city of world importance, host of the 2008 Olympics, make any such distancing or othering implausible.

China's twentieth century saw the emergence and eventual hegemony of a modern nation-state and a familiar set of scientific values and secular institutions. Though many writers presume that in its early years (1949–1978), the People's Republic of China was static and isolated, neither truly modern nor contemporary with "the free world," we are more inclined to see socialist modernity as having many basic features in common with the midcentury world of liberal democracies.[33] One important formation common to both the "first" and "second" worlds was a vast public commitment to progress, development, and a utopian vision of what human societies could achieve. This modernist chronotope sought to discipline time and space into a vast world picture with a troubled, but logically necessary teleology.[34] In the Chinese midcentury world, after 1949, the modern telos was often spoken of as "true communism," imagined as a not-yet-realized state of unrestricted plenty, Marxist internationalism, and advanced technology. After the utopian tenor of Maoist modernism began to recede, however, and especially after Deng Xiaoping proposed that a society of "moderate well-being" (*xiaokang* 小康) should be achieved in China, the certainties of a univocal national modernity and progress became more tenuous.

During the 1980s and early 1990s, "modernization" and "getting on track with the world" were still the watchwords on everyone's lips (though both of us authors at that time were framing research that challenged the hegemony of modernization logics and its narratives of one-way globalization).[35] By the end of the 1990s, a temporality founded in ambitious visions of progress had lost its grip on many of China's lived worlds. American material life no longer appeared the be-all and end-all of modernization as a specifically Asian commodity culture began to thrive along city streets and in the media. Even those with the means to build on and increase their control over daily life became increasingly uncertain about what the future could hold for them personally or for their nation.[36] Meanwhile, many Beijingers already considered themselves to be quite good at the arts of crafting a life of moderate well-being. The old arts of life nurturance, many of them embedded in a conservative habitus and accustomed to certain nonnegotiable comforts (a thermos of boiled water, a thick quilt, fresh food, warm clothing), have been brought into service to organize a post-utopian life.[37]

As China's public culture moved definitively away from socialist asceticism and the collective imperative of service to the people, waves of fads, or "fevers" (re 热), began to diversify the aims of life. From backward-looking fads focusing on Chairman Mao or the model soldier Lei Feng,[38] to the past-denying imagery of "plunging into the [global] sea" propagated by the important documentary He Shang (River elegy) of the late 1980s,[39] from "high culture fevers" on the part of 1980s philosophers and cultural critics[40] to enthusiasms for qigong meditation shared by ordinary city dwellers and elite scientists[41]—everyone was now able to find some popular orientation on the problem of past and future, one of ten thousand possible viewpoints on the problem presented by the decline of a shared modernist teleology.

Practitioners of the yangsheng arts are thus our post-utopian contemporaries, and this is especially clear in the multiplicity of their life habits. Their interests and routines escape the totalizing discourses of vast public campaigns, such as the "One World, One Dream" ideology that dominated Olympic Beijing for a few years before 2008. Moreover, in their practices they dwell on problems of time as they seek to achieve a wholesome aging process in nonteleological personal trajectories. Perhaps there is something particularly "contemporary" about the population we found to be the most enthusiastic participants in the life-nurturing arts in Beijing. These are mostly men and women who have retired, some of them as young as forty-five or fifty, from socialist work units (schools, factories, government agencies, the military) and who are making do materially on limited incomes from state pensions and contributions from their children. They are old enough to remember—indeed, they cannot forget—the Maoist past, when state-mandated disciplines extended to all aspects of everyday life,[42] and they are connected to the neoliberal present through the tense and competitive careers of their children, who no longer enjoy work-unit guarantees or many direct social services from the state. This generation has access to a wide range of media: they read, watch, and listen to all kinds of news, advertising, and public education, and they enjoy fictional genres such as soap operas that recall many past cultures and that narrativize a number of possible presents. Many of them are relieved to have lived on into a depoliticized era in which private desires are quite legitimate, but most of them also worry that collective morality has been compromised by the "selfishness" and "competition" of neoliberal public priorities. They are aware of living in a different rhythm than younger people, often saying they share no language or interests, even with their own children.

In the 1980s, references to "Chinese backwardness" were everywhere. The very generation we speak of here, the midlifers and those later in life who have enthusiastically claimed one of the world's most modern cities as their own[43] and who fill public spaces with the mundane purposes of their own lives not so long ago thought of themselves as suffering from a chronic backwardness as the world developed all around them. This identification with lack was, of course, the predictable other side of that pervasive emphasis on modernization characteristic of the reform era as captained by Deng Xiaoping. Backwardness was the explanation given for everything from failed public services and daily discomforts to corrupt back-door dealings and inegalitarian gender relations. But the language and the stigma of lagging behind is no longer plausible for many Beijingers. Witness the well-pressed and brightly colored silks and satins worn by those who gather in Beihai Park to sing old songs: they are expressing their cosmopolitan good taste and modernity in the present, even as they sing to recover the moments of their youthful years when they wore dark, padded-cotton jackets and cloth shoes, worked to build socialism, and studied Mao Zedong Thought. These days, confidently embodying a mixed temporality, *yangsheng* enthusiasts such as these singers assert their coevalness with moderns everywhere.[44] But this is a coevalness that includes having a past.

Chronic Concerns: Tradition
One scholarly method of taming a proliferation of temporalities is to speak of tradition, conceived as a more or less static reservoir of cultural resources that may be deployed or even "invented" in the context of modernity to sometimes political ends.[45] Those who read about and practice *yangsheng* in Beijing do not generally speak of tradition in this essentializing way. In our experience, they seldom even use the word "tradition" (*chuantong* 传统), but they often see themselves as mining the Chinese past for life-nurturing wisdom.[46] They have been doing so in the current highly mediated manner for only about fifteen or twenty years, so in this sense, *yangsheng* is an invented tradition. The ancientness of the very words *yang* and *sheng* is, perhaps, a convenience as people draw on historical resources to paper over history's major lacunae and ruptures. But we wish to argue that the *yangsheng* we investigate in this study is nevertheless a living tradition, even if (as some would say) it has been brought back to true liveliness quite recently.

The field of Chinese Studies in both Asian and European languages has been faced with a particularly interesting challenge as we frame and reframe what is meant by the concept of tradition (which is, of course, no more stable a category than its accustomed

28

partner, modernity). The cultural heritage preserved in countless archives and embodied in an old and continuous written language now faces Chinese readers, thinkers, tourists, and makers of cultural policy as a vast and unique problem. In fact, we have often heard commentators in the Chinese media refer to "the Chinese heritage" as a tremendous burden: Who will pay for the renovation and maintenance of all the precious temples, palaces, and beauty spots? How can scholars and their students do justice to the vast complexity of thought in Chinese history? How can research in Chinese find a place in global intellectual movements published in more powerful language worlds? Can "folk" customs and cultures find a path between commodity trivialization of culture and the sheer disappearance of every old thing, as those who remember an older way of life die? A now-discredited position on tradition—the Cultural Revolution approach, "Destroy the Four Olds"[47]—still lurks, perhaps, as a temptation for some, given the tremendous demand on Chinese social and psychological resources of the Chinese past and its vast archive. It is not surprising that the television documentary *He Shang* (Death song of the river) was so appealing in the China of the late 1980s; this masterpiece of manipulative editing culminates with images of the long, silt-laden Yangtze River, winding through the entire breadth of a country impacted and befuddled with "old culture," finally merging its dirty yellow waters with the refreshing blue vastness of the Pacific. At that time, the Chinese generation that expected to join their expertise and cosmopolitan sophistication with that of the world's techno elite was referred to as "plunging into the sea." Presumably these hopeful young people, armed with modern science and globally marketable skills, would be able to leave "Chinese culture" behind.[48]

The rhetoric of *He Shang* is not ultimately different from that of empiricist history and anthropology, however. In both, the past is "othered," made into an object of contemplation or a landscape to be viewed from the comfortable standpoint of the analyst's secure position in modernity.[49] The rich and comparatively well-preserved Chinese past is made available, in this othering logic, to be summarized,

29

essentialized, and spiritualized. From Arthur Smith's *Chinese Characteristics* (1894) to Lucian Pye's *The Spirit of Chinese Politics* (1992), we
have seen Western scholars, confident in their cultural superiority,
deliver into English a static Chinese tradition. Some versions of this
modernist historiography encourage cultural appropriation, treating
Chinese tradition as a resource that can remedy "our" (read "Euro-
American") alienation and shallowness. Thus, scholars propagating a
new transnational "Confucian" Chineseness argue for business practices that are more collectively responsible, suggesting that Chinese
people somehow understand better than Americans and Europeans
how to make "Asian"—or any—contracts work. And successive generations of young readers in the United States seriously consider how
they might live in accord with the relativism of the *Dao de jing* (*The
Way and Its Power*, in Waley's classic translation) or gain confidence
through the practice of Asian martial arts that are taught by old men
and billed as ancient.

Not unlike these approaches to the Chinese past, *Ten Thousand
Things* freely appropriates tradition to present-day ends. We do not
claim to offer here a historical study that could defeat the reifications
and essentialisms of mainstream Chinese culture studies, though we
try to avoid oversimplifying past thought or rendering it static and
timeless.[50] Especially in Chapter 2, we discuss the newly popular literature that propagates Chinese medical wisdom. As a contribution
to the huge field of self-help works available in Beijing, this literature's new twist on the *yangsheng* tradition is frankly appropriative
of the past.

But tradition in this study runs deeper than that. Through Zhang
Qicheng's wide reading in the medical and metaphysical Chinese
archive, we ourselves select, very pointedly, pieces of text that are
of present-day use—to us, to our readers, and, we argue, to practitioners of *yangsheng* in Beijing's parks. Without proposing any
determinate relationships (the "influence" of intellectual history, for
example), we juxtapose terms, concepts, and poetic extracts from
past sources with the lively cultural concerns of China's contemporaneity. The aim is to put ancients and moderns in dialogue, not

just through reading, but through learning. This form of presentism may be a historical sin, but we have good company in our misbehavior: not only anthropologists who persist in deploying the study of difference as (North American) cultural critique,[51] but also the translator-commentators who insist on finding modern theoretical and philosophical riches in ancient Chinese writing.[52]

More important to us, in our conversations with *yangsheng* enthusiasts, we began to hear deep currents of resonance with Chinese discourses that an empiricist historiography would have long ago declared to be dead (even if subject to resuscitation as "invented tradition"). Though the retired workers and teachers, soldiers and bookkeepers with whom we most often spoke seldom cited the classics in so many words, we have occasion to point out, especially in Chapter 3, that the commonsense values they reported have much in common with ancient wisdom. Their crafted daily lives recall the self-cultivation (*zixiu* 自修) that has been theorized in Chinese philosophy since at least the Han Dynasty (206 B.C.E – 220 C.E.), and their self-conscious orientations toward life processes respond to a living tradition of knowing the Way. (Response itself [*ganying* 感应] was much theorized in China's classic philosophy as the interresponsiveness of the ten thousand things, understandable and predictable with the help of a—far from dead, even now—*yinyang* logic.)[53]

Though we found much that was classical to appreciate in what our interlocutors in Beijing had to say, we nevertheless hold that the knowing of a tradition goes beyond the verbal and does not alter historically in the same way or at the same pace as explicitly narrativized ideologies do. Dipesh Chakrabarty, commenting on largely critical studies of invented traditions in Japan—while thinking of India, another country with a massive heritage "problem"—clarifies:

> If even invented traditions need genealogies for their own effectiveness, no such genealogy can ever consist of an inventory of ideas alone. Ideas acquire materiality through the history of bodily practices. They work not simply because they persuade through their logic; they are also capable, through a long and heterogeneous history of the cultural

training of the senses, of making connections with our glands and muscles and neuronal networks. This is the work of memory, if we do not reduce the meaning of that word to the simple and conscious mental act of remembering. The past is embodied through a long process of training the senses.[54]

Ideas acquire materiality in bodies, and bodily practices have long and heterogeneous histories. Chakrabarty's writing recalls Marx's famous dictum that "the forming of the five senses is a labor of the entire history of the world down to the present."[55] Certainly, in the Chinese context, such historicity of the body and its life cannot be thought apart from the continuities of the Chinese language. The fact that third-century or fourth-century B.C.E. thinking about the seasons and the sensations was expressed and remains legible in words that are still in daily use facilitates memory in Chakrabarty's sense. Some ancient/modern words and phrases, as we will see in the world of *yangsheng*, invite the making of connections to glands and muscles and neuronal networks. Others are consumed as—at least—metaphors for the otherwise little-theorized experiences of tasting food, resting after exertion, or chatting with friends. In calligraphic mode, the concepts that are materialized as the writer's effort and dispositions flow out and manifest in ink on a surface are, in *yangsheng* "readings," further realized in bodies, entered into the bloodstream of lives. To appreciate the powers of tradition in modernity fully, a process of living in and constantly remaking both a flow of meaning and breaks in that flow becomes central. It is both a privilege and a burden for Chinese contemporaries that they have such a deep fund of resources on which to draw as they craft a living tradition and embody myriad daily lives.

Chronic Concerns: Collaboration

The writing of this book has been collaborative in a special sense. We authors work between anthropology and philosophy, between literary interpretation and practical strategies, between American and Chinese scholarship, between Judith Farquhar's and Zhang

Qicheng's habits, training, idioms, and writing styles. In doing collaborative field research, both of us also moved between our shared scholarly world of Chinese medicine studies and the street-level views of Beijing's ordinary city dwellers. As we have moved across these various great divides, some familiar terrain has been sacrificed, but much has been gained. The anthropology we here offer, for example, somewhat shortchanges historical and sociological contextualization, even as it preserves anthropology's populist and interpretive commitments. At one point the two of us undertook, for example, a long written exchange on the anthropological notion of resistance; for a while it seemed important to ask whether hobbyists gathering in public spaces might constitute a form of popular opposition to instituted state power. Once we had understood each other's positions on the subject, however, we both decided that this book can do without the problematic of resistance. Further, the philosophy we undertake has ignored most grand narratives in favor of selective appropriations of the language of China's great writers, hoping to speak to contemporaries in intimately philosophical ways. Zhang's usual style is to offer, as a philological historian, the best and most accurate readings of difficult ancient texts. But as we selected materials for discussion here, we preferred the places in his writing where he reaches out to contemporaries with mundane advice and engaging poetic language. As we developed a style of reading and commentary that draws at once on the very different talents and training of an American ethnographer and a Chinese philologist, we found that there was much we could not attempt. Some of our familiar projects had to be abandoned: neither Zhang's tendency to provide close commentary on Chinese medical and metaphysical works nor Farquhar's penchant for extensive literary and theoretical interpretations could be fully indulged. Neither of us is very conversant with the other's most-studied archive, so we rely on each other to invoke authorities. Both of us see *Ten Thousand Things* as a worthwhile continuation of our own scholarly projects, but here we have had to find a different voice (or, to be more exact, several different voices) than the voice of authority our home disciplines and accustomed idioms normally afford. We write from a space of encounter where deep global differences and inequalities produce frictions between knowledge worlds.[56] Part of this friction appears when we translate: Zhang Qicheng has struggled with post-Cartesian ideas such as "habitus" and "embodiment," and Judith Farquhar despairs of translating *wanwu* or *jingshen* well. The very nature(s) to which we anchor our perceptions of the healthy and the socially good differ—the ancient Daoist cosmogony that gave rise to the myriad things by way of *yin* and *yang*, heaven and earth, contradicts evolutionary science. Zhang feels no need to reconcile this inconsistency; both accounts can be true, for his purposes. Farquhar worries about an asymmetry between Chinese metaphysics (which sounds like myth or religion) and the equally unprovable assumptions of the modernist sciences (which are seldom addressed in theory, since they are assumptions). Operating in still distinguishable conceptual worlds, we constantly encounter objects that do not travel well into the thinking of our expectant readers. But we have enjoyed negotiating this uneven terrain; it has been full of surprises and has given us at times great pleasure. Some of this enjoyment, we hope, enlivens the book.

Though the book is written in English (there will also be a Chinese version), we have sought to avoid the domination of one Anglophone interpretive voice. Such a monotone tends to relegate work on Chinese philosophy and medicine to the domains of religion or spirituality, the New Age, and the fringe humanities. The English language is not well suited to capturing the simultaneous concreteness and dynamism, the down-to-earth practicality and truth, of Chinese worldviews. In any translation project, in fact, the first and largest element that is lost is the historical conversation within which the translated text originally made a contribution. Translators are often required to restore the social context of textual references in footnotes, as we sometimes do here. A deeper problem for translation, however, worries us more.

Objects themselves, and thus objective worlds, differ fundamentally between languages. Much of the friction in the encounters noted above is ontological: what Zhang Qicheng calls "the three treasures of the human body: *jing*-essence, *qi*-energy, and *shen*-spirit," for example, simply cannot be conformed to the body known to biology or even to the ordinary embodiment of our American readers. Though we argue in places that unfamiliar forms of being are actually not so strange as philosophers might make them out—*qi* is not hard to experience, once you start attending to it—we nevertheless can see that an English text that treats *jing*, *qi*, and *shen* as commonsense nouns is in danger of appearing quaint or "merely cultural."

Our tactic for addressing this friction has been to multiply texts, to show many contexts in which the usual objects referred to in Chinese simply work. An empirical engagement with many forms of life (which must, of course, include the liveliness of texts, discourses, conversations) is, perhaps, a turn away from the great Western philosophical questions, especially those that have maintained a mind-body divide. The only way we see to get beyond the dualisms, essences, and self-serving comparisons of the usual East-West divide, however, is to multiply forms—even our method, then, insists on the ten thousand things.

To this end, we have adopted a style that sometimes combines and sometimes distinguishes our two authorial voices while also giving due recognition to the many speakers and writers we cite. Translations into English (all by Farquhar) have striven to reflect the style of the Chinese originals, sometimes preserving the oddness of unfamiliar logics, objects, images, and histories. Our coauthored commentary seeks to assist Anglophone readers to appreciate these linguistic and practical differences while finding in them—we both hope—something common and valuable. In Chapter 3, where we quote at length many Beijingers as they talk about their *yangsheng* practices, we have distinguished the comments of "JF" and "ZQC." We two interviewers have heard different tensions and promises in these diverse remarks and see no need to homogenize our contributions to the chapter. In Chapter 4, a long essay by Zhang is the topic of the chapter, but the discussion of it is coauthored; the chapter nevertheless has a bias toward Farquhar's reading of the essay.

Chapter 1 is even more Farquhar's, describing as it does a city life that Zhang decided, as we talked about the chapter, that he has no need to articulate; Beijing has been his home since the early 1990s. But as he edited drafts of the chapter, he added his own sense of the relationship between the contemporary city and its residents' ways of nurturing life. And Chapter 2 presents viewpoints on *yangsheng* from a variety of recent popular publications. One of these works is by Zhang, and another is by a colleague, Qu Limin, who helped us in our research in 2003. We have privileged these two sources in the coauthored discussion. This Introduction is the result of many discussions over several years as drafts of book chapters moved between us, in two languages. The Conclusion returns to the overarching questions of embodiment and historicity, to the myriad things, and it includes a record of a conversation we had over a meal as the writing was drawing to a close.

In the course of gathering materials from the popular health literature for use in Chapter 2, we came across the following remarks by Zhang Qicheng's colleague Qu Limin:

> Basically, the Inner Canon is a book that teaches medical theory (or, the Way of medicine). Its opening chapters speak of nondesiring and vacancy, then it turns to the four seasons and the interactions of *yin* and *yang*—this tells everyone that the secret of a healthy longevity rests on whether one's emotions and the *qi* and blood of the circulation tracks are moving smoothly, and whether life's phases of emergence, development, retreating, and storing are all in order. If they are, it is just as the *Book of Changes* ("Uses of the Undivided") says: "If you see a host of dragons with no leader, this is auspicious."[57]

Qu does not explain why this quote about dragons from the *Book of Changes* helps us understand the virtues of classical medical systems. Nor does she explain why a host of dragons, with no one dragon first among them, should be an auspicious manifestation. She seems to think the relevance and significance of the reference are obvious. And perhaps they are obvious, or at least suggestive, to her Chinese readers. In a Beijing where one can readily visit several versions of "Nine Dragon Screens" and where cartoon images of dragons thundering through vast cloudy skies are quite common, a rippling mass of dragons is not hard to visualize.

The twisting and turning body of the dragon is a materialization of the alternating positive and negative, fast and slow dynamics of *yin* and *yang*; dragons share the space between heaven and earth where humans find their home; they have a special affinity with the courses of the winds and waters (the *fengshui*) that determine the quality and generativity of human life. And as anyone who has seen a dragon dance in a Chinese New Year parade knows, dragons *play*—with a flaming pearl, with each other. All this makes dragons a nice figure for human lives of "healthy longevity." But this multitude of leaderless dragons, appearing with their ever-changing lines of flight and their irreducible multiplicity, also invites the viewer into an enchanted space. No authority limits the myriad ways that can be followed by dragons; embodied life is not just flesh and effort— it is also high spirits and simple pleasures. A life well nurtured might turn the everyday into the flight of a dragon, one among many.

Beijing's back alleys (*hutongs*) inside the second ring road have been crowded for decades, ever since the workers, soldiers, and cadres needed to run the government began to crowd into the city's low-rise housing in the 1950s. Life spills into the walkways and lanes, and the practical needs of many for sleeping and cooking space or for a place to hang laundry and storage for tools must be met in the cramped spaces between buildings thrown up in the courtyards of once-elegant single-family houses.

The amount of commercial activity on the streets varies, and in the year of the Olympics, it was rather restricted. But the daily or thrice-weekly corner markets and the not always licensed offerings of vendors of services and notions to early morning park-going crowds are hard to repress. Though many ordinary services and sales have moved inside or—in the case of food—to windowed stalls facing the street, Beijingers still like to shop on the street.

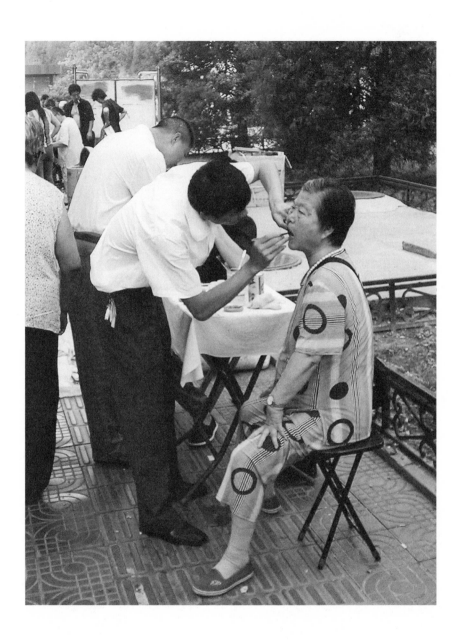

With the exception of the wholesale redevelopment of the Qianmen District, the back-alley neighborhoods in Beijing are being modernized piecemeal, sometimes with city development grants. The houses that crowd major arteries are often torn down in order to be reconstructed farther back and supplied with a shop front. Sites of historical importance are often built from scratch in Qing Dynasty style, supporting a major industry of construction skills from an earlier period. And some ruins are preserved as such and made into points of interest for tourists. In the third picture, a piece of the old wall of the Imperial Palace has been preserved as an archaeological excavation, with lavish documentation mounted on the walls.

The alternative to living in crumbling downtown low-rise housing is living in vast high-rise housing estates in the neighborhood of the fourth and fifth ring roads. Complexes of twenty or thirty buildings always provide a bit of parkland among their towers (including a lot of thirsty grass, despite Beijing's chronic water shortages); living in the suburbs entails hours on buses to get to work or downtown activities, and even the longer train lines are very time consuming. In older neighborhoods in the city, a piecemeal revival of tradition is evident everywhere, producing hybrid streetscapes that combine lavish Qing ornamentation with the bland utilitarianism of the four-to-five-story structures through which the city grew between 1950 and 1980. In the new Central Business District of eastern Beijing, a few courtyard houses are carefully preserved as high-rises soar all around them. And in a new walking park near the Forbidden City, public sculptures invoke a traditional Beijing of civilized and leisured public life.

CHAPTER ONE

City Life

Cities are not natural forms. Our very notion of what a city is seems today to be inescapably bound up with complexity, diversity, difference, degradation, even chaos. Cities seep out at the edges; they appear to be irreducible to any ultimate principle or determination. It is not surprising that social thought, though repetitively drawn to the theme of urbanism, seems to have trouble conceptualizing cities. This is because modern cities are not entities; they are more like multiplicities, accidents, or events.

—Thomas Osborne and Nikolas Rose, "Governing Cities"

The streets of Beijing teem with life. This is a cliché about Asian cities, but it is also common to think of cities in general as places of intensified and burgeoning life. It is not just that by definition a city gathers many people in one place; rather, the essence of the city is spoken of as dynamic, a site of constant movement and rapid change; as heterogeneous, supporting many kinds of people and forms of life; and as intensely social, providing constant occasions for casual or significant contact with others. The life of the city is partly a direct result of population density, but the life of any particular city—its pleasures and hassles, its habits of daily encounter, its forms of rumor and gossip, its ways of making livable places, its mundane rhythms—cannot be accounted for solely in quantitative terms. Like any *gathering*—a concept and a process we emphasize throughout these pages—formations of life in cities arise in part, but only in part, from deliberate action. Practitioners of *yangsheng*, the arts of nurturing life, know this. In their *yangsheng* practice, they produce cultivated forms of space and time for their own lives and the lives of their communities.[1] In this chapter, we describe *yangsheng* practice in space, arguing that its form has much to do with the urban conditions from which desiring and enjoying people construct dynamic, heterogeneous, social, embodied lives.[2]

Our focus in this chapter is on the practical cityscape within which everyone, from "old Beijing" residents to the most transient tourists, finds themselves orienting to a Chinese past and a global future (while orienting at the same time to a global past and a Chinese future). We trace the life of the city, especially the everyday activities through which Beijingers people and civilize their city and their nation.[3] In this effort to appreciate local viewpoints on the urban experience, we have found the fiction films of Chinese director Ning Ying especially revealing, and we discuss parts of these films here.[4] Ning's "Beijing Trilogy," especially, theorizes by way of film narrative and imagery the city's contemporary historical moment.[5] Her vision is a poetics of urban Chinese experience at the millennium; situated and critical, her work seeks both to clarify and to show the complexity of the social entrapments and degrees of freedom lived by Beijing residents. As ethnography does, Ning Ying's films eschew prediction while analyzing the ambiguities and multiplicities inherent in every present. We have enjoyed reading her in a kind of ethnographic-theoretical partnership.

Though Ning Ying sees herself as a Beijing voice, we write here as non-Beijingers. Perhaps for this reason, we are more willing to see hope in the quotidian life of the city than she is. Zhang Qicheng moved to the city from the south as a student in the 1980s, and Judith Farquhar has visited for a mixture of short and long stays since 1990.[6] Along with many who were born and bred in the city, we have witnessed major changes in the structural face of Beijing and the practices of its everyday life. For different reasons, we have both spent much of our time in the city without much dependence on the expanding cosmopolitan spaces—what Marc Augé has called "non-places"—of four-star hotels, night-spot bars, high-end

shopping malls, and fusion-cuisine restaurants.[7] Despite the aston-
ishing rise of a consumerist middle class in urban China, such "non-
places" remain rather irrelevant to the great majority of Beijing's
residents. Parks and city squares, streets, stores open to sidewalks,
the courtyards of apartment blocks (*shequ* 社区), schools, hospitals,
work-unit housing complexes, shared offices, sidewalk markets, and
small apartments are the more salient forms of urban space both
for us and for the people we have interviewed, the Beijingers who
practice the arts of nurturing life. Just as Walter Benjamin found
it necessary to describe the historical character of the Paris of the
arcades—"the capital of the nineteenth century"—we feel there is
much to be learned from an engagement with the lived city of Beijing's *laobaixing* 老百姓, the mixed-by-definition "common people
of China."[8] This is a city and a polity continually produced in the
everyday life of a population that thinks of itself, with considerable
historical resonance, as "the people."[9]

As much as any city in China at the moment, however, Beijing
is global, cosmopolitan, and oriented toward the future. Everyone,
from the top leadership right down to the most menial laborer, is
aware that the millennial city of Beijing is and must be a kind of
performance for the world. This was especially the case in 2008
before and during the Olympics. But the officially generated image
of the city is neither simple nor ahistorical, combining as it does
an aestheticized Chinese tradition and a pumped-up hypermoder-
nity, retraditionalized back alleys in the shadow of world-famous
high-rise office towers. Ongoing work to produce and display both
tradition and modernity is heterogeneous and conflicted, both for
policy makers and planners and for ordinary people whose lives are
structured by the affordances of space, but who also insist on using
urban space according to their own diverse purposes.

Thus, in keeping with our emphasis on the heterogeneity of the
ten thousand things, we seek to recover, through a reading of built
space and urban practices and an attention to cultural texts and
casual lore, arenas of unique, multiplicitous, and creative sociality. Every city is made up of polycentric spaces and overlapping

histories.[10] We think the specificity and historicity of the Chinese and Beijing urban arenas are especially visible in the *yangsheng* practices going on daily in public places. These practices are an articulation of a situation—not the 1920s, not 1936, not Shanghai, not New York—in which multiple cultural and social forces converge and overlap. The embodied lives of Beijingers, taking place in rapidly evolving spaces, speak history and locality. They do so in ways that present themselves to our observant appreciation, but ultimately escape our writing grasp. Nevertheless, attention to some details will help us to see the difference.

Ultimately we aim with this chapter to put the reader in Beijing at the millennium, and, in a sense, to put Beijingers there, too. The life-nurturing residents of the city—experts and amateurs alike—with whom we have been engaged over the last decade embody, continuously, through all kinds of action, a historical moment and a unique place. Their practical achievements and frustrations, their philosophical reflections and aesthetic choices, weave together to make particular conditions and to offer ongoing challenges. The people we have gotten to know in this research are gathering lives and disposing bodies in the rapidly changing space of the city.[11] Here we characterize that space as it continues to become a habitation for contemporary people. To this end, this chapter takes a rather winding path, beginning with an appreciative description of street life and "urban charisma" in Beijing. Focusing on how public space is used and how (crowded) private space has evolved, we invoke both thinking about cities and the usual practices of city life in this place at this time. The chapter then turns to a discussion of the relationship between official planning and urban life, adapting Henri Lefebvre's remark that "the city is an oeuvre" while remaining open on the question of who the artists of the emergent urban might be. Within these two frames, descriptive and historical, we then provide more detailed observations about the neighborhood in which we worked, the West City District, through a morning walk and an evening stroll. These versions of walking in the city allow us to introduce some particular practices of *yangsheng* life nurturing, especially those that are done in public. (A more intimate and in some cases more domestic view of *yangsheng* is in Chapter 3.) We then widen the frame again to consider the spatial, cultural, spectacular, and hygienic politics of the city that were evident during the Olympic era, from the time of the Olympic bid in 2000 to the summer of 2008, when the games were held in Beijing. As we show there, Beijing's population enthusiastically supported the Olympics project and obligingly performed both Chineseness and modernity for both actual and imaginary visitors. But in the section that follows, we show that there were pleasures and anxieties, routines and achievements, that developed during this time on trajectories only indirectly connected to the city's self-conscious globalization. The films of Ning Ying help us make these points about the subjective life of the contemporary city. The chapter concludes with a reflection on the management of ruins.

In a sense, then, this chapter is an idiosyncratic tour of Beijing's spaces, times, and (life-nurturing) bodies. Much is left out of it, and perhaps too much is kept in. The miscellany we offer here signals the heterogeneity, incompleteness, and untidiness of the city, but also, like the construction safety sign we mention below, "Take people to be the root," (*yi ren wei ben* 以人为本), it takes the city to be the gathered, contemporary, and variously nurtured lives of its inhabitants.

Street Life

The size and diversity of urban crowds in Asia presents palpable contrasts with North American urban life. An American visitor we know, walking in Shanghai in 1983 (even before the late 1990s increase in automotive traffic), felt quite panicked by the crush of people on a rainy day; the constant jostle of umbrellas was unnatural and unacceptable to him. American students new to Beijing, wishing to maintain their own pace on the crowded streets, develop consciously aggressive strategies of walking or biking in the city. They are not content to amble along more slowly than their own normal pace behind a gaggle of middle-school students or a couple of shuffling elderly people. North Americans are accustomed to wide, tidy sidewalks and relatively few pedestrians in their cities, and their expectations about urban activity are framed accordingly. By contrast, a Chinese friend walking in Chicago slightly after the evening rush hour felt uncomfortable that there were so few people on the streets. It was too early to worry much about crime, but the place felt dead and cold to her. It lacked the *renao* (热闹, heat and noise) Chinese urbanites so value in public life.

It is not just that there are more people on the streets of East Asia's major population centers, for longer hours, but that more kinds of activity seem to take place in highly visible public spaces. In Chicago or Atlanta, Washington, D.C., or Montreal, most walkers in the city are moving between indoor destinations.[12] Though there are districts in these cities with sidewalk cafés and sales kiosks, time spent in and on the streets is significantly devoted to travel, and to highly regulated travel, at that. No jaywalking, stick to the bike lanes, keep to the right. Thomas Blom Hansen and Oskar Verkaaik have noted Richard Sennett's characterization of modern cities as "bland, impersonal, homogenizing spaces that remove the threat of social contact: the mall, the gated community, the ever-moving highway." Hansen and Verkaaik, seeking to understand the "urban charisma" of postcolonial cities, argue that this vision is an essentially North American view.[13] Such a relatively "hygienic" North American expectation about urban life is already part of the habitus of many visitors to Beijing.

Visitors from the "First World" tend to find themselves surprised, charmed, or discomfited (often all three at once) by Chinese street life. Most of Beijing is not bland, impersonal, or homogenizing, especially when one considers both the core of the old city and the suburban districts and the outer counties, where rapid and rather chaotic commercial development is encouraged. Even in 2008, after significant clean-up campaigns limiting sidewalk vending, meant to render the city more beautiful and hygienic for the 2008 Olympics, the great numbers of people doing all manner of things on the streets was still impressive.

In the summer of 2007, Judith Farquhar made the following notes after a few walks through the neighborhood of her hotel near the Drum Tower:

Walking home from visiting with E. about 10:00 last night, I almost stumbled on a little old guy in only his undershorts squatting on the sidewalk washing clothes in a basin. It was only then that I noticed two enclosures made of sheet metal on the sidewalk where construction workers are living (though I can't see what in the immediate neighborhood is really under construction). A bunch of the men were already asleep on mats on the sidewalk outside their metal lean-tos; it must be way too hot and crowded inside those sheds for sleeping.

On the way out earlier in the day I noticed a man helping his aged father take a sponge bath (partly clothed) with a basin in their semi-enclosed front yard abutting the street. And of course this neighborhood has all the other street and sidewalk activity that one associates with Beijing. Bicycle repair stations with tools spread out on oily drop cloths. People squatting on the stoop in the morning washing hair and brushing teeth. An old man dozing in a small front yard with his birdcages. A taxi depot spreads car washing and repairs out all over the sidewalk, as does a motorcycle repair shop. Amid the mess there is often a small table where workers eat their meals. Families also put tables for eating on the sidewalk outside their front doors while all the rest of us go by on our various missions. When there's not food on these tables there might be card games or chess games going on. Or homework. Children play, and adults play with babies, perched on stools in the middle of the sidewalk. A few closely tended pet dogs are allowed to explore. Some people on bikes use the sidewalk instead of the street, at least for the few longer sections not obstructed by somebody's everyday life. Three-wheeler bike carts are parked higgledy-piggledy on the sidewalk; not to mention the vans and private cars, since there is no room for parking along these streets (like so many other streets in the city). There are piles of sand and bricks on the sidewalks for small construction projects inside the buildings; little sand wells for mixing concrete; piles of construction debris that eventually will be removed.

A "Vacant" Lot

Over a period of years, it has been possible to track the transformation of a small vacant lot near the old stone bridge on Di'anmen Street. In 2001, it was a vacant lot with nothing but packed dirt and some old wooden cable spools (used as card tables) ranged outside the south wall of a closed and decrepit temple. Players of card games, Go (*weiqi* 围棋), and elephant chess (*xiangqi* 象棋) gathered there in all weather to indulge their gaming habits in regular groups of neighbors. A couple of years later, the lot's size had been substantially reduced as the temple grounds were closed off for renovations, but card players still gathered there, winter and summer. By 2007, however, the temple had been fixed up — it was eventually restaffed with a few monks and opened to the public — and the adjacent space had been improved as a landscaped vest-pocket park, still unwalled and still in use by gaming locals. One Beijinger I know, witnessing developments of this sort, also mentioned the construction at Xizhimen of a vast plaza over the highway heading west. Several of us had noticed how women's folk-dance group (*yangge* groups, see below) had long occupied the highway verges and underpasses with their evening practice sessions and performances, refusing to let the rushing traffic deter them from using an available space as their neighborhoods were being "urban redeveloped." After talking with a few of these dancers, who insisted that they had a "right" to any such space and used it partly to sustain that right, our friend felt that the users of "vacant" neighborhood space assert powerful claims over space with their seemingly casual play. They essentially dispose themselves to "say" that the space is not vacant, it is in use, and this use must be accommodated as the city develops. In some cases, it has been.[1]

---

1. For a somewhat contrasting argument, see Paul E. Festa, "Mahjong Politics in Contemporary China: Civility, Chineseness, and Mass Culture," *Positions: East Asia Cultures Critique* 14.1 (Spring 2006), pp. 7–35. Festa sees the politics of mahjong and public space as aspects of the moral regulation of mass culture from above.

Also on the sidewalks, people sit and peel or clean vegetables. Washing is hung out to dry on coat hangers dangling from traffic signs. Floor mops are propped up against light poles to dry. Plastic bottle and aluminum can scavengers make their rounds of the (still too rare) trash bins, competing with the junk recyclers slowly peddling their three-wheelers and filling the back alleys with their calls for "old things." Beauty parlors (of which there are four or five every hundred yards in this neighborhood) drape washed towels to dry over bicycles, signs, and wires strung between trees. At a couple of points along the street between the Deshengmen Watchtower and the Drum Tower, city-sponsored exercise parks, with their bright-colored aerobic and resistance machines, are in use in the cooler hours of morning and evening. And even in the heat of the afternoon, groups of kids or retirees gather in shady places just to hang out.

And this is not a neighborhood known for its crowds! Most of the snack-food vending has been moved indoors (some restaurants now have sales windows opening onto the street), and bicycle parking has been significantly reduced since residents grew so much more dependent on buses, the subway, taxis, and private cars. The neighborhood committees still post the daily newspapers on bulletin boards, and people still stop to read them, standing up and stepping sideways from page to page. Some corners or vacant lots are known as locations for pick-up card games, mahjong, and chess. One gets the overwhelming impression of private life lived in public, of tiny apartments squeezing residents out onto the street, of too many objects for too little space. This quality of the street is not just an unwelcome product of domestic overcrowding. It is also *renao*, that desirable quality of commotion, hustle and bustle, collective liveliness, excitement, the activity of crowds, heat and noise, in search of which Beijingers leave their houses.

The street life of today's Beijing is like the *renao* or flourishing (*fanhua* 繁华) activity described in a recent book by historian Meng Yue for early twentieth-century Shanghai.[14] Following Lefebvre in describing the city's culture of "urban festivity," she meticulously traces the energy generated by "a concentration of such urban settings as restaurants, hotels, theaters, shops, teahouses, and singsong palaces, filled . . . with milling crowds of businessmen, travelers, theatergoers, sightseers, small shopkeepers, 'country bumpkins,' rich ladies, prostitutes, and pickpockets."[15] Eschewing generalizations about the universal urban, she insists on the historical specificity of the "polycentric spaces" and "overlapping histories" that converged in Shanghai, producing its particular form of urbanity in the late nineteenth and early twentieth centuries.[16] This Shanghai includes much more theater, vice, and violence than any city in the People's Republic of China since 1949 has allowed, but her vision of a cosmopolitan, "street-oriented" city is nevertheless recalled by the everyday life of Beijing's old neighborhoods, even today.

This comparison of contemporary Chinese cities to prerevolutionary flourishing is not just ours. The Beijing City Planning Exhibition Hall supports its emphasis on simultaneous modernization and restoration with a strong reference to the teeming city of the past. A specially commissioned mural depicting the north-south axis of the center city in 1936 for a long time occupied a custom-made oval room at the heart of the permanent exhibits. In 2010, the oval room was repurposed, and the mural was remounted as a long video crawl. In a classical style, but with modern ambition and thoroughness of detail, the painting depicts streets full of people, animals, and vehicles, lined with stores and theaters and anchored by imperial architecture (by 1936, many such buildings were open to the public). The diversities depicted in this *Heavenly Thoroughfare and Cinnabar Palaces* streetscape are strongly akin to those listed by Meng Yue in her description of 1920s Shanghai. But in the case of this recent mural, they tend to be flattened and romanticized into a vision of a "flourishing" and *renao* city that was nevertheless benign, clean, safe, and well controlled.

There are important differences between prewar cities and today's Beijing, of course, though one feels that city planners are trying to forget many of them. Decades of revolutionary mobilization and socialism left their mark on both the physical form of the city (with its Soviet-style office buildings and ring-road structure) and on the habits of daily life (work-unit and street-committee organization of collective life are still influential).[17] The processes of globalization at work in Chinese cities today are quite different from the colonizing forces that produced nineteenth-century Shanghai. Particular ways of doing business, seeking pleasure, sustaining bodily life, reproducing family ties, and performing duties are activities that make place and pass time in characteristically contemporary, as well as characteristically Beijing ways. They generate forms of life that proliferate over and above or outside of the predictions of city planners or the generalizations of urban sociologists. As Thomas Osborne and Nikolas Rose note, "cities seep out at the edges."[18] These are forms of life that cannot be fully explained by economic rationality, by the pressure of population, or by the imperatives of producing an Olympic Beijing for international consumption. These lives are overfull of unique frustrations and pleasures for residents steeped in a modern Chinese historical experience.

The excess of meaning in everyday life is productive, and in Beijing, this overflow becomes particularly evident in *yangsheng*. *Yangsheng* practice contributes to urban complexity *as* excess. It is more than individual self-cultivation; it is also a form of engagement with and contribution to the cultural form and life of the city. It is more than an effective health regime; it is also a source of unproductive pleasure. It is more than an elaboration of Maoist collective physical cultivation; it is also a forward-looking way of producing a new human nature.[19] It is more than a practice of ancient Chinese medicine and ethics; it is also an appropriation of global concerns with the modern good life. And so on. In the next section, then, we turn to some of the ways Beijingers gather and dispose themselves as neighbors or co-residents, at the same time gathering and disposing their own lives, and in the process inform the development of their capital city.

"The City Is an Oeuvre"

As Henri Lefebvre has put it, "If there is production of the city, and social relations in the city, it is a production and reproduction of

59

human beings by human beings, rather than a production of objects."
It is thus that "the city is an *oeuvre*, closer to a work of art than to a
simple material product": "The city has a history; it is the work of a
history, that is, of clearly defined people and groups who accomplish
this *oeuvre* in historical conditions. Those conditions, which simultaneously enable and limit possibilities, are never sufficient to explain
what was born of them, in them, by them."[20]

The urban life of Olympic-era Beijing, an *oeuvre* produced by
human beings and for human beings, is being deliberately produced
in several senses and at several levels. Not every Beijing neighborhood is so teeming as the Drum Tower neighborhood described in
the field notes we cited at the beginning of this chapter; the life of
its streets does not everywhere indicate a spontaneous overflow of
natural life. Shaped by the heavy hand of a city administration and a
national government who see high stakes in Beijing's international
image, the physical form of the city is deliberately being built as a
relatively purified transnational space, simultaneously ultramodern
and traditional Chinese. The developmental trajectory of all the
planning, razing, and construction always underway literally moves
away the street life we described above, moving in a new spatial
imaginary of modernist simplicity and high-gloss surfaces and apparently losing the urban charisma of the East Asian city.[21]

As Lefebvre says, after many denunciations of the modernist
project he calls "planning thought," "on the ground, the bulldozer
realizes 'plans.'"[22] Similarly, Walter Benjamin noted that Baron
Haussmann, the great architect of Paris's boulevards, referred
to himself as a "demolition artist."[23] And Lewis Mumford, in his
history of the city, remarked that "long before the invention of bulldozers, the Italian military engineer developed, through his professional specialization in destruction, a bulldozing habit of mind."[24]
City planners and architects, responding to the imperatives of China's globally visible development, imagine and then facilitate, on
land once occupied by much humbler buildings, the rapid construction of ultramodern office buildings, highways, performance spaces,
malls, and museums. In these gleaming buildings they aggressively

produce a Beijing that can outmodern any global city, and they fundamentally alter public space. In true postmodern style, Qing dynasty architectural elements are freely scattered about. Nowadays, there are many neighborhoods—the Embassy District, the Wang-fujing Shopping Street, the streets inside multibuilding high-rise apartment complexes, the cities within a city occupied by foreigners and the new rich (Soho at Dabeiyao is an example)—where places for working and resting, shopping and socializing, and even the people on the streets very much resemble the hypothetical and hygienic loveliness of architects' renderings.

This mass-produced quality, in which the street life enabled by planned new construction comes to approximate an ideal imagined by some cosmopolitan middle-class architect, was strikingly obvious on huge signs put up in 2007 both announcing and hiding the construction of a new retro-style, mixed-use development at Qianmen, just south of Tiananmen Square. The Qianmen Historical Culture District now covers acres where low-rise housing was recently razed.[25] The architectural and planning aesthetic of the development claims to have produced a return to the teeming Beijing of 1936, the same year invoked by the mural, *Heavenly Thoroughfare and Cinnabar Palaces*. This year is a cleverly chosen moment before the Japanese occupation, before the complications of "actually existing socialism," but after a great deal of cultural modernization in eastern Chinese cities. Thanks to the miracle of large-scale digital photography, the construction barriers were decorated with huge composite images of the designed future that look quite natural—snapshots of actual pedestrians and vehicles in the Qianmen and Tiananmen areas digitally pasted in the foreground of a not-yet-realized landscape, their feet and wheels sometimes floating ever so slightly above the virtual pavement. Small families with the regulation one child, backpack-wearing foreign college students, businessmen in Italian suits, pretty girls arm-in-arm, one or two white-haired, but vigorous elderly people—these images give a contemporary or futuristic daily-life quality to the nostalgic promises of the new-old architecture springing up in this classically urban neighborhood.[26]

The buildings in the new Qianmen are only a few stories tall, include fairly dense housing, and provide many spaces for commercial activity as well as a wide pedestrianized street to accommodate shoppers. True *renao* was a bit slower to appear. Planners seem to hope that mundane street life similar to what we described in the Drum Tower neighborhood (but tidier) will reemerge. If it does, it will be a further demonstration that even the most "natural" and "spontaneous," even the most "typically Chinese" aspects of urban life are "a production and reproduction by human beings and for human beings," an aspect of the *oeuvre* that is Olympic-era Beijing.

However, as Lefebvre notes, "The eminent use of the city ... is *la Fête* (a celebration which consumes unproductively, without other advantage but pleasure and prestige and enormous riches in money and objects)."[27] Will the Qianmen Historical Culture District ever overcome the theme-park quality so evident in its advance advertising? This nostalgic retrieval of the imagined presocialist capital is consistent with the privatizing trend of Olympics-era planning: new and expensive apartments, as they spread throughout the high-priced real estate of the center city, will probably move more of daily life inside locked doors and compound gates; street life in the district may come to be dominated by isolated individuals moving from point A to point B; gates manned by security guards and multiply locked steel doors will protect a more luxurious private life—developments like these make fundamental changes in the culture of the city, including a containment and reduction of what Lefebvre would see as its unproductive public festivity.

Lefebvre would denounce recent development in Beijing as a regrettable triumph of planning thought.[28] New office blocks privatize and narrow the range of encounters between people; gated forests of high-rise apartments render communities superficially more homogeneous; the beautification and extension of public parkland limits the flexibility of open space; a sentimental and limited view of local history is represented in public sculpture with a complacent official seal of approval. Yet these developments are perhaps no more total a triumph than the uncertain contemporary hegemony of neoliberal thought or bourgeois modernity, those globalizing cultural and practical forms to which urban planning and demolition contribute. If "conditions...are never sufficient to explain what was born of them, in them, by them," as Lefebvre argued, then it would follow that no matter how well we scholars understand the conditions for the future now coming into existence, we cannot predict what urban phenomena will be "born," what kind of city will "seep out at the edges."

Paul Rabinow, with an eye to anthropological method, has extensively explored this dilemma in theory: "If one no longer assumes that the new is what is dominant, to use Raymond Williams' distinction, and that the old is somehow essentially residual, then the question of how older and newer elements are given form and worked together, either well or poorly, becomes a significant site of inquiry. I call that site the contemporary."[29] Duanfang Lu, one of the few China urbanists who base their insights on both ethnography and archival research, has an even more powerful vision of the historical dynamic in the contemporary moment. Drawing on a Freudian notion of the return of the repressed, she accounts especially well for the degree of investment Beijingers have in the modernizing process of regenerating tradition. She argues that "the debris that has been smashed by the previous storm is more than just a residue: it holds the potential to bring about another storm."[30] In her work, to which we will return below, the agonistic, unpredictable, and generative character of new/old urban forms is very clear. We cannot know what will be born of the city's contemporary form.

Those of us who have often strolled in the neighborhoods where evening visiting on front stoops takes place in pajamas and where any open space can be used to offer a needed service at a low price, where homework is done at sidewalk tables and shade trees provide more comfort than air-conditioning in the hot summers, fear that the particular form of "teeming" life we describe here is ultimately doomed. The "Demolish" (*chai* 拆) mark that appears on many nearby structures gives us ambivalent regrets, and we hate to hear the bulldozers of the planners rumble just a few blocks away.

63

But the teeming daily life that seems to be destroyed by any shift into more private, "bourgeois" styles of urban spacetime[31] is also in a strict sense artificial; it has always been contingent on some kind of urban imaginary and deliberate program. Why should it be seen as somehow more "authentic" than the street life now being planned into existence in hypermodern Beijing? To see such relatively long-standing forms of life as belonging unequivocally to a more natural past is to deny the constitutive hybridity and the political character of social and cultural production suggested by Rabinow and Lu. All forms of urban life are artificial in the literal sense, made by human arts: though they are always complex beyond the conscious purposes of planners or users, these activities nevertheless arise from particular conditions crafted "by human beings for human beings."

The masters of demolition notwithstanding, then, ordinary people who are the witnesses of rapid structural change in Beijing take for granted the notion that "the city is an *oeuvre*" of their own making. They make their contribution to its crafting in their daily practices. They claim for their own lives all available spaces in the streets, the vacant lots, the parks. In doing so, they take the modern Chinese concept of "the people" quite literally, peopling the city in a self-consciously Chinese way. Seeking to be "civilized" (*wenming* 文明) in their arts of nurturing life,[32] emphasizing the traditional and historical character of much of what they do to nurture life, Beijingers dispose their bodies as citizens wherever bodily comforts, social gratification, and cultural enjoyments can be cultivated. Thousands of particular lives humanize the streets, each a minor *oeuvre*, every one responding to conditions that are "never sufficient to explain what was born of them, in them."

A Morning Walk

In order to continue to bear witness to the peopling and civilizing of Beijing's space and time, let's take a walk around some of Beijing's parks, beginning early in the morning, at first light. It doesn't matter what the season of the year is, some of the same life-nurturing scenes are visible everywhere and every day. In the coldest months of the winter, some activities cease for a few months or take place only in the middle of the day, when the winter sun has warmed the parks a bit. In the hottest days of the summer, everything is done either in the early morning or late in the day to avoid the heat. But whether bundling up in the winter or rising well before sunup in the summer, a lot of Beijingers daily head for the parks to nurture their lives in public.

One very popular form of *yangsheng* is calisthenics, and no matter which park we start our walk in, in the most wide-open spaces between dawn and about 7:30 we will find groups of middle-aged and elderly people doing group exercises. Calisthenics is a form of *yangsheng* that is usually done in groups.[33] In the wide plaza at the south end of the Houhai lake system, for example, 75 to 100 people routinely gather to do their morning exercises, guided by one or several leaders who call out each exercise in turn, counting off the repetitions.

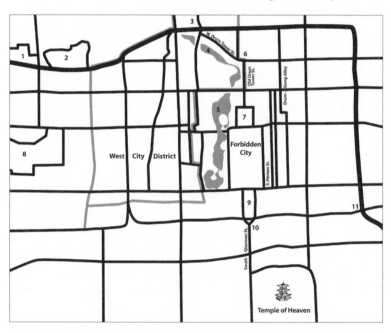

Parks in downtown Beijing. 1. Purple Bamboo Park. 2. Beijing Zoo. 3. Deshengmen. 4. Houhai Lakes. 5. Beihai Park. 6. Drum Tower. 7. Coal Hill. 8. Yuyuantan Park. 9. Tiananmen Square. 10. Qianmen.

Calisthenics groups tend to be large, so some leaders use a microphone or an amplified tape recorder to reach everyone with their directions. Touching toes, twisting at the waist, pounding fists on the lower back and legs, rotating outstretched arms, rolling the head, swiveling the hips—all these and many more separate actions are built into a comprehensive regime that gets bodies moving and keeps joints limber.

Most of those who join daily calisthenics groups are past the age of their greatest vigor. Though they have sought out a public place for this physical activity and join large numbers of others to do it, exercisers do not seem to perform for an audience. The visual aesthetics of calisthenics in Beijing parks has nothing to do with elegance, and for the American who watches, it is odd for something as personal as an exercise regime, with all its unavoidable awkwardness, to be unself-consciously performed in such a public place. Perhaps this is not so different from doing laundry or homework on the sidewalk near home, though.

Moreover, most of the exercises people perform seem so minimal and gentle as hardly to qualify as a physical discipline. Those who prefer this form of *yangsheng*, however, emphasize not physical rigor, but regularity and repetition. Getting out into the fresher air of parks, being around other people, and moving and stimulating all parts of the body for a sustained period (half an hour to forty-five minutes) every day are all activities considered to be good for nurturing life and maintaining health in the course of aging. They are also felt to be enjoyable, not just a technique or a means to a healthy maturity, but an intrinsic element of the pleasure one can take in life after retirement.

It is, after all, retired people who can best devote time to nurturing life. No longer required to get up early and send young children to school or to catch an early bus for a long ride to work, retirees can seek out their own pleasures when they rise early, the result, they say, of long custom. Often combining a daily trip to a street-corner vegetable market with a regular exercise regime or having chats with *yangsheng* acquaintances during a long walk or a bus ride that takes them a distance from home, older Beijingers have more control of their own time than their hard-working grown children or grandchildren. As will be noted below, the relatively young mandated retirement age of forty-five for many women and fifty to fifty-five for most men (at least in Beijing's center city) makes for a cohort of healthy urbanites with time to spare.[34] *Yangsheng* culture provides these Beijingers with meaningful, pleasant, and inexpensive pastimes.

Many retirees can be found, as we walk in the early morning parks, doing other morning *yangsheng* activities besides calisthenics, and in some of these activities they are joined by still-working younger people. Early morning joggers around the Beihai or Houhai lakes, or around Coal Hill, include men and women in their twenties or thirties alongside older, but still athletic men (not many older women jog). As the time comes for the working day to start, the joggers thin out, but other activities gear up. Once we have passed the large group that makes use of the plaza at the south end of Houhai for calisthenics, we can proceed along either shore of the lake, joining the individuals or groups of two or three who take long walks, circumambulating the Back and West Lakes every day. Walking, we found in our 200 short interviews, was the most popular form of *yangsheng* exercise.

But there are so many others. In a children's play area on the southwest side of Houhai, three days a week, we might encounter a group of about forty women who practice folk dances with a teacher; later in the day, preschool children, many of them tended by their grandparents, will be driving go-carts in this space. Not far from these dancers, a small group of choral singers belts out the popular songs of a generation ago, following words handwritten by a fellow singer on a big sheet of paper. In this part of the lake's-edge park, from very early in the day, dog walkers sit alongside the main sidewalk, talking with other dog lovers while watching their tiny pets play and fight (large dogs in Beijing are illegal, or very expensive to license, or both). Smaller groups—three to ten people—of *qigong* practitioners find quiet corners for their slow-moving form of meditation; *taiji quan* and *taiji* sword groups, in slightly larger numbers, utilize wide spaces in the lanes or sidewalks to exercise their art of giving form to space.[35]

Song Lyrics

The songs translated below were among the nationalist and revolutionary anthems popular among choral singers in Beijing's public parks from 2003 to 2007. These versions were taken from a photocopied songbook we bought for two yuan (about U.S. $0.25) in Beihai Park. The cover page reads: *Everybody Sing, Collected Lyrics of 180 Songs*. At the bottom of the cover page are the words "Sing! Be happy! Be healthy!"

Eulogy to Heroes

(*Yingxiong zange* 英雄赞歌, words by Gong Mu)

A song of heroes rolls in the smoky wind, amid green mountains
    it rings in our ears, rings in our ears!
Like thunder on a clear day, striking its metal drums.
Vast ocean waves crash in harmony,
The people's army drives out tigers and leopards,
Risking their lives, heeding not death, protecting the peace.
Why is our battle flag as lovely as a painting?
    Stained by the blood of heroes.
Why is the earth ever as spring? The lives of heroes bloom as flowers.

Heroes leap from the trenches, lightning bolts split the vast sky,
    split the vast sky!
Their vigilant bodies keep us from the quagmire, their hands alone keep the sky aloft.
Their feet tread the blazing, blazing flames of struggle,
Their bodies glisten, glisten, draped in rainbows.

Slowly, as the morning progresses, these regular activities give way to others, equally regular, but recruiting a more shifting population of participants. If we cross the street from the south end of Houhai and go into Beihai Park, paying an admission fee unless we have an annual park pass, we are perhaps first impressed with the park as a tourist attraction. Especially in Olympic Beijing, old city parks such as Beihai are especially well manicured and especially well fitted out with neotraditional pavilions, fragments of palace ruins, and gardens. They still offer many excellent backdrops for the snapshots that accompany all Chinese tourism. But it is easy to see that many of the users of these parks are not tourists at all, but ordinary city dwellers pursuing the nurturance of life. In Beihai, at the north end of the park, for example, there are usually a few ballroom dancers twirling and dipping in couples, poised at elegant arm's length, to the accompaniment of cassette-taped lounge music. The better dancers are clearly very happy to be watched and to have their cultivated form admired. Dancing with them, though, apparently quite willing to look clumsy and uncertain, with fumbling steps and awkwardly placed hands, are other couples (often women with women) trying to learn ballroom dancing by following the lead of the public-park dancing masters.

On benches alongside the lake's edge, groups of women gather to crochet. Many of these are not retirees, but laid-off workers, and their crocheting groups are sometimes organized by neighborhood committees. The purses and hats, doilies and cell-phone pouches they make are for sale; one goal of this activity is to earn a bit of money. Usually, each group includes someone who is very experienced in this art; she shares patterns and helps participants through the tricky parts of the needlework. Judging from the general good cheer among these crocheters, leaders also provide encouragement, and fellow needleworkers provide friendly support for women whose lives have taken a turn for the worse. Crocheters have cheerfully informed us that this, too, is *yangsheng*.

In the Five Dragon Pavilions along the far shore of Beihai, choral singing draws crowds of at least a hundred people twice a week.

Why is our battle flag as lovely as a painting?

    Stained by the blood of heroes.

Why is the earth ever as spring? The lives of heroes bloom as flowers.

Great shouts echo, big guns roar, swelling rivers and surging sea,

    land and sky asunder, land and sky asunder!

Hands grip dynamite, eyes blaze with fire, hot blood surges.

The enemy's bodies rot into soil, heroes in glory rise as golden stars.

Why is the battle flag as lovely as a painting?

    Stained by the blood of heroes.

Why is the earth ever as spring? The lives of heroes bloom as flowers.

Blessings on the Motherland

(*Zhufu zuguo* 祝福祖国, words by Qing Feng)

They say your flowers are truly scarlet,

    they say your fruits are truly bountiful,

They say your earth is truly fertile, they say your roads are truly broad.

Motherland! My motherland! With fiery fervor I bless you,

    may you always be young, may you always be happy.

They say your faith will never waver, they say your flag will never fade,

They say your trials and triumphs will ever endure,

    they say your principles are truly broad.

Motherland! My motherland! Motherland! My motherland!

    Heart bursting and sincere, I bless you, may you always be strong,

    may you always flourish.

May you always flourish. Flourish!

Here there are a few fine amateur vocalists who take turns conducting the lusty efforts of the singers crowded into the pavilions. The songs are mostly patriotic, dating from the Maoist years of the 1950s through the 1970s, when the state culture apparatus produced most popular music and when everyone knew the same inspiring socialist and nationalist songs. This music stirs the soul, especially as it is sung loudly and enthusiastically by Beijingers whose youth was defined by these songs and the collective mobilizations they accompanied. One of our interviewees, Mr. Ma, spoke of his love for choral singing: "When it's most crowded there are as many as three hundred people, everyone sings together, it's really rousing for the spirit [*jingshen zhengfen* 精神振奋]; the mood is happy and worry free [*xinqing shuchang* 心请舒畅]. It's an extremely good feeling. The first time I went, and heard so many older people singing at the top of their lungs, I felt a surge of emotion; tears came to my eyes."

If we were walking on a Sunday morning in Coal Hill Park, as we approached the East Gate, we would be substantially slowed by the huge crowds of singers gathered there. People come from the far suburbs to sing with well-known vocal leaders at Coal Hill, and no technology is available that can bring everyone together. Instead, there are multiple centers, multiple songs all going at once. One sings along with whatever group is nearest and can be heard the best. Everyone who loves to sing knows which park to go to, on which day, to join a group. Purple Bamboo Park and Taoran Ting Park host large groups at least once a week, and every time we have visited the Temple of Heaven Park in the morning, there has been a smaller group singing there.

Other arts also nurture life. When the wind is right, both Houhai and Beihai Parks provide good conditions for kite flying, a life-nurturing hobby that people of all ages—especially men—enjoy. Of course kite flying is a sport, since it takes skill, but it is also an art; the making of the kite is as important a part of this avocation as getting it to stay high up in the air above the lake. Another example of *yangsheng* artfulness: one of our interviewees brought to our second meeting all his favorite equipment: not only his *taiji* sword,

71

Crossing the Snowy Mountains and Plains [*On the Long March*]
(*Guo xueshan caodi* 过雪山草地, words by Xiao Hua)

(Women's voices): White white snow, dark dark night, high plains winter, food all gone. Men of iron are the Red Army, tested and tempered, they fear no hardship. The snowy mountains bow before guests from afar; with grass as their blanket and mud as their tent, they pitch their camp.

(Male leader): White white snow, dark dark night, high plains winter, food all gone. Men of iron are the Red Army, tested and tempered, fearing no hardship. The snowy mountains bow before guests from afar; with grass as their blanket and mud as their tent, they pitch their camp. Wind and rain soaking their clothes only toughens them, eating wild plants strengthens their will, strengthens their will. Officers and men share comforts and hardships, revolutionary ideals rise to the heavens, rise to the heavens.

(Men's voices): Wind and rain soaking their clothes only toughens them, eating wild plants strengthens their will, strengthens their will. Officers and men share comforts and hardships, revolutionary ideals rise heavenward, rise heavenward.

(Male leader): Ah, ah, Eating wild plants strengthens their will, ah, ah, revolutionary ideals rise heavenward, rise heavenward.

(All): Wind and rain soaking their clothes only toughens them, eating wild plants strengthens their will, strengthens their will. Officers and men share comforts and hardships, revolutionary ideals rise heavenward, rise heavenward.

but brushes and ink for landscape painting, catalogs from art exhibits he had visited, and his broomstick-mounted sponge brush for water-calligraphy. Demonstrating, he dipped his sponge brush in lake water—our meeting spot was beside Houhai—and showed off his calligraphy, writing on the pavement "The Red Army fears not the hardships of the Long March" (*hongjun bupa yuanzheng nan* 红军不怕远征难). As the characters traced in water gradually dried and faded, he told us that most days, after delivering his grandson to school on a motorized bicycle, he would drop by Beihai Park, where a master of calligraphy could be observed writing on the pavement in water. Local teachers of this kind—calligraphers, singers, dancers, crocheters—do not need to have formal status (such as street committee sponsorship) to collect followers in informal groupings that together bring civilization—a nurtured life—to the public space of the parks.

The informality of these small *yangsheng* collectivities is attested to by an instance of relative failure that we witnessed over a period of a year around Houhai. When Judith Farquhar was first living in the area and going out early in the mornings for a walk, there was a group of seven or eight doing calisthenics under the trees near former first lady Song Qingling's residence-museum. They had a leader, an incredibly energetic woman in her fifties whose commanding voice and great enthusiasm for exercise recommended her as a calisthenics manager. But her style was strange. In contrast to the relatively relaxed approach of most calisthenics exercisers, she maintained a vigorous pace and a very muscular, punchy gestural style. Her activity looked downright aerobic. And she had a drill sergeant's fervor. One could see in the half-hearted thumpings and swivelings, stretches and bends of her followers that no one really wanted to be like her. But she was maintaining the count, and it was impossible not to comply with her high-energy regimen.

We were not surprised when this group grew smaller and smaller and finally disappeared. Their drill sergeant continued to appear under the trees, running in place and doing her own exercises for a while, and then she took up the practice of shouting *qigong*. This is an exercise that involves standing facing the lake and controlling the

On Beijing's Golden Mountain

(*Beijingde Jinshanshang* 北京的金山上, a Tibetan folk song)

From Beijing's Golden Mountain, radiance shines afar,
    that golden sun is our own Chairman Mao.
So very warm, so very kind, this light of peasant-slave liberation
    shines in our hearts.
On the great road of socialist good fortune we march.
From Beijing's Golden Mountain radiance shines all round,
    that golden sun is our own Chairman Mao.
Intense is the struggle of the liberated peasant-slaves,
    creating the new socialist Tibet. Ai ba zha hai!

I Drill Oil for the Motherland

(*Wo wei zuguo xian shiyou* 我为祖国献石油, words by Xue Wangguo)

Brocade of rivers and mountains, lovely as a painting;
    the motherland is building a great striding steed.
Being an oil worker is so glorious. Wearing my hard hat
    I pace the far horizons.
Shoulders covered with snow of the Tianshan Range,
    face turned toward sandstorms of the Gobi Desert,
Welcoming dawn beside the Jialing River,
    greeting sunset below Mount Kunlun.
I fear not Heaven, I fear not Earth, nor fear their wind and snow,
    thunder and lightning.
I drill oil for the Motherland — wherever oil is, that's my home.

breathing to generate a deep and far-carrying shout. She had a vocal partner on the other side of the lake for a few days, and they would echo each other's calls. Then she, too, disappeared from that spot. Farquhar soon moved away, but returned to the neighborhood later that year for a few weeks. She encountered the drill sergeant leading calisthenics on the other side of the lake, a bit later in the morning, with quite a different group of followers. They, too, were somewhat reluctantly following her orders, and even over the course of a few days of morning walks, their numbers diminished.

These observations support the remarks of many we talked to, suggesting that membership in *yangsheng* groups in the parks is far from compulsory, and leadership status must be earned. Singers, calligraphers, calisthenics leaders, and elegant ballroom dancers find in the parks a place where they can demonstrate their own form of excellence, and many ordinary people with time on their hands are happy to learn from them, follow their steps, and accept their guidance. But participation is optional and for most has nothing to do with a sense of duty. Even those who told us they did the same exercises or life-nurturing activities every single day without fail mostly didn't. As we got to know a few of our interviewees a little better, it was clear that they felt quite free to stay in on cold mornings, to switch calligraphy or singing groups as they pleased, or to walk to quite a different market area than the one where their usual calisthenics leader could be found nearby. In this sense, the new collectives in the parks are not at all analogous to the work-unit (*danwei* 单位) structures of the socialist past. There is no more required lining up in rows for punctual factory or school-yard exercises, no more scheduled singing or choreographed dancing, no more intrusive public-address system. Retired Beijingers are nurturing their *own* lives, for fun.

The fact that they are doing so in public and so often in groups with leaders is significant, however. Some Chinese observers see more continuity than change in the group health practices of the contemporary city. Liu Kang, for example, refers to "the kinds of collective forms and practices still alive today in everyday life and popular culture," tracing the enjoyment of dancing and singing to a

The fluttering red flag reflects the rosy sun, the iron man spirit fills the world.
Mao Zedong Thought guides us, its life-giving strength builds the nation.
We erect oil derricks on vast plains,

    we drill wells in cloud-shrouded heights,

Oil from far underground sees the blue sky,

    the Motherland blooms with the flowers of oil.

I fear not Heaven, I fear not Earth, I gaze on the universe with heroic heart.
I drill oil for the Motherland. Oil gurgles forth,

    flowers bloom in my happy heart.

Chairman Mao's Words are Inscribed in my Heart

(*Mao Zhuxide hua'r ji xinshang* 毛主席的话儿记心上,
words by Fu Gengchen)

The rising sun shines in all directions, Chairman Mao's Thought
shimmers with golden light. The sunshine warms our bodies,
ah, Chairman Mao's radiant Thought shines as the light in our hearts.

The Chairman's Thought spreads all round, the revolutionary people
stand firm. Men and women, old and young, together make revolution,
ah, the people's struggle draws on that very same matchless strength,
matchless strength.

The Chairman's words inscribed in our hearts, need we fear the enemy's
fierce rage? We have set an invincible trap, ah, we will bury those bandits
and outlaws, jackals and wolves, bury them all, bury them all.

history of Maoist cultural mobilization.[36] Once we in the Western academy—no doubt influenced by the journalists and *Life* magazine photographers of the early 1970s—thought of group calisthenics and regimented dance routines as a form of totalitarian oppression. Why would so many people get up so early in the morning to bend and jump in response to commands barked from a scratchy-voiced PA system? Surely this was coercion or "goose-stepping" militarism.[37]

If it was, it seems nevertheless to have worked to produce a habitus that takes pleasure in early morning group exercise. Now, little collectivities form spontaneously and continuously in the parks for *yangsheng* activity; sociability in public and knowing—at least a little—one's neighbors is commonly thought of as a key element in urban ways of nurturing life. This is in part a new form of social intercourse, one less informed by the older dependencies of work-unit life and made more anonymous as people move in and out of once-stable neighborhoods and exercise groups. People still chat easily with each other, but on the whole, they don't know each other as well. *Yangsheng* encounters may be very good examples of what Osborne and Rose refer to (citing Kant) as the "unsocial sociability" of contemporary urban life.[38] But sociability itself, even when not based on long acquaintance, has specifically Chinese meanings. *Yangsheng* practice translates city social life into *renao*, or excitement, *fanhua*, or flourishing, along lines first traced in China's first modern urban thought. As ancient as the category of *yangsheng* is, the contemporary social phenomena thought of and experienced under its aegis present themselves as a new formation of the hygienic city, a city where citizens thrive. Within *yangsheng*, forms of sociality and collectivity, formed as they are by modern urban thought and the imperatives of gathering and disposing populations, as well as by the earlier collective disciplines of governing populations, a particular sense of urban place in the present is made.[39]

We will return to the emergent quality of life nurturance activities again and again in these pages, attending to the particular forms through which the past—of a *yangsheng* archive, of Maoist socialism and internationalism, of a Chinese literate and built tradition—is

Life Magazine

The contemporary era of cultural and economic exchange between the United States and China began with sports. In early 1971, after President Nixon had made very clear his desire to open a dialogue with the People's Republic, the U.S. table tennis team was invited to China for a series of matches in Shanghai and Beijing. The next year, despite predictions that the huge diplomatic challenge of reestablishing diplomatic relations with China would take, perhaps, decades, Nixon himself went to China, accompanied by a large corps of journalists and photographers.[1] A number of important cultural innovations are now dated from the moment of Nixon's visit. Among them are a marked international interest in Chinese medicine and an emulation, in some countries, of the public-health programs that relied in part on barefoot doctors.[2] But perhaps the most influential visual images of Mao's China had already begun to circulate in the United States, appearing in the pages of *Life* magazine's issue of April 30, 1971.

Life sent its Asian bureau chief, John Saar, and one photographer, Frank Fischbeck, with the ping-pong players. Emphasizing the extreme rarity of opportunities to observe and record life inside a country long seen as "closed" in every way, Fischbeck realized that he had an opportunity to publish a unique visual record of much more than sports contests. The twenty-seven-page article resulting from this trip, unusually large for *Life*, included thirty-eight images, with some single photographs spread across two facing pages. The cover, captioned "Children on the march," sums up the import of many of the photos: a double column of Young Pioneers, sporting Mao buttons and red neck scarves, marches solemnly toward the camera, the head boys clearly taking very seriously their responsibility of carrying the national flag and a large portrait of Chairman Mao. They are not quite cute—only one of the children is visibly smiling—and they might even be a little threatening in their disciplined determination (though it is worth noting that in fact their feet are not marching in step). But they are, after all, children. They and their motherland might respond with "that marvelous [Chinese] air of innocence and honesty" to diplomatic and commercial overtures (p. 3).

actively made essential to life in the present. *Yangsheng* in Beijing today is a historical formation with an ever-renewing life, one in which, as Duanfang Lu has argued, "The past always rests upon the present, competes with the present, and at times thrusts forward to shape the future."[40]

An Evening Stroll

Thus far, we have spoken mostly of early morning and daytime activities. An evening stroll in the public spaces of central Beijing reveals somewhat different *yangsheng* practices underway. As dusk falls, many families are cooking and cleaning up from cooking, doing other housework, making space and quiet so younger family members can do their homework, bathing and changing into pajamas, doing laundry, or visiting, sometimes in pajamas, with friends in their own neighborhoods. Later, nearly everyone turns to watching television. These domesticities are not usually thought of as *yangsheng* activities, though some interviewees did argue that television is a wholesome form of relaxation. One *yangsheng* enthusiast we came to know well said that the keystone of her healthful regimes was "soaking my feet every night without fail and eating an apple, while watching TV." But the evening parks are still active. Even those that are walled and charge admission stay open until 10:00 P.M. much of the year, and though there are fewer people entering the gates after dark, a few groups of life nurturers are regular users.

Yangge dancers, for example: this is a folk dance form with a long history, especially in northeastern China; it is sometimes called "fan dancing" or "handkerchief dancing."[41] Done in formation as a kind of line dancing, to the accompaniment of a loud percussion and wind-instrument band, *yangge* is supposed to mimic the motions of manual labor. The shiny sateen jackets and fluorescent-toned fans or scarves of the more organized groups belie this mundane origin, however. The genre was adapted and popularized by Communist Party arts activists in the mid-twentieth century, but what was once a genre of politicized populism is now understood as a healthful hobby and as a "civic" (*wenming* 文明) art. In downtown Beijing,

Saar and Fischbeck take the opportunity of this unusually long photo spread to emphasize, in one two-page array, the "startling individuality" of "the Chinese people," whom they had earlier visualized as "an anonymous mass of gray and regimented humanity" (pp. 26–27). But there is no shortage of gray and regimented humanity in other photos, especially where labor is shown. In an item entitled "For work, exercise, or entertainment, a tendency to fall in line," a large picture depicting morning calisthenics is described as follows: "At dawn, a group of marchers goose-steps repeatedly past a Peking hotel window, apparently engaging in early morning exercises." (pp. 38–39) The association of goose-stepping with Fascism, or at least totalitarianism, is obvious, and the caption also hints, with that curious "apparently," at a certain presumed secretiveness. It is also interesting that the early hour of this physical activity is mentioned twice in the short caption. At this hour, strenuous activity such as "repeated" marching, lifting the legs high and swinging the arms vigorously, however healthful it might be, could not be truly voluntary.

This widely disseminated image archive impresses us as an important source for a number of persistent ideas about everyday life in "Communist China."[3] Perhaps now, with so much tourist and business travel to the PRC from the United States and Europe, the notion that life in China is characterized by ascetic collectivism and resigned acceptance of domination is receding. But when the question of group exercises or basic practical life is raised, perhaps we still associate, too quickly, an imposed quasi-military discipline with Chinese physical activity. Any such impression is belied by the enthusiastic emphasis we found among Beijingers in the 1990s and 2000s on exercise for pleasure.

1. "Inside China," *Life* 70.15 (April 30, 1971), pp. 4 and 52.
2. See, for example, Victor W. Sidel and Ruth Sidel, *Serve the People: Observations on Medicine in the People's Republic of China* (Boston: Beacon Press, 1973); American Herbal Pharmacology Delegation, *Herbal Pharmacology in the People's Republic of China* (Washington, D.C.: National Academy of Sciences, 1975); and Rural Health Systems Delegation, *Rural Health in the People's Republic of China* (Washington, D.C.: U.S. Department of Health and Human Services, 1980).
3. In 1971, the circulation of *Life* was about 7 million in the United States. Wikipedia, s.v. "Life (magazine)."

some evenings one can hear the rhythms and wails of *yangge* music from almost any point. Dancing groups will use any open space to gather (though Florence Graezer and Stephan Feuchtwang correctly argue, we think, that such claims on space work to center and mark culturally significant "places"),[42] and if musicians are scarce, the music can always come from boom boxes.

Though Beijingers do not all agree that *yangge* is civilized, or *wenming*, there is no doubt that *yangge* dancing is healthful activity. The moves are not hard, but they don't include resting, and the constant stepping, the stylized posing of feet, torso, and head, and the waving of arms and hands provide a good workout for the mostly middle-aged women who dance. And in Beijing nowadays, it is overwhelmingly women who dance *yangge*; sometimes there are a few men who follow along on the edges of the group, though unlike the women, they seldom are seen waving a handkerchief or wearing a special costume. And some larger troupes have one man who acts as clown, leading, teasing, and elaborating the dancing of the formation of women. It is typical of the genre that the male clown is almost always a cross dresser, lampooning the looks of an old peasant woman, with a gray wig drawn up in a bun, secured by a scarf, bright red spots painted on the cheeks, and women's platform shoes. This is not the only sexualized aspect of *yangge*; it is hard to avoid the feeling that these respectable mothers and grandmothers are strutting their stuff. A *China Daily* article from 2004 refers to public dancing of this kind as "shak[ing] their groove thing" and says that *yangge* occasions have a "let-loose feel." Everyone seems to have a good time, no one appears embarrassed about not knowing how, and middle-aged dignity is both forgotten and redefined.[43] Because these groups have relatively stable membership, it is clear that lasting friendships are formed within them; as the dancing comes to an end and the musicians pack up their instruments, women go off arm-in-arm, calling out farewells and promises of future meetings to other dancers.

In 2003, we spent some time observing a more diverse and professional folk-dancing class that convened inside the south gate of Beihai Park. This group was led by a teacher who had taken up dancing when she retired. She had joined a number of workshops, some of them convened by Beijing's prestigious song-and-dance troupes, to learn new styles and genres. She was a brilliant dancer, and thirty or so women paid her a small monthly fee (five yuan) to study with her in the park after dark. Each week, this teacher would introduce a new dance and review old ones with the group, drawing her repertoire from all parts of China. She told us that she was out most evenings, either teaching or studying dancing. This schedule was not a problem for her new second husband, because he often accompanied her to help out; he must have enjoyed watching her dance as much as we did. Her followers included some long-standing members, and the amount of socializing before, after, and between the dances suggested lasting friendships between them, as well.

An interviewee of ours who volunteered days at the neighborhood committee offices, keeping their books, most nights of the week led a humbler dancing group in the entryway to Song Qingling's old residence on the north shore of Houhai. The preferred style of this group was disco, though Judith Farquhar is not sure she would have known this either from the music or from the moves if she hadn't been told. Most of the participants in this group were older women who paid little attention to elegant form; the aim was to keep moving in time to the music and in concert with companions. We asked our acquaintance why she bothered to turn up with her cassette recorder every night, especially after we learned that as soon as the disco was over, she would run home to catch her favorite TV show. She replied that not only was the exercise good for her and enjoyable, the neighborhood ladies depended on her. It was a form of *yangsheng* for all of them, and in addition a way for her to continue to serve the people—a responsibility to which she was devoted—after her workday was done.

Across the lake from the disco group, at the same time in the evening, a veritable theme park of *yangsheng* activities is underway. In a small bilevel park built in the early 2000s, around 7:00 or 7:30 P.M., several avocation groups gather. In a pavilion on the park's upper level, for example, musicians and singers of Beijing opera dispose themselves to perform classic arias (complete with gestures); they attract a small crowd of fans. Below them, a larger and very intent group of fast walkers hustles along the paths in a tight loop, counting their steps out loud and intimidating all who might wish to use these paths for anything else. Closer to the lake, ballroom dancers position their cassette deck just far enough from the percussion and strings of the opera singers, coupling up to waltz or fox-trot, or even tango. The resistance and aerobics machines of the adjacent exercise park are always heavily in use. And the dogs are often out again with their doting owners.

By this time of night around Houhai, apart from these two *yang-sheng* enclaves, much of the lakeshore is dominated by bars with outdoor tables. Young Beijingers and some foreigners begin to arrive and drink just as *yangsheng*ers are going home and local people are turning off their televisions and going to bed; the late-night carousing tends to thin out only by 3:00 or 4:00 in the morning. This sedentary activity is not considered life nurturance, and the expansion of nightlife businesses around Houhai has restricted the space that is suitable for *yangsheng* activities. Of course, we heard many complaints, most of them couched in terms of personal and civic (un)health. Once we asked someone who was giving us a particularly long list of *yangsheng* activities if she could name something that was not *yangsheng*; she said, "Well, I'm quite sure that sitting around all day playing mah-jong, as my husband does, is *not yangsheng*." Similarly, members of an older generation do not see the charm or virtue in drinking too much and spending too much money in a lakeside bar. This means that walled parks such as Beihai, Coal Hill, and Purple Bamboo offer more peaceful settings for regularly organized *yangsheng* activities. But they are less accessible to where the largest numbers of ordinary people live; it's harder to rush home in time for a favorite TV show or just drop into a calisthenics group while buying some leeks. The lives and social worlds of old residents and bar patrons tend to overlap without meaningfully encountering each other. Nowadays, these two strains of city life are often polemically contrasted with each other, each giving a certain meaning to the other: Houhai "bar street" is ungovernable urban excess and titillation; morning and evening *yangsheng* is hygienic discipline and internalized civic order. Even a small, but symbolically important area such as Houhai is a spacetime palimpsest of urban (im)possibilities.

Olympic Beijing, China's Beijing

On July 13, 2001, the International Olympic Committee (IOC) announced that Beijing would host the 2008 Summer Olympics. Beijingers were glued to their televisions; most of the city had been anxiously awaiting the announcement. When IOC president Juan Antonio Samaranch uttered the word "Beijing," cheers went up everywhere; in some apartment-building neighborhoods, people opened their windows, stuck out their heads, and filled the streets with a great shout. In public places downtown, large public TV screens had been set up for the crowds that gathered to hear the decision, so a convivial celebration was possible the instant the word was uttered. Within minutes, enthusiasts from all over the city were converging on Tiananmen Square, even though the best-prepared official celebration had been set up at the new Millennium Monument. An estimated two hundred thousand people reveled at Tiananmen throughout the night; foreigners who were present report that they were repeatedly embraced by total strangers in an emotional expression of Olympic internationalism. One American student spoke of the mood in the square as "collective effervescence" and felt that everyone there experienced a dissolution of boundaries of class, gender, nationality, and language.[44]

There is no doubt that Beijingers wanted the Olympics to be held in their city. A Gallup poll conducted in November 2000 found that 94.9 percent of city residents supported the Olympic bid that was pending at that time.[45] Attitudes were undoubtedly influenced by the massive publicity campaign that had attended the city's preparation for an inspection tour in early 2001 by the IOC, but even so, this was an astoundingly high level of support. Notwithstanding the boosterism typical of Olympic-bid propaganda, however, the city's leadership did not go into the Olympic bid process in ignorance. Nor were city dwellers themselves naive about possible negative consequences. Newspaper articles appearing from 1999 forward reflected the anxiety of the Beijing Olympic Committee and the office of the mayor to reassure citizens that problems that had arisen for other Olympic cities would be avoided. When we were both living in the city and routinely reading the Chinese press between January and May of 2001, we saw many long and detailed articles about planned improvements to the city's infrastructure, long-term "greening" projects to reduce dust storms and air pollution, the ambitious new aqueduct canal from the south to increase water supply, and the future even more visitor-friendly face of the city. Citizens were assured that the development already underway in the city was producing permanent improvements with many implications for everyday life. One often heard the phrase "not merely cosmetic."

Changes were underway well before 2001. It is typical in Chinese Studies to identify Deng Xiaoping's southern tour through a number of rapidly developing Chinese cities in early 1992 as a key turning point for the nation. During and especially after this tour, Deng led a policy shift—or an intensification of an older policy—that explicitly encouraged privatization and entrepreneurship; this is the point at which his vision of "socialism with Chinese characteristics" really began to figure in the neoliberal global order. Deng's dramatic and repeated insistence on an economic policy of capitalist global participation that had been developing for over ten years seems to have reassured a growing Chinese business community that they would never again be penalized for investing in private business. Especially in the north and in Beijing, where investment and entrepreneurship had been slower to develop than in Shenzhen, Guangzhou, and Shanghai, the region began to show an enlivened commercial life in the mid-1990s.

Everyone who visited Beijing after an absence in those years remarked on the rapid rate of change, though some of us felt that we saw little alteration in daily hassles, financial limitations, and social intercourse for ordinary city dwellers. True, Kentucky Fried Chicken and McDonald's stores had proliferated, and these were much remarked upon in both journalistic and academic writing.[46] Transnational and cosmopolitan retailers increasingly offered their branded merchandise in large and glitzy new malls. But daily life in the neighborhoods remained little changed during the early and mid-1990s. Keeping clean (or cool, or warm), feeding the family, succeeding in school, saving money for emergencies and old age, bundling up to use the public latrines in the alleys, finding a first job or getting a promotion—these sorts of things seemed just as difficult and complicated as they had ever been.

But the character of urban life seemed to change more thoroughly in the late 1990s. Judith Farquhar was especially impressed when a friend living in a university district asked her to wait while she stopped into a local bank to pay her utility bills online. Gone were the waits at home for the bill collector, the many slips of paper serving as invoices and receipts, the visits to gas company offices to straighten out an account. Many kinds of information and services were at this time becoming available on the Web, and Internet cafés were very numerous and heavily used.[47] At the same time, our more critical friends grumbled that the old shops and sidewalk stands in their neighborhoods had been replaced by overpriced department stores–cum-supermarkets: "Now there's no place to get your shoes repaired or your watch battery replaced," they complained. They also noted with annoyance the slow, but definite shrinkage of street space devoted to morning vegetable markets, bicycle repairs, and snack vending.

In 2001, Judith Farquhar had a chance to talk with filmmaker Ning Ying about her most recent film, *I Love Beijing* (*Xiari nuan yangyang* 夏日暖痒痒). (See the discussion of this film below.) Thinking of the routine hassles, worries, and discomforts that afflicted the characters in the narrative, she praised Ning Ying for capturing something very contemporary about the city.[48] Ning Ying said then that the film had its beginnings one day in 1997 when she "woke up, looked around her neighborhood, and thought, 'I don't recognize this city, it is no longer the Beijing I know and where I have lived for so long.'" In this remark, she provided us with a watershed date. We think it mirrors the experience of many Beijingers, who just as the millennium was being marked were finally able to incorporate some of the practical modernizations of city life into their daily routines.

In Ning Ying's storytelling, however, it also appears that these same cosmopolitans were less secure, less sure of the future, than ever. Even so, the official vision drawn from Deng Xiaoping Thought of a globalized, "moderately comfortable" (*xiaokang* 小康) life of ever-expanding commodity consumption was being retailed by the media and accepted by most urbanites as a relatively unquestioned good.

Insofar as the urban hassles of living in any global city can be reduced, the Olympic era sought to do so.[49] Rapidly fulfilled promises of new subway lines, better bus service, modern housing, a reduction of reliance on polluting soft coal for heat, more shade trees and green spaces, and more effective trash and waste management translated into at least the hope of fewer discomforts for ordinary middle-class and working-class Beijingers.[50] In addition, the new rich could anticipate a number of novel pleasures. Clubs and restaurants meant to entice tourists would also gratify local consumer desires and provide better venues for business entertaining. Upscale shopping malls would allow the fortunate to try on high fashion, eat, drink, be massaged, and go to the movies, all in the same climate-controlled space. (The long-popular urban leisure pursuit of window shopping or, more literally, strolling the [commercial] streets [*guangjie* 逛街], is well facilitated by the huge new malls.) More and better highways, along with a vastly expanded subway system, might reduce the traffic jams in which car owners and taxi riders sometimes find themselves trapped for hours. For everyone, environmental measures aimed at reducing air pollution and minimizing the dust storms that sweep through the city in the spring were making Beijing more habitable, and highly effective cell-phone coverage was already revolutionizing the management of everyday life. Thus, when the Beijing Olympic Committee and the city government proposed lasting systematic changes as part of the Olympic bid, Beijingers saw a better life emerging that would last far beyond 2008.

But a desire for a more developed city and a more manageable everyday life was not the main reason for popular euphoria brought on by the successful Olympic bid. Much more explicit, widespread, and widely shared were expressions of the nationalist gratification that would come with the games.[51] The rhetoric was and remains familiar. After a "century of humiliation" at the hands of imperialist foreign powers in the nineteenth century, after a twentieth century characterized by underdevelopment and political isolation from First World powers, China at the millennium finally emerged on the world scene as a nation to be reckoned with. Of course, this global influence had as much to do with World Trade Organization accession and uneven trade balances as with the symbolics of the Olympics. And citizens are aware of criticisms to be found in the Western media linked to economic issues. But they tend to think that it is churlish for outsiders to harp on just a few themes: human rights, environmental degradation, workplace and product safety. Chinese intellectuals often argue that the repetitive critiques appearing in foreign newspapers, even though they are not entirely misconceived, are ill informed. (We sometimes agree.) China's internal critics recently have focused more on a deepening gulf between rich and poor, chronic rural underdevelopment, inadequate public health care, inflexible and backward education systems, and even on soulless urban developmentalism.[52] But in 2001, intellectuals and other Beijingers could agree that hosting the Olympics might finally persuade the world that China, warts and all, is a formidable world power and a responsible participant in the global economy and political order.

This state-led rhetoric of national modernization and global competitiveness, committed to overcoming China's history of perceived backwardness, has been coupled with a rapid increase in large-scale building. Superhighways gird the city, and gigantic modernist office buildings in glass and steel rise along major arteries, especially in the much-vaunted Central Business District (referred to even in Chinese, adopting the global panache of the English acronym, as "CBD" or *xibidi*). Decrepit older-model taxis and buses were "sent down" to smaller cities and towns and replaced with sleek and frequently washed air-conditioned vehicles. (Ning Ying notes this process of mandatory upgrading as a source of unbearable financial pressure on her taxi-driver protagonist Dezi in *I Love Beijing*.) The city Department of Public Health in late 2007 announced that by the time of the

Olympics, 90 percent of Beijing's restaurants would have to achieve A or B grades on health inspections. Doubtless, this campaign drove many small restaurants out of business, at least until the Olympics were over. Foreign brands of food, fashion, and electronic gear were readily available, though often at prices ordinary Beijingers could not afford to pay. There was a boom in apartment renovation and interior decorating downtown, matched by a suburban proliferation of new townhouses and single-family houses with yards.[53] Cars were everywhere, not just taxis, but also 1.2 million private cars (as of summer 2007). All service personnel were urged to study English, the international language; English tutoring services, free neighborhood classes, and teaching fairs were ubiquitous. One consequence of all this glossy new urbanism was that a global traveler can enter the disorienting nonplaces of hotel/restaurant/office/coffee shop/bar almost anywhere now, leaving the specificity of the city, Beijing's "urban charisma," safely behind.

All this modernization and internationalization brings along its own form of disquiet. Chinese nationalism focuses not only on national strength, but also on national character; political nationalism is accompanied by cultural nationalism. Even as developers (planners, architects, engineers, and so on) in Beijing must show that they can master, even excel at producing the most modern buildings and services, something must be done about "preserving" and reasserting, perhaps only as spectacle, the Chineseness of the capital city. Certainly Beijing's local flavor is what brings tourists to the city, and such desires for Chinese culture must be accommodated. But local critics of wholesale modernization are also numerous, and they frame their concerns in a discourse of local essences in danger of being lost. In keeping with these criticisms, restoration, renovation, and preservation movements have begun to receive intensive investment and meet historically conscious aesthetic goals under the impetus of the Olympic buildup.[54]

Above, for example, we mentioned the Qianmen Historical Culture District, recently completed just south of Tiananmen Square. Its location alone makes this a showplace, conveniently reached in a

Perpetual Motion

The story of Ning Ying's latest full-length feature film, *Perpetual Motion* (*Wuqiong dong* 无穷动), takes place in a single-family courtyard house in one of Beijing's old neighborhoods. Even though there is a movement afoot among the rich to renovate courtyard houses, after many former residents have been compensated and moved out, this compound still reflects a minority way of life. The kitchen is large and modern, converted from several of the bedrooms; the living room and bedrooms, with windows facing the courtyard, are well insulated against the winter cold, though the family servant must cross back and forth through the wintry courtyard to perform her daily tasks. There is a second-story library where the main character's father once wrote and read; New Year's guests go up there to catch a bird that has gotten in. But they visit this dead scholar's study as if it were a foreign country. One well-educated woman looks into an old string-bound book and remarks, "I can't read it." Throughout the film, a certain claustrophobic intimacy is encouraged by the space; one thinks of Luis Bunuel's film *Exterminating Angel*; people are perfectly free to go out of this space, but somehow they are physically unable to do so. Even when the four women who have spent a traumatic New Year's Eve together do leave the courtyard house, they do not go out into a small-scale, socially welcoming neighborhood public space; instead, they stumble along in the middle of a vast highway, on the move, but not sure where they are going. In this film, Ning Ying presents a critical and unsentimental vision of a particular form of urban everyday life, this time that of an elite class who are both postmodern cosmopolitans and uncritical cultural nationalists. More generally, the mise-en-scène of the film poses the horizontal closure of the "traditional" courtyard (fully equipped with the mysterious, disused second story of the civilizational past) against the vacant, flat openness of the road ringed with the distant high-rises of ultramodernity. Perhaps these seem to be the only two choices for Beijingers now, especially since their own lived past, that of Maoism and socialism, is accorded no aesthetic value and cannot be read.

short walk south across the square from the Palace Museum (Forbidden City). As we have suggested, however, it is not yet clear whether anything resembling the district's former street life will reemerge. There are other, less ambitious renovation and restoration projects, already complete, that have sought to achieve a similar nostalgic atmosphere. Old Drum Tower Street (Jiu Guolou Dajie 旧鼓楼大街), for example, was widened in 2005 and 2006, and public financing was made available for its existing one-story houses to add neo-traditional facades; some of these have become boutiques or small cafés, and the sidewalks are both newly shaded with vines on lattices and multilevel sidewalks, thus deterring bicycle and cart parking. Small spaces on the side of the street now welcome leisurely use by children, students after school, outdoor smokers, and the retired and elderly. Not far away, the East City District invested (we hear) 100 million yuan (about U.S. $12 million) in renovating the long north-south Drum-Gong Alley (Nan Luogu Xiang 南锣鼓巷) into a tree-shaded shopping and eating street with the Beijing Theater Academy at its center. In both of these projects, many of the original residents have remained in their small houses, perhaps opening shops or coffeehouses to serve the arty locals and foreign students who are drawn to the charm of these areas, which are by turns both quiet and *renao*. The architectural imaginary of these renovations is "traditional Chinese," which is to say incorporating colorful molded eaves in the manner of Qing imperial palaces, carved window panels of aged wood that filter the light, lintels that need to be stepped over, and matched couplets in calligraphy hanging beside the doors. Ethnic textiles, Tibetan prayer wheels, and religious paintings decorate many interiors, ambiguously incorporating the remote cultural hinterlands of China proper. At the doors of larger restaurants, hostesses wearing *qipao* (旗袍), tight satin sheaths that went out of style when Mao's ascetic socialism came in, welcome patrons.

In these nostalgic redevelopment projects, the history of socialism, revolution, and collectivist institutional design is, without comment, dropped into oblivion. The past that is actively remembered in architectural nationalism leaves out the thirty-to-forty-year history of Maoism, socialist mobilization, and collective social organization. With the selection of 1936 as the year of prototypical Beijing urbanism to be rebuilt in the Qianmen Historical Culture District, and with the late Qing period treated as the source of "typically Chinese" architectural forms, the built world of much of the twentieth century is thus pointedly forgotten.

This gap-ridden historical memory is evident in the superficial forms of buildings, but a closer look may reveal another kind of remembering. Duanfang Lu, in her thorough study of transformations in Chinese urban form between 1949 and 2005, argues persuasively that the collective spatial structures developed in the Maoist era, when work units (*danwei*) organized so much of everyday life, are still an influential resource for new construction in Beijing.[55] We agree and will continue to argue here that a certain habitus inculcated in Beijingers in the collective era remains fundamental to the spatiotemporal practices of citizens and to the places they make. This practical conservatism is perhaps especially true of those citizens who practice the *yangsheng* arts. But there is no denying that Beijing's development discourse and practice has insisted on significant privatization and commodification of what once were commonly used spaces. Even a "Qing dynasty street" such as Liuli Chang, renovated and pedestrianized in the 1980s, before the capitalist reforms really took hold, is short on public bathhouses, inexpensive teahouses, performance spaces, and street food. The places where ordinary comforts can be found in public are ever fewer and ever more costly. The space of the public overlaps ever more completely with the space of consumption. Put another way, in "socialism with Chinese characteristics"—a term that covers a great deal of privatization—the public and the socialist collective are radically distinguished.

It is tempting, when witnessing the thoroughgoing commodification of space in Olympic Beijing, to romanticize the *bricolage* and recycling, the outdoor sociability and long memories of the city's now-disappearing *hutong* (back-alley) neighborhoods. We could be seen as doing exactly that in the opening sections of this chapter. But however charming it may be to witness residents in Beijing's back alleys living at ground level, moving readily between street, courtyard, and private rooms, socializing in a familiar way with neighbors of many decades, it must be borne in mind that the life of the *hutongs* in late twentieth-century China was a hard one. No one with direct experience of living there would really seek to preserve or return to such a life in full. Before 1949, the multiroom courtyard houses where extended families lived were heated by coal-burning braziers or iron stoves set in the middle of rooms, and cooking was done in tiny, partially enclosed kitchens with only space for a coal or wood stove and a chopping block. Cooks sweltered in the summer and froze only a little less than everyone else in the winter. Water was carried in from a neighborhood tap; to be drunk, it needed to be boiled. The latrine opened off the alley and was shared by all the neighbors, lugging their chamberpots in the morning, braving the dark and dirt just before bed. Bathing required a washtub and the heating of a lot of water or a visit to the community baths.

This life had its pleasures, certainly. When large families had servants, they could shift some physical inconveniences to them while flexibly using domestic space to enjoy the companionship of intimates, grow flowers and a few vegetables, and host friends in big-enough sitting rooms or at courtyard tables. Nostalgia for the down-to-earth carnality and abundant hot water of the community bathhouse is a well-established literary and conversational topic. Memoirists in film and literature also speak of rose gardens and scholars' book-lined studies, of children climbing on tiled roofs, and of gathering the fruit of courtyard persimmon trees or grape vines.

But the "genuine old Beijing" form of the good life in courtyard housing and back alleys became more uncomfortable, perhaps to a breaking point, starting in the 1950s, when the socialist government began to transfer cadres and soldiers, skilled workers, and intellectuals to the capital in vast numbers. Under pressure from the diverse and large population gathered in the capital and compulsorily disposed in newly organized work units, five-story and six-story apartment blocks were hastily thrown up, especially outside the second ring road, but also replacing low-rise housing in the city center. The

93

Long underwear

Long underwear begins to appear in Beijing's neighborhood stores in vast quantities and many styles in October of every year. As the weather gets colder, everyone shifts to wearing trousers, and no one would consider going without their cozy long johns. This kind of underwear is especially useful for sleeping in cold rooms; it doubles as pajamas, and you only really need to take it off or change it when bathing (at the bathhouse, or at home after the space has been warmed up a bit). Getting up in the morning, you can throw on trousers and sweaters over these colorful and snug-fitting garments without freezing and even without requiring much privacy. Some favored colors are red, hot pink, electric blue, and pine green; the fibers now used range from silk and cashmere to a variety of polyester fleeces, Lycra-enhanced. Before there were so many consumer goods available in the stores, older women would devote time in the fall to knitting bulky, sweater-style long underwear for the members of their families, using whatever color of wool yarn was most cheaply available in large quantities. One result, once the cold weather came, was a very puffy and overstuffed appearance, even for thin people, who—because indoor heating was so difficult—wore all their layers both indoors and out. One could see the cuffs of knitted underwear, often in an ugly brown or gray, sticking out below the hems of pants and the sleeves of jackets. How itchy such arrangements must have been! The new commodity and consumer regime still requires over-all undergarments in Beijing's cold winters, but nowadays, these are snug and slim, not itchy, but still warm, and they allow fashionably cut clothes to drape properly over them. This new seasonal regime of long underwear is one aspect of modernization and commodification that none of us would reverse.

courtyard houses that remained were subdivided and subdivided again, and in the process, families divided, disputed, and fruitlessly protested confiscations. Most of the unrenovated compounds in central Beijing now house multiple small families in suites of one to three rooms built of cheap materials in the space that was once open courtyard. Extra kitchens extend into *hutongs*, pigeon coops sprout on roofs, along with TV antennas. Usually there is one water tap for all residents of each courtyard. There is no central heating, though recently, electric space heaters have been mandated, at a cost, in some neighborhoods. There are very few private toilets or bathing facilities. Windows are few and admit little light or air; outlets for smoke from cooking stoves are often inadequate. The courtyard space that remains outside the doors of private rooms is a warren of crowded walkways, rather than a court open to the sky. Floors are brick or painted concrete and walls are crumbling whitewashed plaster. Personal and family hygiene under these conditions presents a continuous challenge. Keeping warm in Beijing's cold winters involves a great commitment to cotton-batting quilts, long underwear, and space heaters. People speak with almost religious awe of the (rare) freedom to "snuggle in the nest" of their quilts before getting up to unheated rooms first thing in the morning. There is precious little privacy and considerable tension over tiny shared and sometimes contested spaces.

Given the difficulty and expense involved in achieving a comfortable existence in the low-rise housing along the *hutongs*, it is not surprising that so many inner-city residents are willing to sell out to renovators and move to the far suburbs. (From there, they then are often willing to ride buses back downtown for long distances to get to their old downtown haunts for *yangsheng* activities.) It is hard to argue with the virtues of indoor plumbing, readily cleaned floors and walls, and central heating and air-conditioning. What is more surprising, then, is that there is still a significant appreciation of *hutong* life on the part of some Beijingers. Many who stay, and even many who move, say that they value familiarity with neighbors and local services, they love the much-used spaces and well-known

I Love Beijing

The third of Ning Ying's "Beijing Trilogy" films, *I Love Beijing* (*Xiari nuan-yangyang* 夏日暖洋洋), presents a rather bleak and critical view of the potentials of city life as seen through the eyes of a young taxi driver. The opening sequence sums up an urban dynamic of mobility and encounter in the language of traffic: a helicopter shot from above one of the city's busy intersections slowly zooms in on a mobile tangle of taxis, buses, pedestrians, bicyclists, three-wheeled carts, and small trucks, all contesting for space in the intersection, all moving through the area of the crossroads to head off in one of four directions. Everything moves, but immobility frequently threatens the larger vehicles, while walkers and bikers take advantage of their smaller size to slip through the cracks in streams of traffic, to fill and refill the space of crossing and frustrate the aims of drivers. The camera begins to zoom out again, revealing the stolid forms of the streets themselves and the buildings that line them—cars and buses that have managed to make the turn stream off northward, channeled between tall office buildings. Those heading south into the intersection slow and almost stop, maneuvering for inches of advantage, changing lanes in slow motion, honking horns at walkers and bicyclists. The different capacities for motion of cars, buses, and people under these conditions of crowding, channeling, and tangling of purposes prepare us well for the painful burden of the film's narrative. In it, Dezi, a taxi driver and small entrepreneur, keeps trying and failing to achieve a moderately comfortable life.

As a driver, Dezi is better able to move than some, and he at first seems to exercise a certain freedom in his personal and business life, driving his taxi all over the city, seeing Beijing as a whole in a way that is rare for more spatially constrained city dwellers. His fellow taxi drivers see him as a Lothario, and he does indeed sample various social sectors in his choice of girlfriends. But for Dezi, every choice, either romantic or economic, leads to disappointment, impasse, and physical discomfort. His very freedom of mobility is the cause of terrible loneliness and stress—there is almost no place where he can stop, sleep, eat, urinate, or bathe. Even on the rare rhythms of urban life—a dance group, a street-corner morning market, the vendors and recyclers biking on their rounds through the alleys with their distinctive cries—and they note that all this is lost when they move to an apartment on the outskirts of Beijing.

One resident of two rooms in an alley off Di'anmen Street, explaining her hopes for a new government loan program that would support limited renovations for her house, said: "I know everyone on this street, and have known them since I came here as a bride forty years ago. I hope with this kind of help we can all stay here." At the same time, we talked about whether the mature tree that shaded her tiny walled front yard could be saved from street improvements. This Beijinger and her husband had few strong opinions about the city's development, and in fact, they were happy to be able to spend part of most weeks sharing their son's modern apartment in another Beijing district. But they had maintained a sense of neighborhood belonging that found more hope in renovation than in removal.

There is a different local valorization of *hutong* life, however, one that sees alleys and old houses as a kind of theme park. One ubiquitous medium through which back-alley life is commodified is that of the increasingly relentless *hutong* tours. Phalanxes of bicycle rickshaws cruise the streets around the lakes and the Drum Tower, soliciting footsore tourists for narrated rides through old residential areas. Tour groups both foreign and domestic routinely fill convoys of rickshaws for *hutong* tours. If the members of the group understand Chinese, they can pick up lore about the famous historical figures who once lived relatively graciously in local courtyards; if they don't, they can at least visually appreciate the quiet rhythms of back-alley life under the locust trees. Either way, Chineseness or, more exactly, Beijing local character, is very much at issue.

If in a few decades *hutongs* and *hutong* tours are all gone, there will be several generations of China travelers who will lament the disappearance of the "real Beijing." In theoretically unguarded moments, we could well join them in expressing such regrets. The Olympic-era planners of the new Beijing, the Beijing of the future far beyond 2008, would like to prevent these laments from gaining currency by occasions when he does stop to rest, the social connections that might be enabled by habitation are depicted as conflictual or otherwise completely failed. His only option is to keep driving; to paraphrase one of Dezi's fellow taxi drivers, if you don't drive the streets today, you'll walk them tomorrow. Dezi's divorce—because he is, as his wife charges, "never here"—opens the film, and his remarriage to a rural girl seeking an urban residence permit through marriage to a Beijinger closes it. Thus, as Dezi and his fiancée pose against romantic backdrops in a photo studio for the customary fancy wedding pictures, we can see little by way of a more stable future for him, even though his rural wife has promised to be financially and emotionally undemanding. Dezi's every pose for the photographer, in every costume and before each different backdrop, is uncomfortable for him; he must lean, stretch, balance on one leg, force a smile or a passionate gaze in the interest of maintaining appearances, in the interest of appearing to be freely choosing this romantic liaison.

Eventually, Dezi foregoes his earlier intentions of making it as an entrepreneur with steady clients, and as the film closes, we see his life of driving a variety of strangers—none of them much more comfortable in Olympic Beijing than he is—from place to place, sharing the intimate, but still public space of his taxi with this multitude while looking out at little more than highways, high-rises, and desolate vacant lots. The community imagined here is even more dysfunctional than the group of opera singers in Temple of Heaven Park who populate Ning Ying's earlier film, *For Fun*. In fact, no community or collective future seems to be imaginable at all. But perhaps that's just the point. As shown in the traffic scene that opens the film, a complex urban system of communication—the Chinese term for both traffic and communications is *jiaotong* 交通—works more or less well to insure mobility, but not security, peace, or satisfaction. The individual is the site of greatest freedom to move, but the whole is going nowhere, even as it offers no place to rest.[1]

1. For a discussion of modern Chinese evaluations of stability and movement, see Julie Y. Chu, "To Be 'Emplaced': Fuzhounese Migration and the Politics of Destination," *Identities: Global Studies in Culture and Power* 13.3 (July–September 2006), pp. 395–425.

producing new neighborhoods in an old style. Perhaps they hope that *hutong* urbanism will continue to thrive even when residents have plenty of well-heated and well-cooled indoor space and don't need to go out in public to use the toilet. As we saw above, they may hope to recover an urban good life circa 1936 without either the nonmodern inconveniences or the political turmoil of the twentieth century. To achieve these sorts of goals, planners and leaders theorize and thematize *hutong* life, just as the rickshaw drivers who narrate *hutong* tours do. But our acquaintances near Di'anmen Street, hoping for a renovation subsidy for their tree-shaded two rooms, have a richer view of the *hutong* life they have long been living. Even though they express patriotic views and nationalist cultural interests, their attachment to the neighborhood is not about Beijing's past or future character. Rather, it is about the character of their own long lives, lived quite satisfactorily in a small space on a quiet alley. For them, the Olympics would come and go while they were attending to a longer temporality of improvements in daily comforts gradual enough to leave old friendships and reassuring habits in place.

The People and the City: Beyond Spectacle

In the fall of 2007, the Shanghai City Planning Museum hosted an exhibit of urbanist art from Spain. The large sign outside the entrance announced its title as "We, the city" (*Women, chengshi* 我们 城市). This cryptic, but somehow immediately understandable phrase sums up a position that Chinese urbanites constantly reassert. Landmark buildings and famous plazas signify for tourists and swell local pride, but it is the life that takes place within and around them that make it possible to say "We, the city." As a warning sign often seen on construction sites in contemporary Beijing, puts it, "Take people to be the root / Safety first" (*yi ren wei ben / anquan diyi* 以人为本 / 安全第一).

This idea, that a city is really nothing other than its people, in China, at least, is influenced by a long experience of acting within a politicized notion of "the people."[56] The socialist rhetoric of Maoism took "the people to be the root" (*yi ren wei ben*) of revolution, of building socialism, of making progress toward communism. The class analysis that dominated discourse until the decline of Maoist politics, the aggressive resorting of society embodied in rustification campaigns, Three Gorges Dam construction, and develop-the-West movements, as well as the fine-tuned social surveillance and control mechanisms of urban administration all indicate the centrality of a population politics at the heart of Maoism.[57] It is no wonder that Chinese Marxism has long been seen as emphasizing "the cultural," producing a long revolutionary experiment, making new people through ideological and symbolic transformation and gathering and disposing them in ideologically theorized ways.[58]

The logic of "We, the city" also arises from what Robin Visser has discussed as a continuing tension between (homogeneous, officially mapped) space and (locally and subjectively experienced) place in the city.[59] This, too, is a politicized process in a People's Republic that—like so many other modern states—continues to transform the built city in the service of self-conscious social engineering. If this is the case, a polemical undertone informs the phrase: it might just as well be saying to planners, architects, and city leaders "You think that your great buildings and plazas are the city, and you think you can plan the city of the future. You might even think the central task of urban development is the construction of a modern-*looking* space to present to the eyes of the world. But we, the people, are the true city, and it is our daily activities, our forms of habitation, our place making, and our gathered lives that will truly generate the future of the city and the polity."

The engagement of our research group with Beijingers who practice *yangsheng* in public has persuaded us that this kind of polemic, taking the people as the root, makes sense even to the most apolitical of city dwellers. Whether they articulate it or not, they daily live the tension between the Olympic-era production of space and the ongoing inhabiting of familiar places. Perhaps it is no accident that the populist message "We, the City" serves as the title of a museum exhibit, a complex presentation of the modern urban essence. In the same moment that the museum asserts its representational authority, this title resists the idea that the city is solely a landscape to be presented to a stranger's gaze.[60]

Even tourists feel this tension between space and place: Judith Farquhar was especially reminded of the problem of Beijing as a tourist destination when a very conscientious American cultural tourist, after spending some weeks in the city in 2007, asked her in frustration where he could go to find something specifically and authentically Chinese. What he meant was some example of Chinese culture that was not generated primarily for tourist consumption. This was a hard question; everything historical, everything cultural, seemed to have been freshly tailor made for the international influx of 2008 and as such lacked the authenticity this American really sought. Eventually she doubtfully suggested that *yangsheng* practices might suit, in that they are relatively spontaneous and uncommodified and they generally embody very local relationships between people and between people and public space.

The doubt stemmed from our view that ultimately one cannot distinguish meaningful personal experience from performance for the eye of the other. This traveler's wish for authentic cultural spontaneity was, in other words, in theory impossible to fulfill. In any case, he was going to have to get up early to find his Chinese culture or go to the neighborhoods and parks at a time when he would otherwise want to be having a good meal in a restaurant somewhere. Nevertheless, thinking of the enthusiasm and devotion to routine our research group had found among *yangsheng* enthusiasts in 2003 and after and noting their refusal to spend money on this avocation and their deliberate occupation of relatively nontourist times and spaces, we felt that by seeking them out, this friend might be able to grasp something particular about the Chinese city, something that his digital camera could not quite capture.

It is fairly predictable that any tourist returning to Europe or the United States will have among their photographs a snapshot of singers and musicians performing Beijing opera in public parks. The music is loud and exotic enough to attract the attention of strollers, and few performers object to having their pictures taken, though they do not alter their singing and playing to pose for the camera. This kind of authentic traditional culture is thematized by Ning Ying in the first film of her "Beijing Trilogy," *For Fun* (*Zhao le* 找乐), made in 1992. This sophisticated allegory of a changing Deng-era city highlights continuing dilemmas of tradition and modernity, urban space and place, cultural spectacle and spontaneity. Its story and images can begin to thread together the various observations made in this chapter about *yangsheng* and city life.

Ning Ying focuses in *For Fun* on a group of opera-singing amateurs in Temple of Heaven Park. The film centers on Old Han, doorkeeper and maintenance man at one of Beijing's few remaining opera theaters. He is soon to retire, but as the film opens, he and the two young men who are being trained to replace him must fill in as extras on stage for a lively battle scene. It's not an unusual part of the job, it appears, though not one that requires much acting talent. The next day, Old Han packs up his few belongings and moves back to the one room he and his wife once shared in a *hutong* neighborhood. His tiny room is utterly recognizable for a Beijinger: the coal stove with a kettle steaming on top, the wind-up Maoist-era alarm clock, the portable radio, the thermos bottles for storing boiled water, the thick cotton-batting quilts—all these requirements for daily life are there. Apart from the portrait of his late wife, the room holds little to keep him indoors, however. This small place, the only one he can claim as his own, is of interest to no other living soul, the portrait seems to say; unlike the visible and rather contested spaces of the opera stage and the theater doorman's booth, this is depicted as the very essence of the private.[61] But privacy and retired life hold few charms for Old Han. After some unsuccessful efforts to enjoy a life of leisure in the city, all of which turn out to be too expensive or just pointless, he discovers a group of elderly amateur opera singers in Temple of Heaven Park.

Once they learn of his former career, these opera buffs treat him as an expert on the genre, and Old Han is able to hold forth on the fine points of performance with great satisfaction. He becomes an activist for the group, eventually finding a community hall where they can meet through the cold winter months. This physical structure seems to mandate new social structures: a schedule for performances is developed, late arrival is penalized, and someone must see to the stove and the tea. Old Han's natural bossiness begins to be a problem, and some singers begin to grumble. Around New Year's time the group enters a city-wide show and competition for amateur opera singers. They rehearse a scene, work on their face paint, and score an interview with a television news reporter. Endearing old men with grease-paint stripes on their faces, they charmingly embody for TV viewers the Beijing amateur cultural tradition.

But the performance itself is a failure; Old Han spoils it by shouting angry instructions to his fumbling companions, even while they are trying to sing and act. Naturally, our heroes do not win a prize. Trudging home late at night, Old Han will not concede that, after all, it was "just for fun." Soon afterward, simmering conflicts splinter the group, and they move out of the community hall, which is, in any case, soon to be razed. Old Han wanders through the city, loudly complaining to his only remaining companion, a boy with Down syndrome and a tendency to babble. The city and culture are going to hell, for sure, and the old man becomes depressed.

Finally, in the early spring, he swallows his pride and returns to the Temple of Heaven, rejoining the stragglers from the singing group, back in the same spot near the curving wall of the Qing Dynasty Prayer Hall. As the proximity of the wall seems to say, these Beijingers are always a few steps outside of China's cultural centers; yet unlike the famous tourist sites nearby, they are the aspect of tradition that can never be reduced to a simulacrum. Their cultural lives are inseparable from the whole situation of their personal lives, and in their practice, their memories, however unreliable, are more important than any bricks-and-mortar cultural landmarks. Gamely, they keep on trying their best to get the opera tradition right, together.

In the entire visual texture of the film, Ning Ying reads people's stories in relation to city form and practice. The opening sequence of the film is a long tracking shot down Qianmen Avenue at a pedestrian's eye level, recording the walkers, venders, bicyclers, and trash collectors to the accompaniment of Kurt Weil's theme from *The Threepenny Opera*. Since the film was made in 1992, the location has only become more significant: recall the representation of Qianmen's 1936 street life in the city Planning Museum and the Beijing Historical Culture District that has now been built where Ning Ying's camera once tracked the *renao* street. *For Fun* captures an earlier moment, showing a reform-era kind of place making in the same space. It paradoxically displays an irreducible locality while setting the scene to the sound track of what has become a global, if originally quite strongly European piece of opera music.

When, after the titles, the film introduces Old Han, it becomes clear that his life problem is fundamentally spatial: his dwelling in the opera house—where he at least knew what was expected of him—is taken from him, and he cannot find a socially rewarding place to inhabit. But his problem is also temporal—his productive life is over, and so is the heyday of the opera he loves. He and his friends gather together a little society, a little city of their own, but they find institutionalized collective imperatives too hard to live with. Moreover, the built spaces that once encouraged collectivism are on their way out.[62] Perhaps the totalitarian tendencies of just one individual are the most to blame (here one is reminded of both a Chinese and American historiographic tendency to blame everything on the megalomania of just one man, Mao Zedong). But everyone chafes under the need for rules when the scarce resource of indoor space and scheduled time is at stake. Nevertheless, life outside any kind of collective is not sustainable, and certainly not pleasant; even the proudest old man must eventually return to a city that is shared. In a complex practical series of discoveries, Old Han seems to learn that the knowledge and power he commands are imperfect, but memory and civilization are still always worth arguing about.[63]

As we write, the future of Beijing opera is not clear. Many venues for its performance have closed, but new ones sometimes open. Even as it has become almost impossible to find live performances of complete operas, samplers of classic scenes offered in teahouses and hotel conference rooms grow more common. Opera on television still dominates the programming on a number of channels. A restored granary in fashionable East Beijing runs a production of a famous Kunqu opera staple, *The Peony Pavilion*, with elegantly designed staging as a setting for respected professional singing. And every public park with a little seating and some shelter from sun or wind, even some very small ones, hosts a small group of singers and their minimal band. Under these circumstances, what is the fate or the meaning of the authentic Chinese tradition desired by my cultural tourist friend? Can a cultural performance tradition be anything more than a simulacrum or a spectacle for outsiders to consume?[64]

The *yangsheng* tradition suggests to us that it can be more. As Duanfang Lu has argued in her study of urban form in Beijing, there is creative promise in conservative cultural practices. Quoting Freud in *Moses and Monotheism*, she argues: "Written history itself is an engine of repression, through which unpleasant traumatic experiences are denied and original events are distorted. In contrast, tradition is less subject to distorting influences, hence, '[w]hat has been deleted or altered in the written version might quite well have been preserved uninjured in the tradition.'"[65] Neither Lu nor we would join Freud in trying to correct the "distortions" of official history, and this reading of Freud doesn't go far toward understanding the complexities of Chinese history making. Chinese official history, in fact, tends to emphasize rather than to repress some "unpleasant traumatic experiences" of revolution in a selective narration of the past that seeks to uplift the people by reminding them of their national suffering. It would also be problematic to seek some "original event" as indirectly informing the embodied traditions of ordinary practice.[66]

All that said, however, Freud's distinction between history and tradition remains suggestive. Quite possibly, bodies, spaces, buildings, and everyday talk *are* able to preserve something that has been deleted, altered, or occluded in official histories. We argued as much, with the help of Dipesh Chakrabarty, in the Introduction. And Ning Ying gestures toward this possibility in her affectionate filming of the endless discussions between the singers of *For Fun* as they struggle to determine the "correct" performance of a particular bar of music or combination of hand and foot gestures. They have nothing to rely on but their memories of performing or of witnessing performances. And of course, it is not only the memories, but the performances themselves that have been highly various. Precedent is the only arbiter of an authentic past, but precedent, like the meaning of the city, cannot be reduced to an authoritative unity.

Any claim on civilization is fragile, especially when you consider that nearly everyone in the group except for Old Han's sidekick with Down syndrome is fairly old. This generation is soon to pass. A few Beijingers we have talked with have seen *For Fun*, and most consider it rather sweet, even optimistic, but not particularly relevant to their dynamic, globalizing city. After all, the film figures the future of Chinese cultural life and urban inhabitance only in the person of a child, and he is a mimetic, babbling idiot. The opera houses are closing, few young people seek training in classical music—*For Fun* does not seem to offer much hope for national civilization. In fact, this is not just a problem of the future: the echoing vocal habits of the boy are not so different from those of the aging performers. All are trying to reproduce meaningful culture properly, and all know perfectly well that this is a difficult, always imperfect project.

Ruins

More than Ning Ying does, Duanfang Lu sees generative potential in the shards and fragments of tradition that everyone, from elite city planners and well-known intellectuals to ordinary *yangsheng* practitioners in the parks, refuses to forget, even as they can't quite remember everything. It is no surprise, then, that one part of Beijing's development as an Olympic city hinged on ruins. There has long been debate about the best (most authentic, most symbolically appropriate) ways to handle the ruins of the vast Qing palace complex at the old Summer Palace (*Yuanming Yuan* 圆明园), burned by the British army in 1860.[67] Debates hinge on the protection of "genuine original relics" and the historical authenticity of restoration of sites to their "former glory."[68] Other ruins are also gaining importance in Beijing: one segment of the city wall, at the

Dongbianmen watchtower, has been partially restored. This project is not a reversal of the historic destruction of the city walls in the mid-twentieth century, but—as Lu argues in her chapter on walls—a return of the cultural repressed in a new form.[69] Alongside the rugged masonry of the wall runs a beautifully landscaped park that offers excellent space for kite flying, jogging, walking, and other *yangsheng* exercises.

Even more interesting is a "ruins park" built in the median of North and South Heyan Street, running just east of the Forbidden City. The north end of this long, narrow park retains a piece of the former wall of the palace complex. Walking south from there, there are not many further ruins to be seen, though one monument reveals an archaeological excavation down to the foundations of a former city wall. But there are public sculptures adorning the little plazas and arbors along the way, spaces where *yangsheng* activities can be pursued. One bronze sculpture poses an old man and a child, both in Republican era garb, playing chess; another depicts a girl on a park bench using a laptop, with a young man looking over her shoulder. A young woman plays a traditional zither (*guzheng* 古筝); another reads a book. These young people are dressed in a way that suggests a generic modernity. It is easy to denounce these sculptures as a kind of sentimental realism, incorporating overly obvious symbolism about a rose-colored past and a wholesome future. But it is also possible to read them as a promise to the people from the city-planning and urban-design establishment. Authorized by the past and its fragments, the space of the city is restored and improved so it can be better inhabited by its residents, in all their diversity, with their 12 million mundane purposes. The open-ended sociality of pleasure seeking and life nurturance in the city's public places, the inarticulate gratifications of embodied life in the city: these are goals for a future beyond the Olympics and apart from the tourist gaze. In any case, they can't be prevented from taking space and making place in a city that continues to seep out at the edges.

Gathering in the summer shade or in patches of sun in the winter, retirees living around the back lakes congregate near the lake to play mahjong, chess, cards, and Go. The groups are informal, the conversation casual. Many of those who play in these spots see the same people every day, but attendance for everyone is spotty, and it is not hard for a newcomer to find a group with whom to sit in.

Starting in the late 1990s, the Beijing Commission on Physical Education began to install exercise equipment in small parks and along the edges of alleys and highways. The low-impact machine being tried out by this man and his grandson improves the flexibility of hip joints with a gentle swinging motion; it is one of the most popular kinds of exercisers in the parks. All such machines are painted in bright colors, powered only by users' efforts, and completely unbreakable. They have become an important fixture of the urban landscape throughout China. Calisthenics is also an important style of nurturing life: in these daily "old people's calisthenics," exercisers count off their moves by listening to an announcer with a portable microphone who can be heard through most of the park. Though the exercises are very gentle, most people do them for an hour every day, feeling that this regular bending, swaying, and rubbing is important for staying limber and free of aches and pains.

Small plazas have been built here and there near the shores of the system of back lakes, and such spaces are heavily used for regular meetings of life nurturers. Here, hanky dancers practice their moves early in the morning. Today, they are not wearing the red uniforms they wear when participating in city-wide exhibitions. At the other end of the back lake, a few practitioners of taiji fill the largest plaza with their twenty-four or forty-eight moves. Many learn taiji by imitating the moves of more experienced and elegant practitioners in such open spaces. Novices don't seem to feel embarrassed by their clumsiness in public, and no one minds that they seek no formal teaching. And in a very small space a bit off the path, qigong practitioners choose a quiet lakeside spot for their meditative daily qi work. These had a boom box that played quiet, resonant directions, keeping their slow movements in concert. Some Beijingers told us that qigong practiced in groups is counterproductive; they felt that such regimentation could not allow inner sensitivity to develop. Larger gatherings for qigong would be viewed with suspicion by the authorities (though calisthenics and singing can assemble very large numbers), but this small group poses no problem for anyone.

Hobbies pursued in public, in the fresh air, are everywhere evident in Beijing. The charm of the hand-made kite is as important as the fun of flying it. Here, a kite flyer is about to catch the winter wind above the water with his kite, but first he wanted to show us his lovely creation. Amateur photographers bring their film cameras and big lenses to Coal Hill Park during a flower show, hoping to produce a beautiful picture. A young man finds a quiet spot near an exercise park to practice his erhu, or two-stringed lute. Water calligraphers demonstrate diverse styles on the pavement in Beihai Park. They dip their sponge brushes into a bucket of water and then work quickly to get a few lines down where they can be admired before the water evaporates and the words are invisible again. Most popular hobbies do not require much investment. Many Beijingers make scrapbooks, knit or crochet, carve name seals, collect stamps, exchange good tea or health tonics, and much more. Hobbyists in a postascetic moment in Chinese history are grateful to have the time and resources to indulge personal interests as forms of self-cultivation after retirement.

Parks are full of music and performance. Here, ballroom dancers dip and sway in a pavilion above a lotus pond in Daguan Park. A retro–Qing Dynasty pavilion makes for a good place to show off elegant dancing, and every group like this one attracts some very elegant dancers indeed. Another group takes advantage of the only cool hours on a summer day as the sun rises in the southeast. Some of these dancers in Temple of Heaven Park have come a long way from their homes. Their purses and shopping bags piled together contain the things they will need to spend most of the day in the shade of the park's old trees, singing, strolling, eating the lunch they brought, "chatting of heaven, speaking of earth." Tourists have often seen Peking opera being sung in the major parks. Many who come to listen and perform wear their best clothes for these gatherings several times a week. A more recent phenomenon, and less specialized, is the life-nurturing practice of singing the songs of revolution. So many people come to Coal Hill every Sunday to sing that there are now a number of song leaders around whom many groups gather. Almost everyone knows all the words; the most beloved songs were all learned by heart at school, in factories, or in the army. These crowds share an infectious joy, singing at the top of their lungs, laughing and clapping after particularly rousing numbers.

CHAPTER TWO

How to Live

Study this *Inner Canon*, savor this; under the guidance of sages, explore and attend to the secrets of the body and soul—in this way, we can again perfect human life and complete the central voyage of human life.
—Qu Limin, *The Yangsheng Wisdom of "The Yellow Emperor's Inner Canon"*

Beijingers, especially those who reflect on life nurturance, are veteran givers and takers of practical advice. Most of them belong, after all, to that aging generation who are famous for believing that they know how to live. Chinese grannies are notoriously assertive on subjects such as bundling up in the cold, the best diet in hot weather, the dangers of iced drinks, and the proper color and consistency of their grandchild's excreta. In the context of our interviews, at least those attended by Judith Farquhar, practitioners of *yangsheng* happily seized the opportunity to instruct a foreigner, surely unaccustomed to life in a north China city, in the arts of everyday life.[1]

In the interviews to follow in Chapter 3, we listen to this kind of friendly advice with an ear for echoes of metaphysics and cosmology, and we return to these canonical depths in the philosophical echoes of Chapter 4. But there is no denying that *yangsheng* advice is usually couched in a language of very concrete everyday practice. Nurturing life hinges almost entirely on the quotidian: the timing of meals or walks, the wearing of proper clothing, the techniques of household management, the proprieties of neighborhood sociability. *Yangsheng* wisdom often takes the form of rules of thumb. Its philosophy is less about freedom, transcendence, or providing theory for practice than it is about continuity, simply living on in a state of moderate well-being (*xiaokang* 小康). It advocates a craftwork of the well-formed life, not a quest for the ultimate meanings of life and death. "The secrets of body and soul" that Qu Limin promises to elucidate in the epigraph to this chapter are all meant for use, or "savoring," in a practice. The rhetoric of this popular health guru is grand: it charges readers to craft a more perfect and complete life. But her books nevertheless acknowledge and valorize the many mundane routines that must be undertaken in such a project of crafting.

In our participation in *yangsheng* activity in Beijing, we sought to read everyday practice and to attend to ordinary talk about it. Fortunately, there is also a large literature, and this chapter is devoted to a reading of it. The popular health literature is too large and wide ranging for any thorough treatment here, however. Rather than attempt a comprehensive description, we follow two waves of health-advice books evident in the first decade of the twenty-first century: first, there was a series of books more or less sponsored by the Ministry of Health, under variations of the title *Get on the Health Express*. The culmination of this wave, arguably, was a contentious little book called *Health Is Not an Express Train*. As the popularity of the "Health Express" campaign receded, a new fad emerged from 2007 forward: senior doctors of traditional medicine (some of them fabricated by commercial publishers) authored popular guides to classical literature and lore about healing, prevention, and the management of everyday life. The very successful works for a general audience by Zhang Qicheng and Qu Limin (neither of whom is publisher-manufactured) that we will discuss in this chapter appeared as part of this latter genre.

After considering some characteristics of this publishing history below, we focus particularly on forms of temporality assumed and advocated in popular health works. The "express train" series made an issue of time in its ruling metaphor, after all, suggesting that "health" might be a destination and that self-care practices might be especially fast and efficient in getting people to it. But it appears that both ordinary practitioners doing their daily exercises and specialists in traditional medicine agreed, after a while, that health is not the objective of an instrumental technique, but a daily, ongoing practice. As we will show here, the classics had much to say about the principles that should govern the ordinary "rising and resting" (*qiju* 起居) of a wholesome life. In understanding the special temporalities of the classically oriented self-health books, we have found works that comment on the medical classics (especially the first-century C.E. *Yellow Emperor's Inner Canon*, or *Huangdi neijing* 皇帝内径) especially clear and inspiring. So, apparently, have consumers; these works have sold millions of copies since 2007.

We attend in this chapter, then, to the everyday life of a popular health literature and the circulation of its common sense. The transit that takes place in this arena between the Chinese heritage of written thought and the practical technics of the good life is not a flight between the sublime and the mundane. Rather, it is a much more intimate movement between various articulated principles of life and the various habits that come to be inscribed through embodied experience. In order to understand how life-crafting common sense is propagated and appropriated through media products such as books, however, some background is in order. People consume these materials in the context of a significant withdrawal of state-provided medical care, a reform-era publishing boom, and a literate public that keeps its own counsel as it reads health propaganda and meets the experiential challenge of staying well.

Privatizing Health Care

As the *yangsheng* movement was gathering steam in Beijing court-yards and parks, a series of life-nurturance and health-care "fevers" (*yangsheng baojian re* 养生保健热) appeared in the popular media. Titles such as *Finding Yourself Is Better Than Finding a Doctor* and *The Family Yangsheng Canon* were common, reflecting a breathless new interest in self-care and healthy living. The imperative tone of some of these books, such as *Illness Is Self-Created* and *A Healthy Maturity Depends on You*, reminds us, however, that Ministry of Health policies have for some time been designed to shift the burden of health care from the state to the family.[2]

By the early 1990s, the socialist health system had mostly abandoned the direct delivery of medical services through government hospitals and clinics in favor of minimally subsidized institutions, fee-for-service management, and private and public forms of health insurance.[3] At the same time, the one-child policy and a still-impressive public health apparatus dating from the 1950s had—at least in reform-era policy-makers' eyes—produced the demographic "crisis" of a large "aging population." If the "diseases of modernity"—cancers, cardiovascular disease, and diabetes, for example—begin to occur at American rates in China's aging population, it was argued, the medical services "burden" for the nation would be huge. A newly privatized, but still centrally regulated publishing industry was encouraged to fill, with self-health information, a space long ago created for public-health propaganda. It is not a surprise that the emphasis in these media products was on the individual and the private family as the reform era advanced toward ever more radical decollectivization. What did surprise some observers, however, was the great popularity of health information and rapid expansion of the self-help media sector, especially after the turn of the twenty-first century.

The *Finding Yourself Is Better than Finding a Doctor* handbooks and their like have been especially popular with families experiencing a pregnancy, raising a small child, or caring for elderly parents. Organized for rapid consultation as needed and incorporating techniques that can be easily and cheaply used at home, these books address the widespread complaint we have been hearing since the 1980s: finding a doctor and paying for clinic and hospital care is expensive, inconvenient, and sometimes humiliating. (Of course one hears the same complaints in the United States, though institutional conditions are different in many respects, and health insurance is more common and works differently.) Medical charges have soared during this period, and even when people have a health-cost reimbursement scheme, they must always pay in advance for care. Hospitalizations, which can run to the many thousands of yuan, must be paid in full before the patient will be admitted. This almost universal payment procedure is experienced as akin to bribery, on top of which, many attest, some doctors expect gifts if they are to attend seriously to any particular patient.[4] Beijingers commonly remark, punningly, that the physician's "white-coated angel" (*baiyi tianshi* 白衣天使) has become the "white-eyed wolf" (*baiyan lang* 白眼狼). The image captures well the fears besetting families, ill or potentially ill, who not so long ago expected to receive decent medical care at low cost from a nurturing state.

Though state subsidies for health services had been eroding for some time already, it was in the mid-1990s that the current dramatic neoliberalization of the Chinese economy really took off. State-supported institutions, forced to raise fees in the face of declining subsidies, were widely perceived as not only expensive, but overcrowded, neglectful, and dirty; the many new private clinics and hospitals were beyond the means of most people. The Ministry of Health began to encourage a new era of health propaganda that turned from educating people to use professional care intelligently—an important emphasis in earlier socialist health-care propaganda—to educating them to care for themselves. The *yangsheng* movement is obviously related to this policy emphasis, and many elderly people in Beijing told us that they looked after their own health so as not to become a burden either to their children or to the state.[5]

The new health-information regime, when viewed in the most utilitarian light, especially targets the prevention and management of chronic complaints. And chronic disease—as its etymology reflects—is a formation of time. Those who suffer from or are at risk for[6] heart disease and diabetes, some forms of cancer, arthritis, or fibromyalgia, senile dementias, and so forth must learn to manage little disciplines and comforts, pains and pleasures, in the medium of daily life. Looked at in this way, then, a self-help literature that should train people to evade the evils of chronic disease shades into a literature of wellness. It is also, unavoidably, a biopolitical discourse that concerns itself with the disciplined and regulated health of the population.

As has been reflected in a series of World Health Organization definitions of health "beyond the mere absence of disease," twentieth-century approaches to national and global medical policy have long expanded their view of the aims of public health to focus in some sense on the nurturance of human life. Almost all authors in the self-health genre we discuss here cite WHO policy. This worldwide emphasis on healthy environments and a hygiene of health behavior has offered to Chinese policy makers and publishers a clear invitation to propagate the language and the logic of *yangsheng*.

The popularity of *yangsheng* in contemporary Beijing can readily be seen as an effort to avoid the high cost of privatized medical care and as a form of "docile" compliance with the regulatory aims of a biopolitical state. But as we will see in Chapter 3, what is cultivated in Beijing's parks and alleyways are not lives of quiet desperation. One hears in so many voices a great emphasis on the *pleasures* of life nurturance in itself; this testimony must be taken seriously. Even the *yangsheng* literature, with its many items of concrete advice, leads beyond the conveniences (and the risks, and the experts, and the policy makers) of the biopolitical state toward a kind of enjoyment that exceeds the utilitarian.

Mediated Life

The reform era in China has seen the emergence of a vast discourse on how to live. In the privatizing and commercializing 1990s, building on a foundation of public-health information propagated by the Ministry of Health since the 1950s,[7] television and radio programmers, magazine and book publishers, and masses of online publishers found an enthusiastic and lucrative market for practical health advice. There are several cable television stations in Beijing wholly devoted to health and wellness; newsstands are stocked with five to ten weekly or monthly magazines and one large-circulation daily newspaper dedicated to health news. Medical experts, psychologists, and even philosophers now provide lectures and workshops for neighborhood organizations, clubs, and businesses. The advertising mediascape is dominated by commercials for tonics, supplements, and other commonly used patent medicines, most of these invoking some kind of medical authority.

There is almost no form of knowledge or commonsense lore that is *not* found in this genre of information. It ranges promiscuously across domains—medical (both in biomedicine and in traditional medicine), psychological, moral, legal, hygienic, aesthetic, and recreational—with a dizzying fluidity and considerable miscellaneousness. The essential meanings and powers of such a sprawling literature, as it addresses contemporary Chinese embodiment (habits, spaces, discomforts), are difficult to pin down or to summarize. Too many aims are accompanied by too many means; attractive advice contradicts persuasive information, all available at the same time in similar sources. For every urging toward a daily glass of wine, there is a warning about the dangers of drinking alcohol; lactose intolerance is noted as a generalized danger, even as frequent milk drinking for all is advocated. The dilemma is familiar to American health consumers. Aerobic or isometric exercises? Cardiac or resistance training? What combination? Whose advice can be taken as gospel? Like self-help literature in many places, the broad topic of health in the media brings to life a hydra-headed monster of information that cannot be stabilized into a reasoned program for daily life. "Consumers" of health information in these circumstances have no choice but to pick and choose according to their own lights.

One thing this literature does share, however, is an improving impulse. With their step-by-step advice, "how-to" books both propose goals and intervene in practice. If you want to keep healthier houseplants, here's how it's done; if you want to master French cooking, here are some ingredients and techniques; if you have high blood pressure, here are some ways—dietary, mental, pharmaceutical—to bring it down. How-to advice presumes a great many commonsense objects: tools, materials, bodies, social expectations, even motivations toward good outcomes are posited without being rigorously defined or otherwise theorized. Authorities speak, presumably from experience, and readers compare written advice with their own experience, adjusting the message accordingly. No one needs to argue for or against the value of a project; a flourishing philodendron, a well-made crepe, or lowered blood pressure simply is or is not a desired end for the how-to book's reader as she self-selects in the bookstore or on the Internet. There is, in other words, a vast sea of the taken-for-granted indexed and touched upon by books about how to live.

As noted above, we are especially interested in the temporalities of life as a process: not just the historicity of nurtured lives, but the qualities of Beijing life morning and night, winter and summer; lives that last long (*shou* 寿) or lives that are ended or spoiled too early (*sang* 丧). The timing and rhythms of life are much discussed in the how-to health advice literature (though death and dying are not much thematized). Our selection of materials in this chapter emphasizes the timing and goals proposed by these discourses on "how to live" and, to some extent, by their readers. *Yangsheng* practitioners often self-consciously craft their daily lives according to principles of "rising and resting" (*qiju* 起居); we will discuss these below. Many people try to live in accord with longer trajectories of aging well (*changshou* 长寿, the time-honored Chinese cultural principle of longevity). They seek to embody past and future in wholesome and enjoyable ways that are both Chinese and well-suited to our global and urban times.

Express-Train Medicine

The Chinese-medicine-inflected common sense evoked by the term *yangsheng* was not at first the dominant mode of information in the health-care fads that swept China's urban mediascapes in the 1990s. Much of the information available, especially the information sponsored directly by the Ministry of Health and authored by its staff and paid consultants, emphasized biomedical public-health advice and spoke more about a medicalized notion of health than about life in any broader sense. Conditions such as high blood pressure, diabetes, senile dementia, osteoporosis, and various forms of cancer took center stage in a discourse on prevention and management. Lifestyle advice emphasized good nutrition, moderate physical and mental exercise, limitation of smoking and drinking, avoidance of stress, and regular medical consultations. In the hands of a few experts, there was also a rather bizarre emphasis on drinking milk. Time itself was rendered as a kind of to-do list (walk 1000 steps, exercise half an hour a day, cook pork longer, live 100 years).

Up until about 2004 or 2005, more archaic versions of *yangsheng* information appeared only in a scattering of the available how-to books. These works were distinguished by their charmingly "traditional" covers and by their tendency to explain a few founding principles of classical cosmology in an opening chapter (for example, *yinyang* and five-phases dynamics) before turning to more concrete advice from the Chinese medical *yangsheng* tradition. Some remained quite classical in orientation, assembling, for example, useful quotes from very ancient canonical works and explaining them in ordinary language. Others were more purely practical: recipe books for Chinese medicinal foods, family massage handbooks, advice on caring for children or the elderly in seasonally appropriate ways. Most of the works that emphasized Chinese medical health-and-wellness techniques adopted a familiar language of nationalist pride in the cultural heritage, along with a style of rhetoric that sought to advance (still-contested) claims of legitimacy for traditional medicine.

In 2003, while we were doing research in the parks of the West City District, Beijing's bookstores were flooded with books in the series spawned by *Get on the Health Express*. The information in these books had been appearing since 1995 as columns in one of the city's most widely read newspapers, the *Beijing Evening Journal* (*Beijing Wanbao*). The first book in the series was edited by a large committee and presented articles under the bylines of three medical experts, along with a list of "the ten behaviors of complete health." It first appeared in August 2002; by the spring of 2003, it was in its sixteenth printing and had sold over a million copies. Over the next two years, the original version continued to sell very well, and a number of more specialized sequels and quite a few similar-looking books with equally catchy titles appeared (*The Red Treasure Book of Health* [*Jiankang hongbao shu* 健康红宝书], *Health Is Not an Express Train* [*Jiankang bushi kuaiche* 健康不是快车], and so on). All of these emphasized basic public-health good sense and included very concrete advice for keeping blood pressure and cholesterol low, avoiding diabetes by controlling diet, getting regular exercise, quitting smoking and drinking, and getting plenty of sleep. In bookstores ranging from the multistory book-and-media malls in the city's major shopping areas to the smallest neighborhood bookstalls, these brightly colored books were displayed near entrances, cash registers, and at the front of health and how-to sections.

The moment had a very particular historical character in the evolution of ideas about health and lifestyle. In August 2003, Jin Dapeng, the director of Beijing's Department of Health, wrote the following as a preface to the second volume of *Get on the Health Express*:

> In 1947, the World Health Organization laid down the following definition of health: not just the absence of disease, [health] is a state of complete well-being in people's bodies, minds, and societies. This kind of definition includes general concepts from biomedicine and sociology. In 1986, the First International Conference on Health Advancement made the famous Ottawa Declaration. This declaration had five essentials [*jingshen* 精神]: 1) Establish and improve health policy; 2) Create a beneficial material and social environment for health; 3) Encourage the active participation of the masses and social groups; 4) Raise the level of health knowledge and technical ability among the masses; 5) Reform the institutions of health care to meet the health needs of the people better. At the same time, an innovative public-health policy was proposed—an appeal for a great advancement in mass health....
>
> Entering the twenty-first century, the sudden global appearance of the infectious disease SARS made a very deep impression on our memories and taught us a lesson; we learned many more things than we had in more ordinary times. The whole society now has a precious [*shaoyoude* 少有的] common knowledge of disease prevention and health advancement. This book is published against this very special historical background.[8]

As this preface to *Get on the Health Express* makes clear, the sudden expansion of self-health regimes as a media craze in the early 2000s was closely related to public-health crises brought on by SARS in

2003 and avian flu in 2004. The contemporary urgency and popularity of health information was a product of this global crisis, which was widely believed to have its roots in Asia. In this moment, government policy took the lead in both public-health action and popular health education. In Beijing, both epidemics were accompanied by aggressive infection-control measures that at times restricted free movement in the city, altered housekeeping and food-handling practices (perhaps permanently), and stimulated very elaborate discussions of bodily vulnerability and the causes of illness.

Residents of West City District, where we did our interviews, when asked how their neighborhoods had handled these alarming states of emergency, often noted with pride that there had been "not a single case" of SARS or avian flu in their part of the city. Asked why that was, they explained that the air is cleaner and healthier around the lakes of the western downtown areas and that people there know how to take care of themselves. They referred often to the kind of immunity from invading pathogens that Chinese medicine explains as a relation between wholesome, "right" *qi* and dangerous or "evil" *qi* (*zheng/xie* 正气/邪气). If a wholesome lifestyle "rightly" maintains the body's specific vigor, pathogens cannot gain a foothold. Though the technical complexities of right/evil *qi* relationships in Chinese medicine are probably of little interest to the ordinary practitioners of *yangsheng* with whom we spoke, these Beijingers nevertheless saw considerable utility, in the face of globalizing disease plagues, for those everyday health-promoting regimens that, they argued, had long antedated the SARS crisis.[9]

But definitions of health were themselves at stake. As noted above, the *Health Express* books often invoke ambitious midcentury WHO definitions of health. The inspiring vision that "health is more than the absence of disease" had served worldwide since the 1980s as a powerful charter for information regimes that sought to alter everyday "health behavior." The assumption was that most people have pathologically bad habits and are therefore "at risk." Public-health information therefore should motivate them to change their ways with its promise of "complete well-being in body, mind, society." But as we noted, the style of advice included in the *Health Express* books focused on preventive biomedicine and avoidance of disease, rather than on any vision of total wellness. Much of the advice took the form of prohibition: restrict salts, fats, tobacco, and alcohol. Then add some daily disciplines: get out and exercise; avoid worry and stress.

Here, for example, are "the ten behaviors of complete health" that make up the fourth and last chapter of the first *Get on the Health Express* book. While the first three chapters (on healthful eating, exercise, smoking cessation, psychological well-being, and lifestyle diseases such as diabetes) often argue that practical disease avoidance is just a part of a gratifying lifestyle, and thus a form of positive experience, this list is notably remote from experience:

Behavior one: Take a vitamin
Behavior two: Take a psychological assessment test
Behavior three: Do some kind of aerobic exercise
Behavior four: Assess your physical constitution
Behavior five: Get a set of health checkups
Behavior six: Drink a glass of milk
Behavior seven: Take a body mass index test
Behavior eight: Get a flu shot
Behavior nine: Take a calcium pill
Behavior ten: Take an aspirin

Here we have a list of activities that is not only very disparate, it is almost entirely unpleasurable. Vitamins, calcium pills, and a daily aspirin are the kind of medicine that is tasteless and produces no other appreciable experience.[10] Getting a flu shot and an array of physical checkups evokes the hassle and inconvenience of dealing with Beijing's overextended medical institutions. Few Chinese adults really like milk. And the self-testing of psychology and body mass implies that the truths about our bodies and minds are unknown to us, not a part of our experience. Experts must be consulted, even if only through a magazine survey. Only Behavior three, "Do some kind of aerobic exercise," suggests an immediate alteration in daily experience. Those with experience of jogging or step aerobics might see this as advice that could deliver genuine enjoyment, but in our interviews and observations, few who practiced *yangsheng* sought to work up a sweat. So it is plausible that even this advice was read as a rather onerous discipline.

This list is quite a typical text for the biomedical self-health genre. Advice is often provided in tidy, numbered lists that highlight the instrumental character of the *Health Express* project. Even though many of the participating writers waxed philosophical here and there about the meaning of life and the satisfactions of regular exercise, there is no mistaking the utilitarian message of the health educator: change your bad habits to avoid disease. Discipline your daily life according to rational principles known to experts; this is the scientific way to defer the inevitable process of decline with aging.

Reading and Experience

Most people we interviewed didn't think their habits were bad. They quietly failed to accept the most common premise of the worldwide public-health message: that modern populations are in poor health and at high risk for the hidden killers of high blood pressure, high cholesterol, high blood sugar, and carcinogens. Very few spoke of efforts to exert control over their impulses to smoke, drink, and eat fatty foods. A number of the Beijingers with whom we talked about food preferred the familiar logic of experience in their dietary choices: I eat the fatty, salty foods I like because this is a way to be happy, reduce stress, be an authentic Beijinger, and so forth. In Zhang Qicheng's occasional efforts to persuade friends and colleagues to avoid smoking, he has sometimes been told that tobacco smoke improves the body, just as wood smoke improves the taste and texture of smoked meats. Again and again, when we asked Beijingers who practice *yangsheng* about the sources of the health information they found most reliable, they spoke of their own experience of trying various procedures, and they noted the advice collected from the experience of family and friends as by far the most useful.

Once Judith Farquhar took a cartoon-style book about medicinal foods to share with a friend (our interviewee Zhu Hong). This good cook in her early sixties liked to watch health-related shows on television, and she often spoke of the medicinal value of some of her favorite foods. In looking over the book, which compiled a lot of expert knowledge about particular foods and combinations (drawn both from nutritional science and Chinese medicine) she turned only to those foods about which she already had opinions. Speaking to her visiting friend, she remarked, "You see? This book agrees with your sister-in-law that turnips are good for warming the stomach in the winter." Using this method of reading, she also quickly found pieces of advice that, on the basis of her experience and that of her friends, she could not credit. She put the book down, having lost interest.

It is understandable that readers pick and choose the elements that recur with the greatest consistency or that make the most sense in the context of their daily lives. But the *Health Express* subgenre had, we think, a particularly troubled relationship to the reading and living habits of Beijingers. Most successful immediately after the global SARS crisis, these books quickly began to seem a little shrill. Their advice was simple and could be restated in different, more urgent terms only a limited number of times. It was, moreover, focused on a form of self-regulation that was designed to control problems most people did not acknowledge as real.

When in 2008 we found so few *Health Express* books available in bookstores and noted that their once-prominent visibility had been taken over by a series of works much more centered on Chinese medicine, we asked a Chinese medical friend with contacts in publishing why he thought this change had taken place. He said, "It's obvious, isn't it? Western medicine has only the same few kinds of advice to offer: restrict fats and salt in your diet, get some exercise, avoid stress.... Chinese medicine, on the other hand, has massive amounts of very detailed advice about how to live. We could go on forever with the helpful hints. Those Western medical books ran their course; now it's the turn of Chinese medicine to show how much richer our knowledge of health really is."

Who buys these books? Do they read them? In our experience with residents of Beijing's West City District, very few of them read books for pleasure or collect books in their overcrowded rooms. Books and magazines are, however, passed around between acquaintances to a much greater extent than they are among intellectuals, who maintain personal libraries. But a great many ordinary city dwellers read. In our survey of 200 people, we asked where respondents found health information: many mentioned health magazines and newspapers, and quite a few mentioned mass-market books. Two of our interviewees, middle-aged, retired men who had made a specialty of *yangsheng* practice, were collecting and systematically studying self-health books because they planned to write their own; a policeman in his thirties spent his spare time studying the classics of Chinese medicine to support his rather dismal theories about human nature; a hobbyist who found his *yangsheng* pleasures in painting and calligraphy showed us a treasured handful of fine-arts how-to books; and a single, middle-aged woman whose house Judith Farquhar visited several times had a well-thumbed collection of *yangsheng* books that combined pop psychology with metaphysical cosmology.[11] When asked, many acknowledged that they might buy a *yangsheng* book as a gift for an elderly person or for a pregnant friend, even if they didn't read these books themselves. There is a great deal of casual, piecemeal reading that accounts for the impressive sales figures of the new Chinese medical *yangsheng* books.

Authors and publishers know quite a bit about their reading publics and design their products to meet their habits and desires. What publishers know is usually expressed as detailed information about what formats, what forms of authority, and what health topics sell the best. Most of the books in the *yangsheng* self-health genre are organized to meet the needs of a reading public that seeks mainly to get through daily life more or less well. The "moderate well-being" promised by the development policy of the Deng Xiaoping era expresses well the state of health and happiness aimed at by recent public-health literature and media products.[12] In the design of popular health books, much is presumed about the modest everyday needs and reading pleasures of a vast book-consuming public.[13] Such assumptions about the "natural" and particularly "modern Chinese" aspirations for bodily and practice life could be quite wrong, of course. But the books do sell—in the millions, in some cases—so here we seek to explore what in these works appeals to the hopes and habits of modern urban readers as they organize their daily round of activities.

Writing for Reading

The authors of *yangsheng* books have much to say about how their readers are expected to read and why they should read. Zhang Qicheng, for example, in the preface to the 2008 book in which he provides readings of the *Yellow Emperor's Inner Canon*, refers to reading even in the table of contents, which provides a short abstract of each chapter:

> Chapter 1: Entering the Marvelous World of *The Yellow Emperor's Inner Canon*. *The Yellow Emperor's Inner Canon* has passed down many riddles to us. Today, we can lift its veil of mystery. We will read and dwell upon [*kanyikan* 看一看] the value of the *Inner Canon* in today's life, and we will read and dwell upon what kind of meaning the *Inner Canon* has for the health and longevity of mankind.[14]

Here, by using the casual and friendly form of the verb *kan*, i.e., *kanyikan*, Zhang invites readers to *enjoy* the *Inner Canon*. He anticipates their hesitation, their possible fear that this ancient language will present only "riddles" to their ordinary eye. Yet the form of reading he says is possible is relaxed, reflective, and offering up significant meaning "for mankind." A veteran of reading the classics for pleasure with this phrasing, he suggests that it will be easy to share the rewards of the traditional medical canon.

Near the beginning of Chapter 1, Zhang takes up the theme of reading, but writes in a more authoritative voice. He invokes "National Studies," the heading under which much contemporary scholarship on the Chinese heritage is currently being propagated:

> China's age-old culture, its traditional learning, and the so-called Five Books of National Studies are essential reading for every one of us Chinese; in fact they cannot be ignored. Speaking as the head of a

university library, I can responsibly say that there are many books that today do not bear rereading, but we certainly must read the canonical ancient works. I think that if we were only to read and appreciate five canonical books, we could still grasp the rich and profound essence of National Studies. The first of these is the *Book of Changes* (*Yi jing* 易经), the second is the (*Dao de jing* 道德经), and the third is *The Yellow Emperor's Inner Canon* (*Huangdi neijing* 皇帝内径). Together, these are referred to as the Three Great Esoteric [*qi* 奇] Classics; together with the [Confucian] *Analects* (*Lun yu* 论语) and the [later] *Canon of the Sixth Patriarch* (*Liuzu tanjing* 六祖坛经) they make up five classic books. I call these the Five Classics of National Studies.[15]

In arguing that the *Inner Canon* is part of a program of "essential reading for every one of us Chinese," this introductory paragraph is consistent with a widespread cultural nationalism in today's China that extends far beyond the worlds of scholarship. National cultural policy encourages expressions and valorizations of Chinese heritage, and hosts of cultural workers, hobbyists, artists, and Internet commentators reflect on what Chineseness could mean or be under contemporary conditions of globalization. (At the same time, cosmopolitan groups such as scientists and contemporary artists deny any particular value or character to "Chineseness," even when they consider themselves patriotic.) Thus, when Zhang Qicheng urges readers to "read and appreciate" a selection of canonical works as an expression of their Chinese belonging, he can be sure of reaching a sympathetic and cooperative audience, an audience that would like to "grasp the rich and profound essence" of National Studies. Reading the *Inner Canon* is, thus, partly a personal pleasure and partly a civic duty.

Qu Limin's massively popular recent works on *yangsheng* develop the theme of reading even more fully and suggest that even where the rather abstruse *Inner Canon* is concerned, duty and pleasure are indistinguishable. Her forward to *The Yangsheng Wisdom of the Yellow Emperor's Inner Canon* opens by arguing that unlike biomedical works, this ancient classic speaks of ordinary shared realities (the cardinal directions, the seasons) and does not hide its truths behind impossible esoteric language. In the paragraphs that follow, she promises much from a reading of the classic: "study this, savor this, under the guidance of sages, explore and attend to the secrets of the body and soul—in this way we can again perfect human life and complete the central voyage of human life."[16] Also arguing that the insights of ancient medicine arise in part from the life of the body itself and suggesting that the wisdom of ancient medicine can lead us back into accord with an "ever so natural" (*ziziranrande* 自自然然的) personal embodiment, Qu concludes with an irresistible invitation to read:

> As we now turn to reading the *Yellow Emperor's Inner Canon and the Treatise on Cold Damage* [*Shanghan lun* 伤寒论, the first-century C.E. "clinical canon"], there will be a certain degree of difficulty, but this conversation and reading absolutely do not seek to bestride all culture. The genes of our beautiful and sublime [*kongling* 空灵] Chinese characters are flowing in the bloodstream of every one of us Chinese; if we can enjoy the solitude of the process, we can read the *Inner Canon* as if we were reading the poems of Li Bai or Du Fu. Like them, the *Inner Canon* has insight, a generous spirit, and moving music. Like them, it has all the beauty and virtue possessed by Chinese culture: it establishes authority and orderly rule, stresses harmony and stability, emphasizes realistic proofs and transformation through instruction. It not only leads us to pace the void of the cosmos, to experience the absurdities and lacunae of the remote past, it also leads us to turn continuously inward, toward those almost unknowable dark places, ceaselessly delving into what is most difficult, until we can find in every moment the true heart throb of our life..."[17]

The reader Qu and Zhang envision, then, is not only a crafter of the everyday, but at the same time a philosopher, one who seeks to find the significance in his or her own everyday, embodied life and also one who seeks guidance to find the right way, or Way (*dao* 道), to live. Authors who write and teach within the current Chinese medicine and *yangsheng* fever both presume and help to bring into existence a public who knows how to read, can enjoy reading even historically remote texts, and is in search of the personal and practical significance that can be gained from exploring, as a reader, the Chinese heritage. As we note in the Conclusion, this public, which has been partly produced by the how-to literature, is turning to National Studies and Chinese tradition in droves. The centrality of health books in this broader movement suggests a certain bodily engagement in being Chinese and in having a Chinese past.

The nature of the reading imagined here contrasts strongly with the uses of health information imagined by the expert authors of books of the *Health Express* genre. Zhang and Qu do not see the canonical works they explicate as boiling down to rules for the disciplining of a biological body, host to "risks" and "hidden killers." The classics are not plundered for rules of thumb, then cast aside with other pieces of useless dross from the past. Rather, these authors reflect on reading at length as itself a manner of nurturing life. Attentive engagement with the "moving music" of the classics, a willingness to savor and be transformed by "National Studies"—these are wholesome activities in themselves. Millions of book buyers since 2007 seem willing to give this life-nurturing reading a try.

Possibly the Chinese medical classics will prove a media flash in the pan. Our publishing friend quoted above may turn out to be wrong about the longer shelf life of classical Chinese medicine in the publishing world. But his observations about the greater richness of the Chinese medical corpus in providing advice for a wholesome everyday life strike us as correct. Chinese medical knowledge could, in fact, go on forever with the helpful hints, although we might find some of these tips for everyday living rather bizarre or impractical. But as the new wave of philosophically inclined books suggests, the Chinese medical archive invites readers to embed their habits in a more broadly conceived time (the heritage) and space (China). Zhang Qicheng and Qu Limin, along with the authors of books such as *Great Physician Liu Comments on Yangsheng*; *Human Life and Yangsheng*; *The Book of Changes Wisdom of Avoiding Sickness*; *Quotations from Daoist Yangsheng*; and *Mysteries of Buddhist Yangsheng*, expect that the reading public is yearning for a richer fund of values and a more deeply meaningful context for their "moderate well-being."

But no one produces a *yangsheng* book that does not articulate with the little challenges of everyday embodied life in the modern city. And few books would sell to an audience presumed to be interested only in contemplating timeless and placeless truths. So we now turn to a consideration of how the currently popular philosophical Chinese medicine books connect to the lives of their curious, practical, thoughtful, nationalistic, diversely educated, rich and poor, old and young, casual or urgently needy readers.

Longevity in Theory and Practice

The recent Chinese enthusiasm for life-nurturing theory and practice owes partly to the presence in Chinese cities of a large aging population. Though retirement age tends to be early by United States standards, and many who practice *yangsheng* are not weak or ill, it is nevertheless widely felt that the culture of nurturing life is a particular specialty of older people. As a consequence, there are many self-health works that directly address the topic of "long life" (*changshou* 长寿).[18]

Scanning bookstore shelves, for example, one sees titles such as the following: *Good Health and Long Life Are Up to You*; *Ninety Tips for Good Health and Long Life*; *Longevity and Yangsheng*; *How to Use Yangsheng to Live 100 Years*; *How to Cultivate Self and Nurture Nature to Live 100 Years*; *Long Life through Medicinal Wines*; *The Yangsheng Way of Long-Lived People*; and, a personal favorite, *The Everyday Happy Way to Live 100 Years*. The rhetoric used in these works to speak of long life is predictable for a self-help genre: if you regulate your life in wholesome ways, then you will live long. Good personal habits may or may not actually defer death (many environmental hazards are unavoidable, and the causes of many deadly diseases are unknown), but the popular literature is unanimous in its promises: you can take charge of your own health, you can prevent disease, and thus, you can live long. To live long is, moreover, unquestionably a good thing.

The idea of *changshou*-longevity has a long and humble history in Chinese discourses, predating the recent demographic tilt toward senior generations, the shift in modern populations toward the "diseases of civilization," and the privatization of health care. Folk imagery, for example, offers the ubiquitous vision of three auspicious old men representing wealth, prolific fertility, and longevity. To see what elements of the good life are most obvious for Chinese people, even today, it would only be necessary to consult the New Year's prints that proliferate at Spring Festival time: along with the goldfish that symbolize surplus, the flowers and old coins that symbolize wealth, and the many-seeded pomegranates that symbolize fertility, one often sees "Grandpa Longevity." Unlike his companions, the tall and rather austere gods of family blessings and profits, the god of longevity is short, round, and cheerful. He leans with one hand on a long staff shaped like a *ruyi* scepter, indicating both his advanced age and his position as a lordly patriarch. The name for the *ruyi* carving means "everything as you wish." In his hand, he often holds a large, ripe peach, recalling the peaches of immortality cultivated by the gods in the orchards of paradise. The god's broad, wrinkled face, thick lips, and long ears are said to be modeled on the looks of the sage Laozi, traditional founder of Daoism (whose name, incidentally, means "the old one"). And invariably, his forehead bulges with accumulated wisdom, reflecting the surplus stored up from a life lived well.

Old age is a self-evident good. Several interviewees, seeking to help us find others to interview about life nurturing, suggested that we seek out neighbors they thought of as the best exemplars of a life lived well. One of our helpful friends, in referring us to these elders, also pointed out: "Having such old people in our neighborhoods is a good thing, it speaks well for the nation and our culture." In 2003, our group interviewed a retired Daoist monk in his eighties; he was a *yangsheng* theorist, and we were particularly interested in his sophisticated system of teaching health habits for long life. At first, however, Judith Farquhar thought of him as quite debilitated by old age; he could not move around his apartment very well, and he initially appeared fatigued and inarticulate. Once he got going on the technicalities of Daoist *yangsheng*, displaying his active intellect and warm engagement with students and colleagues, his liveliness was much more marked. Even so, in the United States, he would have been seen as an ill old man, well "down" the path of decline. But as we walked away, Zhang Qicheng and our Beijing graduate students all agreed that this old Daoist was quite youthful: his skin was "that of a sixty-year-old," and his intellectual passion demonstrated ageless good spirits (*shen* 神), the sign of a life well lived.

In keeping with the taken-for-granted quality of *changshou* for commonsense Chinese values, few writers in the popular literature interrogate the idea of longevity. In a genre of writing that compulsively examines every term, *changshou* on the whole goes undefined. But the potential for premature death or for debility in one's latter years tends to be kept before the reader's eyes. A quote from the first chapter of the *Inner Canon* is, for example, endlessly cited wherever longevity is mentioned in the popular literature:

> The people of ancient times who knew how to cultivate the Way worked within *yinyang* and harmonized the numbers; their eating and drinking was measured, their breathing was even, and they worked without haste or anxiety. Thus it was possible for their bodily frames and their *shen*-spirits to be at one, so that they lived out their natural spans of life, only passing away when their hundred years had been fulfilled.
>
> People of our times are not like that. Wine is their drink, caprice is their norm. Drunken, they enter the chamber of love, through lust using up their germinal essence, through desire dispersing their inborn vitality. They do not know how to maintain fullness, they entertain untimely thoughts, they covet short-term gratifications, they resist life's joys, and their daily habits are not regular, so by the age of fifty, they are all worn out.[19]

One could hardly wish for a more useful classical quotation for founding the principles of modern *yangsheng* in ancient wisdom. This lament about a degenerate present not only incorporates many long-standing principles of propriety and self-cultivation, it also promises long life as the natural outcome of a life lived well. At the same time, it quite logically threatens exhaustion and early death for those in whom "caprice is the norm." A classical vision of the careful husbanding of bodily and environmental resources, along with a commitment to moderate and regulated expenditure of powers, is clearly at the root of this criticism. Life can be long only if the timing of living is properly measured.

In Zhang Qicheng's 2008 commentary on this passage, he remarks on how familiar it is as a genre of complaint about "these modern times" (though it was originally written at least as early as the first century c.e.). Given the relative timelessness of the problem of degenerate ways, this important classical text argues—still and always—for the value of the life-nurturing arts. If, two thousand years ago, philosophers of life saw their contemporaneity as corrupt and diverging from the Way, then our own contemporary criticisms of foolish lifeways cannot be just a response to modernity. At the beginning of the chapter in which he interprets this quotation, Zhang asks:

> The first chapter of the *Yellow Emperor's Inner Canon*, "On the True Heavenly Essence of Ancient Times," records the Emperor Di's first question about life: What is the basic reason for the great difference between the healthy longevity of antiquity and now? Is it that the times are different, or that the way of *yangsheng* has been lost? Is it a cause traceable to the Way of Heaven, or to the Way of Man?
>
> Regarding this question, most people would blame external conditions, thinking that certainly it is because modern society is very different from before. But has the way of the world really changed? Qi Bo's answer [to the emperor's question] is that the way of the world certainly has not changed, and the Way of Heaven has not changed; it is each of our individual daily lives that has changed, living habits have changed, lifestyles have changed.[20]

And they had already changed in the classical period, when the Emperor Di and his teacher Qi Bo were—as the narrative of the *Inner Canon* would have it—putting the finishing touches on a medical-philosophical synthesis for their times. Classical *yangsheng* was always already turning responsibility for healthy longevity toward the person, with all his or her foolish desires and untimely thoughts, with his or her exhaustible stores of germinal essence (*jing* 精) and inborn vitality (*zhenqi* 真气 meaning "true *qi*" or "original *qi*").

Surely, the contemporary Beijingers whose reflections on daily habits we will hear in Chapter 3 recognize, and many approve, Qi Bo's advice in this passage. But we note that there are some features of this ancient polemic that might puzzle some readers, though commentators in Chinese have not noted any contradiction. For example, in the last sentence, all mixed together in the breach, as it were, are a number of things that seem to be seen as life's natural satisfactions. Knowing how to maintain fullness,[21] entertaining timely thoughts, seeking long-term rather than short-term gratifications, yielding to life's joys, and maintaining regular life habits are all aspects of the good life that the libertines of the present have foregone with their short-sighted hedonism. This is their loss; presumably, living in a measured way and regulating the times of life in good habits is a way of yielding to life's (true, lasting) joys.

There is an even clearer vision, or perhaps a deeper analysis, of the joys of the nurtured life, also from the first chapter of the *Inner Canon* and extending its argument. This passage, too, is very frequently cited in advice about long life in the contemporary self-help literature:

> It is from calm, indifference, emptiness, and nondesiring that true *qi* arises. If essence and spirit are harbored inside, whence can illness arise? When the will is at rest and wishes little, when the heart is at peace and fears nothing, when the body labors but does not tire, then *qi* flows smoothly from these states, each part follows its desires, and the whole gets everything it seeks. Thus it is that the lordly one is able to savor his food, shoulder his responsibilities, and take pleasure in his passions. High and low do not envy each other, so the people of his domain are called simple and honest. Compulsive desires cannot engage his gaze, and the evils all around him cannot afflict his heart. Thus it is that he can live to be 100 years old, and nothing he does can weaken him.[22]

Beijingers often advise each other to find health by limiting desires. Their most common advice, "don't get angry," is consistent with "calm, indifference, emptiness, and nondesiring," as well; "the evils all around him cannot afflict his heart." There is, however, an apparent contradiction between all the caprices of the first paragraph, the excesses that lead to premature debility and death at fifty, and the last sentence above: "nothing he does can weaken him." How can these opposed pieces of advice exist in the very same chapter of the *Inner Canon*, one right after the other?

As students of Chinese medicine, we note an obvious physiological consistency in the vision, however. Underlying sexual and alimentary excesses and other forms of hyperactivity such as overwork is the uneven flow of *qi* resulting from careless expenditure of *jing*-essence. When *qi* does not flow smoothly, states of excess and deficiency develop in the self—indeed, by *yinyang* logic, you could not have one without the other—and the natural needs of the body's systems are starved, or flooded, or both.[23] The *jing*-essence is not properly gathered, and *shen*-spirit, the most volatile product of the *qi*-transformation activity that is physiology, goes a little wild. A *shen* ungrounded in *jing* manifests as spirits that are too high, manic behavior that demands, but cannot get sustenance for its overvolatilized activity. The functions of the heart system, the particular organ devoted to the control of *shen*, are failing; one's heart is too much on one's sleeve, as it were. *Shen*-spirit is not properly harbored inside. If it were, it would be "possible for their bodily frames and their *shen*-spirits to be at one"; people's eating and drinking would be measured, their breathing would be even, and they would work without haste or anxiety. Even more important as a persuasion to adopt the nurtured life, the lordly and healthy one is "able to savor his food, shoulder his responsibilities, and take pleasure in his passions.... Compulsive desires cannot engage his gaze, and the evils all around him cannot afflict his heart.... He can live to be 100 years old, and nothing he does can weaken him." Key to this holistic satisfaction is living in moderation, harboring life's resources. Aging would not be a weakening, and normal passions would not turn into ever more demanding and transgressive desires. Pleasure would be an everyday thing.

These classical passages demonstrate well the philosophical appeal of the *Inner Canon*—widely known as the "theoretical classic" of medicine—for moderns; no wonder there are so many self-health books that explicate this Han Dynasty classic. But *yangsheng* is an art of everyday life, trading in techniques, rules of thumb, small routines. The most popular traditionalists in the self-health field need to be good at building bridges between classical language and modern Chinese, between the abstract and the concrete, between theory and practice. Qu Limin's best-selling two volumes of lectures, *The Yangsheng Wisdom of the Yellow Emperor's Inner Canon* (*Huangdi neijing yangsheng zhihui* 皇帝内径养生智慧) are very good at this. When she speaks of *changshou*, she always refers to "healthy longevity" (*jiankang changshou*). And she recalls the passages cited above in the context of arguing—predictably, as we have seen—that health is a personal responsibility:

> The second major argument of the *Yellow Emperor's Inner Canon* is: a healthy longevity does not depend on other people, it does not depend on medicine; it depends entirely on yourself. Many people have the mistaken idea that once one falls ill, one must entirely rely on doctors and medicines, and more and more they cannot believe in themselves. They would rather believe that some stomach medicine can resolve their stomachache, but they are not willing to change their bad habits of overeating and overdrinking.
>
> The *Inner Canon* doesn't really speak much about medicines; it includes thirteen prescriptions, and these are very simple ones. Without a doubt, it is telling us, a healthy longevity is a process of gathering up *jing*-essence and accumulating *qi*, and what it depends on is eating well, sleeping well, digesting and breathing well, and having the ability to control one's desires—only this kind of person is healthy.
>
> Basically, the *Inner Canon* is a book that teaches medical theory [*yili* 医理] (or the way of medicine [*yidao* 道]). Its opening chapters speak of nondesiring and vacancy, then it turns to the four seasons and the interactions of *yin* and *yang*—this tells everyone that the secret of a healthy longevity rests on whether one's emotions and the *qi* and blood of the circulation tracks are moving smoothly and whether life's phases of emergence, development, retreating, and storing are all in order. If

they are, it is just as the *Book of Changes* ("Uses of the Undivided") says: "If you see a host of dragons with no leader, this is auspicious."[24]

There is much classical (but, for some of us, puzzling) common sense condensed here. Links between gathering essence or *qi* and controlling desires, between smoothly flowing bodily substances and self-mastery, are taken for granted. The impossible states of nondesiring and vacancy are mentioned without further comment. Qu Limin goes on:

> [The *Inner Canon* says,] "wantonness [*yin* 淫] is the chief [cause] of the 10,000 afflictions," "*qi* is the first [cause] of the 100 illnesses." This is to say, excessive sexual activity and excessive emotion are intimately connected to the state of our bodily health. This actually tells us that many things can influence the state of our health, including moods and mental state.... Chinese medicine is able to affect every aspect of life; what it guides is the Way of medicine in human life. The so-called Way of medicine is not content simply with curing diseases; it seeks to provide guidance for all aspects of human life.[25]

The promised guidance, it is implied, would help one chart a course between excess and deficiency. Salient advice of this kind is found elsewhere in both of Qu Limin's volumes of lectures on the *Inner Canon*. In brief, but earthy examples, she mixes cosmic principles, medical theory, and grandmotherly lore. Here's an example:

> We Chinese have a saying, "Eat turnip in the winter, ginger in the summer, no need to get a doctor's scrip." Why do people say this? In the summer, our *yang qi* rises and floats toward the surfaces of the body, so the inner parts of the body develop a pattern of cold-damp; [under these conditions], the spleen-stomach system is at its weakest, and our digestive functions are thus also at their weakest, so in the summer, we want to eat warming and heating, lightening and dispersing things such as ginger and can't eat moistening and tonifying things—our body's insides don't have the power to digest them. But when winter comes, our *yang qi* is entirely retreating, and the inner parts of the body develop a pattern of inward heat, so we can eat moistening and tonifying things.

Thus, eating turnip can clear [heat] and cool [the inside], and make *qi* flow along its pathways [*qingliang xunqi* 清凉顺气]; it can help our body maintain a condition of coolness, with easy and smooth circulation.

This kind of reasoning can be inferred from everyday life. We need only to grasp these detailed issues in daily life for many bodily problems to be resolved. This, too, is an aspect of the *Yellow Emperor's Inner Canon*'s Way of nurturing life.[26]

Much could be said about this kind of advice, not least emphasizing its utter familiarity. Even the technical terminology from Chinese medicine (lightening and dispersing, moistening and tonifying) can, with a bit of reflection, be understood through the idioms of ordinary experience. Food preferences in hot or cold weather, linked to processes of both tasting and digesting tangy or starchy, warming or energizing food, should respond to changes in inner and outer weather. And the *yinyang* logic of life's phases of "emergence, development, retreating, and storing," which Qu Limin mentions in the more theoretical parts of her lectures, is the principled framework that links weather to digestion, the qualities of foods to the character of human bodies. The Way is coherent, and medical reasoning and the authority of the *Yellow Emperor's Inner Canon* can show us this coherence. But all this is just a supplement to the everyday ways our bodies can tell us, if we attend to their seasons and rhythms, how to live.

Measuring the Tempos of Life

Yet both the *Inner Canon* and modern experts remind us that the times are out of joint. Even ancient lords allowed hedonism and selfish desire to lead them astray; in our own high-pressure times, perhaps especially now, achievement of healthful satisfaction requires deliberate effort, regulation, cultivation. Self-health literature of all kinds certainly argues as much; as we noted above, the rhetoric of health advice, biomedical or traditional, presumes that people do not instinctively know and want to do what's good for them. This is an ancient dilemma, about which the philosophers wrote a great deal. Is the Way such that humans will naturally live in accord with its generative power, following the pathways of what is cosmically so of itself (*ziran*)?[27] Or do they need actively to cultivate the good, nurturing their lives toward those moderated satisfactions that could last a hundred years? Parts of the classic Daoist works attributed to Laozi and Zhuangzi could be read as making no distinction between a go-with-the-flow form of "nonaction" (*wuwei* 无为)[28] and complete indulgence of desires for short-term payoffs. But other aspects of Daoism, especially those linked with the East Asian medical and scientific traditions, converge with a Confucian ethical tradition to advance a more activist approach to the crafting of good lives.

Zhang Qicheng, in his lectures on the *Inner Canon*, takes an activist position about the task facing moderns wishing to be healthier and happier. In his 2008 mass-market book *The Great Way of Yangsheng: Zhang Qicheng Lectures on the Yellow Emperor's Inner Canon (Zhang Qicheng jiangdu Huangdi neijing yangsheng da dao* 张其成讲读黄帝内经养生大道), he urges life nurturance from the perspective of a mainstream philosophical tradition that he himself has continued to synthesize while considering the past, the future, and the tasks of Chinese medicine. His central understanding of *yangsheng* action can be summarized with the word *he* 和, usually translated as "harmony"; it is perhaps more properly read, however, as a philosophical abstraction, "harmonics," or as a verb, "harmonizing." When harmonizing is understood as the weaving together of many streams of activity and as the management of a relation between *yin* and *yang* tendencies in the dynamics of life, it becomes quite a complex concept.[29]

In Zhang's second lecture, for example, he begins with one of the passages we cited above ("the people of ancient times who knew how to cultivate the Way") to lay out the "general principles of *yangsheng*: work within *yinyang*, harmonize the numbers." In order to explain why these general principles, which he also calls "this Dao," are "not abstract, not empty, but are really and truly expressed in every person's most ordinary everyday life," he first expands on the idea that "*yangsheng* is nothing other than healthy everyday habits." Then he provides a lengthy introduction to the logic of *yin* and *yang* ("The *yangsheng* thought of the unity of heaven and man:

work within *yinyang*").[30] This is necessary if readers are to understand the character of *yangsheng* action, even the most everyday kind, and the necessity of "harmonizing" in a world made up of ten thousand things.

His explanation shows that *yin* and *yang* are so intimately interactive, their antinomies so complexly nested in ranks of ever more finely differentiated lights and darks, potentials and actuals (every *yang* aspect incorporates *yang* and *yin* aspects, every state of initiating entails its imminent completion, every completed thing holds within it the seeds of a new initiation), that the achievement of harmony is far from natural (pp. 24–26). Perfect yinyang homeostasis may be possible, but it is not stable or lasting, so harmony could not be the default position in life; rather, there are always overflows and shortfalls, always hiccups in the tempos of life, jerkiness in the movement of things. If the labile excesses and deficiencies of the interplay of *yin* and *yang* are to be made symmetrical and regular (if "*qi* is to flow smoothly, each part following its desires, the whole getting everything it seeks") and life is to last 100 years, things at many levels must be placed in proper relation to each other: man and nature, individual and society, self and other, heart-mind and body-person must be actively harmonized (pp. 29–31).

When the lecture reaches the point of explaining what is meant by "work within *yinyang*, harmonize the numbers," Zhang hints at one of his lasting interests: the connection between Chinese medical *yangsheng* and the numerology of the *Book of Changes*. It makes sense that these somewhat distinct traditions could be unified by the language of harmony. Under the section heading "The *Yangsheng* Methods of According with the Dao of Heaven," he argues:

> The phrase "harmonize the numbers" uses the word *he* 和; the meaning of this word is to "accord with" or "conform to" the numbers. The numbers are methods, techniques; methods and techniques can all be expressed numerically. With respect to Chinese medical *yangsheng*, the *yangsheng* of the *Yellow Emperor's Inner Canon* includes a lot of numbers. It tells us various methods, and if we conform with these methods, all will be well—this is the general principle (pp. 27–28).

Though this book is framed as lectures on a classic philosophical-medical work and most often takes the form of commentary on less than transparent passages of classical Chinese, Zhang fulfills the promise of this early paragraph in some later chapters, advising on methods and techniques and showing how the general principles outlined in the first few chapters can be "expressed in ordinary everyday life." Chapter 5, for example, "The Stages of *Yangsheng*," is introduced in the table of contents as follows: "How many stages can human life be divided into? How many cycles? Are a person's *jing*-essence, *qi*, and *shen*-spirit all the same in each stage of life? As people age, can they still protect the true *qi* endowed by Heaven and maintain flourishing energy?" ("Contents," p. 4).

This chapter, after explaining several systems by means of which, in the *Yellow Emperor's Inner Canon*, life is divided into stages (by tens or by sevens and eights), turns to matters of more immediate interest: the "demon times" of life, for example. Demon times are periods of particular vulnerability, when everyone should be especially vigilant about maintaining healthy habits.

> The "demon times" of each day: It is when you first wake up from dreaming in the morning that you enter on the first demon time of the day (6:00–9:00 A.M.). This is the point at which things like heart disease, stroke, bronchitis, emphysema, asthma, and even cancers begin to act up in your body.... [He gives an example of heart symptoms occurring more often in the morning, cited from WHO research.]
>
> Another "demon time" during the day is just at dusk; at this time, in heart conditions the probability of recurrent symptoms is especially elevated. Also, if you drink liquor around 7:00 P.M., the time needed for the liver to eliminate alcohol is longer than at other times of the day, so it's especially easy to become intoxicated at this time and thus to harm the liver. (p. 140)

There are demon times in each week (Mondays), each lunar month (about the fifteenth day), and every year (the hottest and coldest spells); even on the scale of a life, there is a demon time, middle age, when physiology is turning away from its youthful vigor, but the pressure of social responsibility is at its highest (pp. 141–42).

How, concretely, would a person trying to nurture life "harmonize the numbers" of the phases of life? Zhang has suggestions keyed to the different phases, derived from his reading of the *Inner Canon*. For each of these phases—youth, adulthood, middle age, and old age—he provides advice first about mental and emotional self-cultivation and then about food, activities, rest, sex life, and so forth. For the elderly, for example (males over sixty-four—a multiple of eight—and females over fifty-six—a multiple of seven), there are four main areas to which to attend:

> 1. psychologically and spiritually, be content with ordinary joys, stay happy and contented, be open-minded and generous, modest and mild; put the best construction on people's intentions [*shanjie renyi* 善解人意], be young at heart, stay confident, assiduously use your mind, keep meeting challenges.... You should love living, regularly read books and newspapers, and study some kind of specialized knowledge and skills. As allowed by your state of bodily health, do more good deeds, give full play to your interests [*fahui chure* 发挥余热] in order to make new contributions to society. Handle all conflicts calmly and tolerantly, maintain harmony in the family, manage social relations with care. Following your own personality and interests, meditate to clear your mind, spend time chatting with many friends, fish by the side of the lake, walk among the trees to listen to the birds—getting the most pleasure out of life benefits healthy longevity. (p. 147)

It is perhaps a bit strange to American readers to hear in this advice the assumption that so much control can be exercised over the emotions and that a life of self-control is the best path to getting the most pleasure out of life. As we will see in Chapter 3,[31] however, the life of the feelings is widely seen as subject to deliberate cultivation and nurturing; people truly believe that they can resolve not to get angry and can succeed in that resolve. On the whole, contemporary Chinese common sense does not presume an expressivist model of subjectivity and interpersonal communication. This very common kind of advice suggests that personality is not rooted in any kind of ineluctable or wild nature. Zhang Qicheng's contribution is to urge the active coordination of the times and numbers of natural life, or even the Dao, with the dispositions, emotions, interpersonal relations, and even the simple pleasures that smooth the flow of actual everyday life.

He goes on with simpler and ever more obvious advice for the elderly: "2. With respect to eating and drinking, focus on the five great principles: diversity, blandness, low quantity, slowness, and warmth." In the discussion that follows point two, each of these principles of diet and eating is explained, sometimes with reference to the *Inner Canon.* Where food and eating habits are concerned, there is plenty of room for a mixture of scientific nutrition information and principles of daily life derived from the Chinese medical literature. Zhang here advises, even before explaining his five great principles, the "three mores and three lesses": more protein, more vitamins, more fiber; less sugar, less salt, less fat. This is public-health dogma. But this emphasis on the composition of the stuff one puts in one's body is less marked when he turns to the five great principles: "diversity" and "blandness" can be expressed in a nutritional language (calcium and vegetable oils figure here), but they are also connected to the orderly coordination of the powers of food with the regular functions of visceral systems. Thus, for example, "the spleen-stomach systems of the elderly are weakening, their digestive powers are not strong, so it's not appropriate for them to eat fatty or overly salty foods." This consensus advice is easy to agree with, but we can also hear in it the effort to coordinate quantities and qualities of food with the numbers and qualities of the life phase in question, that of the elderly. The principles of "low quantity"—eat less, more frequently—as well as eating slowly and sticking to warm foods, are justified in the same number-harmonizing manner. The point is not *what* you eat, all your life, for superior health; it is *how* you eat—eating in a manner that accords with the evolving activities of a *yinyang* physiology.

The question of the timing or appropriate coordination of everyday life choices with natural developments is both most obvious and most mundane when health advice turns to the management of everyday life. The term is "rising and resting" (*qiju* 起居); this is the translation we prefer to the conventional one of "everyday life."

3. With respect to life's times of rising and resting [*shenghuo qiju* 生活起居] one must focus on appropriate care. The life of the elderly should not be arranged to produce a lot of tension, nor should it be entirely idle; further, it should not be without all regularity. It should be scientifically based, in accord with the physiological condition of aging people. Living conditions should be made very quiet and clean, with good airflow, plenty of light, neither too damp nor too dry, and should have the conveniences of living. One also should assure good sleep, but not stay in bed; lying around in bed harms the *qi* of *shen*-spirit and influences the flow of *qi* in the [four sectors of] *qi*, blood, and protective and nutritive *qi*. It's a good idea to go to bed early and get up early. Avoid drafts and the cold, maintain even warmth. Because elderly people's kidney-system *qi* is declining, bedchamber matters [i.e., sexual activity] should decline as years increase. Watch out for overwork. As much as possible, one should do the physical or mental labor to which one's strength extends, but you shouldn't become excessively fatigued; [as the proverb says,] "The body wants some work, but not to be worn-out." Elderly people should keep up good habits of hygiene: wash your face often, comb your hair, soak your feet in hot water. Ensure regular bowel movements and urination.

4. In order to avoid getting sick and to recover well from sickness, participate in appropriate sports and exercises. Old people often have weak bodies and many illnesses, and they can develop many chronic conditions. But they should still establish an optimistic spirit and the confidence to fight disease; even those with illnesses can extend their years and find much joy in life. Use a happy mood and an optimistic outlook to fight disease courageously. Actively coordinate treatments, support right *qi* and expel evil *qi*; keep right *qi* fully adequate. Have regular health checkups and engage in preventive activities in a timely way. Get more involved in meaningful activities; distribute your attention widely. Do appropriate sports and exercises. In general, the

amount of exercise should not be a lot, and the movement should be slow and measured. Exercises appropriate for the aged are *taiji quan*, "five animals" gymnastics, *qigong*, eight-stage exercises, jogging, walking, swimming, ping-pong, badminton, old people's calisthenics, and so forth. All you need to do is measure your strength as you go, strictly avoid contention and competition, and don't let your mood become tense or agitated. (pp. 147–48)

The vision is one of a regular life, every day pretty much like every other, peaceful, tidy, comfortable, and sociable. Such a life is not for everyone; perhaps this vision of uneventful routine, well under control, is especially attractive to a generation of Beijingers who have lived through very eventful times. Moreover, only retired people would be free enough from external demands to craft the regularities of "rising and resting" mentioned here.

Here, Zhang's rhetoric of advice giving—which is rather a departure from his usual scholarly commentary, even in this mass-market book—implies strongly that for every desirable habit mentioned, there are plenty of elderly people who do not live in accord with this Way. Middle-aged people, moreover, don't have so many choices available to them, though Zhang's advice for the middle years does include suggestions for regulating mood, food, and exercise. Still, those we interviewed about *yangsheng* who were not yet retired complained that they were chronically sleep deprived and often forced to eat unhealthy fast food; they found mental equilibrium hard to maintain amid workplace worries; and they had no time for exercise.

This disconnect between desirable health habits and the (im)-possible arrangements of life in modern times recalls the much more ancient lament of Qi Bo as he explains to the Yellow Emperor that "people of our times are not like that." Zhang Qicheng and the many others who join the chorus of self-help discourses with concrete advice for "rising and resting" remain optimistic, however: if "people of our times" could adopt even some of the many techniques of "working with *yin* and *yang* and harmonizing the numbers," it might be easier to achieve a healthy and happy longevity.

The Four Times of the Year

The seasons present a problem of tempo that is especially clear, especially closely connected to the rhythms of the Dao. Weather and its oscillations, the climatic regularities of warming and cooling, growing and dying back, provide both the best example of *yinyang* processes and the most proximate to bodily experience. Everybody shares the weather, and no one can really control it. Our most taken-for-granted human arrangements—food, clothing, shelter—help us sustain life in relative comfort even when conditions are extreme. The *yangsheng* literature, suggesting that such arrangements demand a certain amount of fresh deliberation, provides all manner of seasonal advice. Titles we have noted over the last few years, for example, include the following: *The Complete Book of Yangsheng for the Twenty-Four Solar Calendar Terms*; *Yangsheng Medicinal Cuisine for the Four Seasons*; *Seasonal Medicinal Tonics for Building Strength*; *Seasonal Medicinal Cuisine for Preventing and Treating Cancer*; *Yangsheng Health in the Four Seasons*; and the *Family Manual of Supplementing Yangsheng in the Four Seasons*.

These works present specialized knowledge in accessible terms and with a practical bent. The temporality of *yangsheng* techniques is also made very clear in less specialized introductions to the healthful management of everyday life. Consider the range of concerns in a little book—one of ten in an attractively packaged set entitled *The Complete Book of "The Yellow Emperor's Inner Canon"*—under the title of *Yangsheng: The Yangsheng of the Four Time Periods*.[32] Each of the four sections of the book is divided into six topic areas. Thus, "Springtime Yangsheng," section 1, offers short articles on the theory of springtime *yangsheng*, methods of nurturing heart-mind in the spring, methods of nurturing body in the spring, methods of nurturing with food in the spring, methods of nurturing with medicines in the spring, and prevention of and recovery from diseases commonly seen in the spring. The same six topics are explored for each of the other seasons. Under each of the six headings, the advice becomes very concrete. Here are some examples of theories and practices suitable for wintertime:

IV.4.1. Foods often used to nurture life in the winter:

Winter weather is cold, the *yang qi* of the natural world is in cold storage and *yin qi* is ascendant. In eating, we should emphasize warming and bolstering foods in order to restrain *yin* and protect *yang*; this is necessary to build up [*yiyang* 贻养] *jing*-essence and *qi*. We must eat more foods containing sugars, fats, protein, and vitamins, and it's a good idea to increase consumption of animal viscera, lean meats, fish, eggs, and the like. At the same time, we should eat enough vegetables for nutritional balance and to avoid weight gain.

(1) Staple foods: In the winter, polished nonglutinous rice and wheat flour are the main staples, but one should accompany them with the other staples such as yams, sorghum, and corn. The nutritional value of these other staples is high; they prevent weakening and promote fitness in the elderly, and they improve and advance development in children. [1] Sweet potatoes: Also called red yams, white yams, or sweet yams; sweet in flavor, bland in character. Functions are to bolster and supplement spleen-stomach-system functions, smooth bowel movements, produce fluids, and satisfy thirst (when used fresh). Useful where the spleen-stomach system is depleted and weak, energy levels are low, stools are dry and constipated, or there are intermittent fevers with dry mouth. Contains sugar, protein, carotene, vitamins B_1, B_2, and C, calcium, and phosphorus. But eating too much makes people feel overfull and acidic [*fansuan* 泛酸]....

(2) Meats: In winter, besides eating lean pork and chicken, you can also eat warming and strong-flavored meats such as lamb, dog meat, and venison. [1] Lamb. Sweet in flavor, warming in character. Its function is to bolster *qi* and nourish blood and to warm the spleen and kidney systems. Useful in cases of impotence brought on by kidney system *yang* depletion, chronic lower back pain, intolerance of cold, excessive nighttime urination, clear and protracted urination, feelings of cold due to postpartum blood depletion, midabdominal stomachache, stomachache due to blood depletion in the circulation tracks, depletion-cold of the spleen-stomach system, loss of appetite or diarrhea, chronically cold extremities, exhausted spirits, and lack of energy.[33]

The section on main foods excerpted here is followed by an even more detailed discussion of cooked dishes especially suitable for the winter season; there are recipes for fish slices with stir-fried lamb, pork kidneys with fennel, steak and kidney casserole, and turnip and lamb soup (pp. 190–92).

In the examples above, facts about physiology and pathology drawn from the technical world of Chinese medicine are very noticeable. The spleen-stomach system, heat and cold disorders, damaged fluids, *jing*-essence, and *qi* are invoked alongside the organic composition of foods drawn from nutritional science. The overarching logic generating this wintertime advice is that of *yin* and *yang*. This orientation toward the systematic knowledge of traditional medicine is not surprising in this series of books, which claims to introduce the wisdom of the *Yellow Emperor's Inner Canon*, nor is the additional inclusion of biochemical facts drawn from nutritional science unusual in modern Chinese public health literature. But if we reflect for a moment on how a reader would consume this kind of hybrid text— always, as we have argued, looking for bits of information that can be recognized as both probably true and practically useful—the seasonality of the body takes on a great deal of substance. Just as weather is directly experienced and a topic for commonsense talk, the correlates of the great Chinese medical categories of *yin* and *yang* are experiential and commonsensical. Comfort food warms at a time when cold can strike as deep as the inmost viscera; it's a good idea to store up some calories while the world is chill and dormant.

In a sense, the substance almost determines the category: if we're eating lamb, this must be winter. The sweet potato vendors have reappeared on the street, so cold weather is on the way. It's natural and (in this case) desirable to stay in bed later when winter *yin* ascendance is forcing *yang qi* inward. As one source cited above argues, "this kind of reasoning can be inferred from everyday life. We only need to grasp these detailed issues in daily life for many bodily problems to be resolved."[34] There is a productive interaction, then, between formal health knowledge and everyday inclinations toward comfort and satisfaction. But just relying on experience and following short-term or instinctual desires won't quite do. We must grasp the detail, we must be careful to "harmonize the numbers": the temporal/substantive shifts of the four seasons, the twenty-four solar terms of the year, the twelve phases of the day. The history of Chinese knowledge about time and qualities of bodily life has much to teach us. If we attend to the seasons—as known both personally and collectively—many bodily problems can be resolved.

Just to continue the example of winter habits, from the winter theory section of the same introductory book:

> In the three months of winter, the myriad things close up and go into storage mode; this is the cold winter season when ice covers the earth; one must respond to the characteristics of the winter season, going to bed early and rising late, coordinating waking hours with the daylight. Don't carelessly expend *yang qi*, guard and store your spirits within, and don't lightly share your thoughts, keep your own counsel, as if you were keeping secrets. [In general,] rigorously protect [yourself] and don't expend [your] energies; act as if you have actually gotten all that you desire and stored it up inside. Hide from the cold and seek out the warm, don't let the skin respire too much or allow *yang qi* to be dissipated; this accords with the reasoning of protecting, nourishing, and storing *qi*. This kind of advice is emphasized in winter; people should regulate their mental life [*jingshen*], their eating and drinking, their use of medicines, and their exercise through all manner of techniques, focusing on "nourishing storage," especially protecting and nourishing the *yang qi* of one's own body. If this isn't done, [it is as the classic says:] "go against this principle and the kidney system will be injured, there will be debility and retraction in the spring, no resources to support rebirth." This is to say, if in the winter we don't attend to "the way of nourishing and storing," the *yang qi* of the kidney system will be injured, which will then influence the capacity for new growth and development in the spring, even to the point of making the four limbs weak and shriveled and seriously damaging general health.[35]

Here, a rather instrumental idiom is adopted, treating *yangsheng* as a form of preventive medicine. If winter storage isn't carefully managed, the active regeneration of the myriad things in the spring will lack resources, be compromised, manifest as illness and debility. People who do not carefully harbor their precious *yang qi* in the winter are at risk, vulnerable to the bad consequences of mismanaged timing.

But Zhang Qicheng goes beyond the logic of preventive medicine, expressing the common ground of seasonal experience and bodily vicissitudes as a capacity for pleasure:

> The *yangsheng* of the seasons in one year, the *yangsheng* of the monthly phases of the moon, the *yangsheng* of the four temporal turning points of the day—these are all versions of one another. The general principle is that of following along with heaven's timing [*tianshi* 天时], making heaven and man accord as one [*tian ren he yi* 天人合一], keeping in step with the regularities of the yinyang changes of heaven's phases [*tianshi* 天时]. As that very famous Chan poem of the Song has it, "Spring has its blossoms and fall its moon, summer has cool breezes and winter has snow. When head and heart do not depart from these, human life is sure of good seasons." When we speak of the weather of the four seasons, and the characteristics of the divisions of the year, each of us can really divide our own lives into the four seasons of spring, summer, fall, and winter; the thing is to be without digressions or antagonisms, this is how one modulates one's spirits, this is the key point of the *Inner Canon*'s chapter "The Great Discourse on the Four Times and the Modulations of Spirit."[36]

Clearly, making heaven and man accord as one is not just a matter of managing the numbers of the myriad things and the phases of the Dao for consistency's sake or to fulfill some kind of moral imperative. Living with the seasons is even more about having "*good seasons*." Attending to the proper rhythms of rising and resting is a way of "modulating one's spirits" (*diao shen* 调神). The *yangsheng* of timing is not about denying desires or limiting pleasures, but balancing them, finding the right mix. As Zhang says, the classics show us how to produce and fulfill our desires in relation to the real patterns of natural process. The aim of harmonizing the numbers is not less pleasure, but more: more reliable, more substantive, more lasting, more conducive to extending a full, but not overly full life.

Rambling through bookstores and listening in on lectures about *yangsheng* in Beijing, we have encountered several levels of rhetoric—and Zhang Qicheng has himself generated several—about the value of the life nurturing arts. Certain hard realities inform every argument: all experts acknowledge the costs of the recent privatization of medical services and the inevitabity of a stark "responsibilization" of individuals at risk. Families worry about meeting the needs of their elderly members, now so much more numerous than the young. Ministry of Health experts bring scientific light to the darkness of people's naturally bad habits and poor health. The "Health Express" promises a revolution of wellness—and a way of avoiding hospital bills—through the cultivation of evidence-based preventive medicine. Commentators on classic medical works go further than this, offering not only wellness, but a deep and pleasurable coherence when life is lived in accord with the Dao. Ordinary city dwellers, interviewed in parks, reliably provide a short list of reasons to practice *yangsheng*: for long life, for fun, to avoid illness. And theorists in government institutes keep returning to the overarching, postutopian promise of the reform era: moderate well-being for all.

We do not believe that Beijingers who enjoy the life-nurturing arts are especially confined, repressed, or determined by these conventional discourses. In our experience—and in our survey and interviews—people insisted on elaborating their own opinions and describing their own strategies, gathering the resources and considering the principles for their crafted lives in extremely eclectic ways. In the face of a strongly individualizing logic of biomedical health management, newly released from all kinds of collective imperatives and denied a number of city and work-unit social supports, practitioners of *yangsheng* are still gathering in groups and comparing notes. Many we spoke with about how they chose the elements of a healthy life insisted that their own and their friends' experience was their best guide. Chatting with the regulars before and after calisthenics, or *taiji*, or lake swimming yielded the most useful advice, as Ms. Wu, among others, attests in Chapter 3.

No wonder Chinese medical writers highlight the experienced efficacies of traditional medicine. Confident that the dietary, seasonal, and "rising and resting" techniques and habits they advocate actually do work to improve everyday life and deliver lived wellness, their advice is backed with the authority not only of tradition, but of experience. Experience is, in fact, presented by these experts as a deep, continuous current in the life of the Chinese people. Originating in ancient times, yet adaptable to a very modern present, Chinese medical *yangsheng* is valuable, these writers argue, because it has long been so markedly effective in making life in East Asia proliferate. But given the many points of convergence between the knowledge systematized in Chinese medicine and the practical lore shared on street corners and in parks, Chinese medical teachers hardly need to impose an authoritative view; they need not be insistent about the instrumental efficacy of turnips in the winter or taking naps in the summer.

Instead, or in addition, they can promise enjoyment and significance. Recall Qu Limin's phrasing of this promise, quoted in the epigraph to this chapter: "In this way, we can again perfect human life and complete the central voyage of human life." Why does she say "again"? Perhaps she refers obliquely to her understanding that the history of *yangsheng* is not a simple story of an unbroken health mainstream throughout the several-thousand-year history of Chinese medicine and philosophy. She is, after all, trained as a historian, as is testified by a technical and academic historical work on *yangsheng* that Zhang Qicheng coauthored with her.[37] She knows that the *yangsheng* movement in contemporary Chinese cities is in some sense a new enthusiasm, an invented tradition, even though many of its ingredients are genuinely ancient. This "again" gives her words an even more polemical tone. It is as if she is responding to a crisis in life and meaning: the central voyage of human life requires some immediate intervention from a time-honored form of refined experience if it is to be perfected.

It is because experience can be or must be refined, because life is best when self-consciously crafted, that books and experts are not only needed, but desirable. In fact, they deliver significant pleasure. Again, recall that Qu Limin persuades us (in a passage quoted above) that the ancient Yellow Emperor and his medical minister Qi Bo and their poetic vision of the body, of time, and of the social order are essential to the well-lived life:

> Like [poets Li Bai and Du Fu], the *Inner Canon* has insight, a generous spirit, and moving music. Like them, it has all the beauty and virtue possessed by Chinese culture: it establishes authority and orderly rule, stresses harmony and stability, emphasizes realistic proofs and transformation through instruction. It not only leads us to pace the void of the cosmos, to experience the absurdities and lacunae of the remote past, it also leads us to turn continuously inward, toward those almost unknowable dark places, ceaselessly delving into what is most difficult, until we can find in every moment the true heart throb of our life.

Culture, especially writing, is everywhere and enthusiastically consumed. Magazine kiosks offer periodical wisdom on every imaginable topic, used-book fairs and markets attract the culturally inclined who want to save money and find out-of-print materials, and neighborhood committees still post the daily newspaper for passersby to read. Neighborhood committees not only make news and culture available to residents in their district, they produce many texts of their own. In the last picture, Lili Lai studies a scrapbook documenting a street committee's cultural enrichment activities over the last year.

CHAPTER THREE

Daily Life

Religion rests its case on revelation, science on method, ideology on moral passion; but common sense rests it on the assertion that it is not a case at all, just life in a nutshell. The world is its authority.
—Clifford Geertz, "Common Sense as a Cultural System"

The surfaces of daily life present themselves as a mosaic of people, tasks, talk, gestures, minor choices, and predictable or surprising encounters. This chapter, too, is a mosaic. Each piece (each person, each task, each voice, each object handled, each chapter section) makes its own demands on our attention. But any appearance of larger patterns requires an act of narrative, analysis, or will. Time fills up and takes on form as a function of our purposes: today, I must finish making that jacket; tomorrow, I look forward to attending a nephew's wedding; one of these days, I'm going to clean out the closet. The multiple meanings of our lives are made from pieces: my father would have loved this movie; if I call on Mr. Zhang, he might help me find a job; that griddle cake looks delicious, but fattening. I can see something essential about *yangsheng* here. We need not turn to existential angst to see the work of meaning-making in practice; it is, after all, always underway. "The meaning of life" may be a classic philosophical problem, but the phrase raises too many unanswerable questions; as some of the images associated with Chinese words for life suggest (see Chapter 4), the many meanings of *a life* or of any number of concrete lives can be caught only as they are produced, gathered into form in the continuum of practice.

The observable parts of usual practice, when viewed with the literal eye, are hardly worth writing about. But for each individual, and for their families and friends, larger, more coherent narratives are at work in the fabric of everyday life: long-term strategies, persistent worries, a sense of duty, bodies of useful knowledge, habits of finding significance in behavior and words, desires, and disappointments—all these and more give form to the experience of daily life in an infinity of particular ways. Interviews or direct observations reveal a limited amount about idiosyncratic personal experience. Perhaps the most interesting kinds of significance in everyday life are not shared, even with intimates. Moreover, the most powerfully formative conditions for life—the structures and categories of languages, the deep-seated metaphysical assumptions dimly visible in idioms and proverbs, the biological processes of daily existence, long-inculcated habits, and built environments—usually fail to draw the attention of actors themselves.

As we discovered in our field study of *yangsheng*, however, interviews and everyday chat can give us *common sense*.[1] When people describe their daily activities, they may not be telling the literal truth about what they actually do every day. When they give us advice about diet or exercise, this may not be advice that they themselves follow. We can be fairly certain, however, that they are at least trying to make sense. They report particular approaches to crafting significance and offer particular insights about why life should be lived in certain ways. The materials from which this common sense is crafted are not invented by individuals; rather, they are first and foremost a shared heritage of language and lore, education and experience, limiting conditions and imaginable freedoms. But each individual has connected the sense-making resources of a language, a mediascape, a physical and economic environment, to his or her own life in unique ways.

It is this craftwork, this linkage of common resources with personal aims, this concern for achieving, in the present, a particular well-lived life, that impressed us most during the interviews about *yangsheng* that we conducted. We interviewed thirty-five Beijingers at length, and they rewarded our historical and cultural interest in *yangsheng* mainly by being interesting people, each facing her or his own situation with courage, creativity, and activism. Sometimes they surprised us with unusual opinions or especially penetrating insights, but more often, they echoed the kind of lore we found in our reading of the popular literature discussed in Chapter 2. The particular combination of interests and concerns was unique to each person, of course, and every interviewee seemed intent on educating us about a personal synthesis of *yangsheng* practice. As we listened, we marveled at the self-confidence of these Beijingers, their certainty that they had worked out in their experience some correct principles of long life and happiness. Certainly, they were aware of what the experts had to say and in many cases could use technical language well. But as we sat by the lakeshore, or in teashops, or in family sitting rooms, talking, we realized that these were the experts on life. Or at least their own lives.[2]

In this chapter, then, we weave together excerpts from interviews conducted in 2003, notes from continuing contact with those life-nurturing city dwellers since then, and our own commentary on what we thought we saw and heard. We also include some literary and historical background that helps us make sense of this material. One goal of this chapter is to multiply the voices through which Beijing's contemporary daily life can be perceived. In reproducing a generous sample of this plurality of voices, we hope to resist temptations to overgeneralize about Chinese culture, healthy living, or the generation of retirees who remember a less orderly past. Instead, we present in this long chapter a dispersion of tactics and evaluations as a few different people seek to make their daily lives wholesome and respectable. The resources they draw on are very similar, but their orientations toward the nurturance of life are far from identical.

The chapter begins with two interviewees whose remarks touched on most of the themes with which this chapter is concerned. Neither of these people enjoys any fame at all beyond their own circle of family, friends, and neighbors. But they are in a sense exemplars of a certain holistic *yangsheng* ideal. Then, in five thematic sections, we introduce the viewpoints of other interviewees as they focused their *yangsheng* knowledge and activities toward particular ends. In the midst of much daily miscellany, these comments take up the following themes: *yangsheng* as active social contribution; avoiding anger; *qi* work (*qigong* 气功) and *qi* transformation (*qihua* 气化); overcoming desire; and balancing the bitter and the sweet. With this multiplication of voices, we seek both to maintain the tonalities of everyday common sense and to respect the coherence of individual lives. Our own contextualizing and speculative commentaries in this chapter are meant to indicate how we heard what people were telling us and how we sought to recover the principles according to which they said they were living. Our comments are sometimes combined, but more often separated as the observations of authors Zhang Qicheng (**ZQC**) and Judith Farquhar (**JF**). For both of us authors, there was much more in the interview material than we have been able to highlight, but we have not wanted to upstage the residents of West City District, whose comments are central.

Yangsheng *Common Sense: Two Exemplary Beijingers*

The two interviewees with whom we begin presented us with the ideal image of the healthy and cheerful practitioners of garden-variety *yangsheng*. Both were enjoying their liberation in retirement from onerous duty and stress, and both actively crafted their health and happiness through a variety of life-nurturing practices. They said they were content with their lives, and as we got to know them (in both cases, beyond the interview context), we became persuaded that they were indeed happy, satisfied people.

> ***Zhu Hong*** *is a widow, sixty years old at the time of our interview, who had spent many years nursing her ill husband; he had been hemiplegic for twelve years as a result of a work injury. He died in 1998. She lives on a few hundred yuan a month supplied by her two sons, and we believe she was the "poorest" (in economic terms) of our thirty-five interviewees. She came to the interview with her good friend, Chen Zhihong, and the two of them joked and laughed throughout the several hours we spent together.*

I think the significance of *yangsheng* is that it's good for your body. For example, after I started exercising my body, my urinary tract problems didn't recur. Also, my spirits are good. Now I can't afford to see a doctor, even for an examination, so I have to nurture my own life well—*yangsheng* is better than everything else. If you don't get sick, on the one hand, you can avoid medical costs, and on the other hand, it's good for society. Having more long-lived elderly people is good for a society's image, and it's also good for the nation. In our neighborhood, we have two people over ninety years old. . . . *Yangsheng* makes you happier, and this is very good. Plus, if you save medical costs, that's more money for other important things.

You should find your own happiness, and don't go looking for reasons to be sad. Don't work too hard. My work is light. Don't get mad. This advice is good for body and health, spiritual enjoyment, elevating mood, and extending life. Watching TV is good, too.

ZQC Zhu Hong's way of talking about *yangsheng* makes little distinction between happiness and physical well-being, between the rationality of avoiding doctor bills and the hedonism of feeling good by cultivating happiness or "finding enjoyments" (*zhao le* 找乐). For her, this is all one package. The good life includes freedom from worry about the future, for example, the concern that one's children might have to take on a heavy burden of nursing care for her, similar to the care she provided for her disabled husband over many years. (Note that the benefits from the mining work unit that had paid her husband's disability compensation were discontinued on his death.) Her good life included finding many small pleasures in the present; indeed, it had been her enthusiastic endorsement of daily foot soaking and her description of how to cook the Beijing specialty *hutazi* (a vegetable crepe) that first charmed us. And she also expressed a concern for the public good and for the "image" of her society and nation. Though Zhu Hong, unlike some of our interviewees, was not actively involved in collective work, she still had strong views about the nature of a civil community and the ways in which the quality of individual lives contributes to it. For example, she admires the long-lived neighbors she mentions and wanted to introduce us to them for an interview. In general, then, she has a rather holistic view of health that includes pleasure, personal responsibility, avoidance of medical care, and a sense of the broader social good.

JF It is also interesting to note that in her way of talking about these life virtues, Zhu Hong speaks of *yangsheng*, health, and the good life as a personal *project*. She feels that she can actively cultivate her life, successfully banish anger, refuse to think about unpleasant things, and—one senses from this optimistic way of talking—successfully guarantee an old age free of illness. An American reading this material notices an interesting absence, especially when we consider that these comments come from a sixty-year-old widow with a very low income. There is no sense of being or becoming a helpless victim of an inexorable aging process or of social forces beyond one's control. Zhu Hong shows no sign of fearing the process of aging, nor does she seem to turn to a language of lack or loss, grief or anxiety, subjugation or powerlessness. All of these pessimistic approaches to the aging process are quite common among older people in the United States and even more common in the idioms of formal knowledge about "aging," as in the social sciences.[3] Of course, to speak of the dark side of getting older and facing illness and death would run counter to Zhu Hong's policy: "don't go looking for reasons to be sad," and "don't get mad."

One might suppose that she does have some secret worries, nighttime terrors, and feelings of grief as older friends and relatives drop off. But we should also take seriously her insistence that this is the best time of her life: now that her ill husband has died, she is free to nurture her own life and enjoy her own gratifying pastimes, including her neighborhood and her friends. Put another way, now that her freedom to craft a life is no longer limited by the needs of her husband, she is confident that she can actively make her own health, her own happiness, her own social goods.

This sense of project is consistent with the theme of activism developed in relation to other interview materials discussed in this chapter.

Ultimately, if we are to understand the kind of personal and collective agency imagined—and thus mobilized—by contemporary Beijingers, we will have to turn to the metaphysical questions taken up in Chapter 4. In a cosmos characterized by unceasing change, constant generation and regeneration, every level of reality is at all times open to intervention. When nothing about life is carved in stone, the imperious external and internal structures that appear to limit the "agency" (in a narrow sense) of the human actors conceived by Euro-American social theory can appear as just more arenas for tinkering. We are not here proposing that *yangsheng* practitioners either seek or find some ultimate plane of freedom. Beijing's city dwellers are quite well aware of the limits of their powers to change their environment and improve their conditions. But these limits are not seen as utterly fixed; because the constraints on daily life are always shifting, ordinary activity can find ways to redefine, bypass, or leapfrog the most immediate confining structures. At the very least, many believe, one can always craft a positive everyday life for oneself. Zhu Hong refuses to be victimized by worry or anger, and she does not see her body as subject to inevitable "natural" decline. She has confidence in the efficacy of her own activist outlook to keep difficulties at bay.

Zhu Hong's understanding of *yangsheng* is consistent with that of many others who emphasize exercise, fan dancing, climbing in the hills, seeking out simple pleasures (*zhao le* 找乐), living on a regular schedule, and avoiding anger. But we think it is important that she pointed out spontaneously that the value of *yangsheng* is not confined to the individual, but also benefits the nation and society. "Having more long-lived elderly people is good for a society's image, and it's also good for the nation." Her comments are fairly representative, typical of the approach of many older Beijing residents to the relationship between their own lives and public duty and civic life. Again and again we have heard Beijingers speak of the simple achievement of living long as a public contribution, and most of her contemporaries would agree with her. This way of thinking is founded on the assumption that the nation is not a separate entity

179

from its people, and perhaps in it there are echoes of the difficult challenges that have been met and overcome by the Chinese people. Having survived so much in good health, people imply, is not only an index of a sound nation, but the very substance of national soundness. This view is certainly more typical of the older, post-Mao generation than it is of younger people more engaged in China's reform economy. But it does offer suggestive insight into a specifically modern Chinese habitus that extends beyond the individual.

Our second "model" yangsheng *practitioner is **Li Jianmin**, a sixty-one-year-old retired factory worker who brought samples of his calligraphy and painting to our interview, as well as his sword to demonstrate* taiji *swordplay, his equipment for water calligraphy, and his choral-singing songbook.*

Now that I'm retired, I'm taking up a lot of hobbies that I have always loved, but didn't have time for. From a young age, I always loved to sing. I would always sing at home while I was doing housework, but while working at the factory, I never had time. From last year, because it's convenient when I take my grandson to school at Jingshan Primary and meet him there at the end of the day, I have been participating in the Beihai Wulongting Retired People's Choral Group. Tuesdays and Thursdays, 9:30 to 11:30. I usually go both days every week; when it's most crowded, there are as many as three hundred people, everyone sings together, it's really rousing for the spirit [*jingshen zhenfen* 精神振奋], the mood is totally happy and worry free [*xinqing shuchang* 心情舒畅], it's an extremely good feeling. The first time I went and heard so many older people singing at the top of their lungs, I felt an upsurge of emotion, and tears came to my eyes. I brought a book [here today], a selection of 100 years of twentieth-century Chinese songs. [When we asked, he checked off the ones he liked the best.]

The significance of *yangsheng* is: if your body/health is good, you can do everything, and there are benefits for your family and the society. Without body/health, you can't do anything. Nowadays, seeing a doctor is too expensive, but if you pay attention to *yangsheng*, you can minimize illness and lessen the burden on your children. *Yangsheng* includes *taiji*, regulation of food and drink, sports and exercise, mountain climbing, and so on.

When I exercise, I feel that my body is healthy, my mood is carefree, my life is happier and healthier, my energy is charged up, and I am saving medical costs....

I think for people who live in the world, if you can move, you should exercise. With exercise, you definitely have to keep it up; if you're not steady, then it will certainly be useless, so to keep doing it, you have to have willpower. In the winter, I, too, like to nestle in my warm quilts, but as soon as I think that it is for my health, for my body, I then climb out and go do my exercises.

JF Even though he's retired, Li Jianmin is a busy man. During the school week, he and his wife look after one of their two grandsons; their two-room apartment in the Drum Tower area is closer to the child's school than the apartment near the airport where his parents live, so the child stays with them during the week. Every morning, Li Jianmin takes his grandson to school on his bike or his motorbike and then goes on to a nearby park for *yangsheng* activities such as singing, pavement calligraphy, and *taiji*. He also seems to do much of the shopping for the household while he's out, bicycling long distances to find good bargains, and he finds time for calligraphy and painting on paper, as well. On our first interview, he brought catalogs from art shows he had visited—he is particularly fond of the Europeanized ink paintings of Xu Beihong.

When asked what sorts of things he would include in the category of *yangsheng*, the list of activities Mr. Li provided was quite conventional: *taiji*, exercise, nutrition. But he clearly thinks of his various artistic pastimes as life-nurturing activities, too. This was made clear in the simplest way: having been told that we were interested in *yangsheng*, he brought with him to the first long interview the various tools of his life-nurturing hobbies. He was happy to demonstrate his calligraphy for us on the spot, and after the interview, he went away and wrote a short poem in cursive script to present to us a couple of days later. He spoke glowingly of the enjoyment he gleans from doing these activities. Listening to him talk, and in later visits to his house, we felt that he was living testimony to the healthful effectiveness of an artistic life.

These artistic interests were not new to him, as he told us. Even while working as a heating-and-cooling technician, he had joined in the calligraphy and *taiji* clubs organized by his factory work unit. With his relatively long experience of *yangsheng* skills, one might expect him to adopt the air of a master and become a local leader of some kind. But this is not his style. In speaking of his pavement calligraphy, for example, he was more interested in telling us about a particularly skilled practitioner in Beihai Park whose work he liked to observe than he was in claiming any particular ability for himself. And he was attracted to the large singing group in Beihai because of the feeling of merging together with others in song. I came to think of Li Jianmin as an everyday collectivist, comfortable in social groups, serving the people (and especially his immediate family) in whatever way comes to hand, and claiming no special virtues for himself. This kind of humble approach to getting through life, combined with an obvious capacity for taking great enjoyment in little things, seems the very picture of health.

American readers may find it odd that such an apparently generous and pacific person should take pleasure in singing the violent martial songs we reproduced in Chapter 1. Another song that Mr. Li noted as a favorite is the following:

Great Broadsword March
The great broadsword sweeps off the heads of the demons,
Twenty-Ninth Army brothers, the Anti-Japanese War is here today.
The guerrilla army of the Northeast ahead of us,
   the people of all China behind us,
Our Twenty-Ninth Army is not alone.
Pick out the enemy, then wipe them out, wipe them out!
Charge!! The great broadsword sweeps off the heads of the demons—Kill!!

JF was at first a bit shocked by this anti-Japanese rhetoric, and on several occasions asked Li Jianmin whether singing such songs could "have a bad influence on China-Japan friendship." At times he insisted that "these are just songs, fun to sing, and they remind us of our youth." At other times, especially when influenced by 2005 commemorations of the end of the Anti-Japanese War, he saw these lyrics as important ways of remembering Japan's crimes against the Chinese people. But in understanding his tastes and those of the many other retirees who sing such songs in the parks, it is important to bear in mind that these are *songs*. The tune, the meter, the ring of the lyrics all combine to make up their charm. They are also the music of a bygone era, when Li Jianmin and his age mates were young, idealistic, and vigorous. Even I, however, a more or less pacifist foreigner, when singing along with the "Great Broadsword March," whole-heartedly enjoyed shouting out "Charge!" and "Kill!"

Perhaps the release involved in these songs is also a form of *yangsheng*. It is in any case a way of exercising little-used parts of the self. Particularly charming was Li Jianmin's remark, "for people who live in the world, if you can move you should exercise." In this respect, he, like Zhu Hong, seemed committed to making a project out of life, to carrying life to a higher level, both more disciplined and more joyful. Just being able to move is not enough: one should dance and sing. Just being able to read and write is not enough: one should read culture and write calligraphy.

ZQC Choral singing is a common *yangsheng* activity in Beijing. Those who participate in it are mostly retired people, though there are also a number of middle-aged participants. This is not only a kind of exercise (*yundong*), it is even more a form of nostalgia; it is a deeply felt remembrance and arousal, and it is also a powerful way of sharing the fellow feeling (*ganqing*) of a generation. Laozi said, "He who wants to live long should 'return to infancy.'" I am reminded of the phrase "return to spring" that is often heard in the world of Chinese medicine. As winter turns to spring, trees and grass come back to life. Thus, the phrase "a return to spring at the clever hands [of the doctor]" (*miaoshou huichun* 妙手回春) is a figure for the highest level of medical skill, allowing a return to life even from the brink of death. It also figures *yangsheng* and its ability to reverse aging and return youth. Many of the older people we spoke with in Beijing had experienced this "return to spring" phenomenon and become "like elderly children."

In practice, these phrases mean two things: one is that the body is returned to health. If in the past there was some illness, it is either cured or the symptoms are much lessened. The other sense of the term is that the spirits are improved, morale is improved, and one feels happy in his or her heart/mind. These "elderly children" are thought of as resembling actual children, at least in that they have returned to a kind of spontaneous wisdom that allows them to get over any small frustrations in their daily lives quickly. There are none of the negative connotations of a "second childhood" in English; rather, it is an achievement of age to recover spontaneity and uncomplicated pleasure.

Among Li Jianmin's interests is a practice worthy of some attention, and that is his use of writing and calligraphy as a form of *yangsheng*. Though he says he had long been interested in calligraphy, earlier in his life, he had not thought of calligraphy as a form of *yangsheng*. While still working, he wrote mainly because there were calligraphy contests sponsored by his work unit. But now he speaks of his writing as good for *yangsheng*. Note, though, that he chooses to practice calligraphy in public, with water on pavement, even though he does have space in his house to spread out and ink words on paper in private. He often goes to a plaza near Wangfujing to practice his pavement calligraphy. At the time of our interview, he demonstrated at our spot by the edge of the lake. Dipping his large sponge "brush" into the water of the lake, he wrote "The Red Army fears no extremity or hardship" in cursive script on the stone pavers. He also showed us a piece of calligraphy he had done earlier on paper, listing the four characters "fortune, longevity, health, stability," as well as some poems by Chairman Mao and a painting of a horse in the style of Xu Beihong. Judging from his manner as he shared these things with us, we felt that he was a person who enjoyed much inner satisfaction. But in addition, because this kind of calligraphy and painting takes energy and engages movement of the hands, feet, and the whole body, it certainly is a form of exercise. Certainly, many famous calligraphers and painters in China have lived to a ripe old age.

Reflecting on the lives and attitudes of these two interviewees, Ms. Zhu and Mr. Li, we remain impressed with their optimism, their enjoyment of simple daily pleasures, and their active crafting of the times and spaces of life. They were both in their early sixties at the time, which may be too young to worry much about a bleak future of true old age and illness. Perhaps they feel that this stage of their lives, while they are still fairly vigorous, is meant to be an enjoyable interlude: onerous duty is in the past, and uncontrollable physical or economic pressure has not yet become a problem. Perhaps their most obvious characteristic, however, is their ability to conduct the good life with such simple and inexpensive tools. They rely on their own resources, and even though neither of them speaks much of spiritual life, it is clear that they understand the meaningful depths of *yangsheng* in practice. The ways in which these two Beijingers talk about *yangsheng* and everyday life may sound rather banal; but it is in the living of this common sense that we can perceive a real achievement, one that is both unique to each person and understandable to anyone. Common sense, indeed.

Yangsheng *as Active Social Contribution: Su Jinqing, Qu Zhixin, Cui Xiumin, and Zhou Xiao*

We located most of our interviewees through an initial survey process in which we sought help from street and neighborhood committees. Thus, it is not surprising that some of those who turned out to be interested in *yangsheng*, interested in talking with us, and interesting to us as individuals were active in their local neighborhood committees. When we turned up in 2001 asking for interviewees, these local public servants volunteered to be interviewed while also helping us locate others who would be willing to participate in our initial survey. As we explored questions about *yangsheng* with these neighborhood committee staff members, we found their particular combinations of social contribution and life cultivation very engaging. Four of them were so interesting that we sought longer follow-up interviews, and those four are presented below.

These individuals are not especially exceptional; rather, they express a kind of citizenship that is often encountered in the older, well-organized neighborhoods of central Beijing. In the West City District, we contacted the ten street committees that serve the district; each street committee oversees the work of a number of smaller neighborhood organizations. Though these latter small offices are for most city dwellers the most proximate arms (or fingertips) of the state, and such committees have sometimes been seen as a site of government surveillance and control, they mainly function to provide community services. In 2003, during the SARS epidemic, and in 2005, amid fears of avian flu outbreaks, they also coordinated public-health surveillance and reporting. The most evident activities of street committees and neighborhood associations these days are offerings such as dance classes, calligraphy clubs, after-school programs for kids, and home visits for ailing elderly people. They also try to coordinate and control trash management and the hygiene in public latrines. Certainly, not all of the local workers who volunteer in the many neighborhood committees are interested in *yangsheng*; but nearly all of them would have something interesting to say about the meaning of their lives in the service of the people.

Su Jinqing is a fifty-four-year-old retired electrician active in his neighborhood committee. In response to one of our questions, he says he doesn't pay much attention to the relationship between food and health. He was raised in a village "where if you could eat your fill, that was good enough. Sometimes we would buy a little meat or fish, but that was for the children.... Nowadays, my eating habits are simple; I'm not a picky eater, I eat whatever there is, and whatever I eat tastes good."

I feel that the food I like to eat is the best, the food one likes to eat is the most nutritious. I don't know what foods have any special benefits for the body. Just eating one's fill is good. What you want to eat is exactly what your body needs. Just eat it; it will be good and do no harm. I have no dislikes or allergies [*wo bujikou* 我不忌口]. But it's also not good to eat foolishly [*buyao huchi* 不要胡吃]....

Before, when I went to the office, I would ride a bicycle, but now I mainly walk. There is no pressure in my work now. The best thing about my daily life is its boring routine, its blandness [*pingdan* 平淡]. I'm very happy, smiling and laughing all day, nothing to upset me. . . .

I was born as a child of bitterness, and before, I never paid any attention to *yangsheng*. The most important is to find one's own happiness [*ziji zhaole* 自己找乐], get plenty of exercise, don't get upset. Whether it's work or just daily life, both are a kind of joy. . . .

What is the significance of *yangsheng*? It's a kind of cultivation of knowledge. Move more, exercise more, be in a carefree mood. I'm a person who has accepted Mao Zedong Thought; I esteem what Chairman Mao said about the great public without [any] private [*dagong wusi* 大公无私]. In contemporary society, don't despise anything, that's the only way to have good health and good spirits [*jingshen* 精神]. *Yangsheng* is not for oneself: this way of thinking is very important. One must do more good works. If you do good works, your mood will be happy. If you go out on the street and see an old person fall down, and you don't help, you'll feel uncomfortable in your heart. There's a lot of selfishness in society today—it's an economistic society. In the past, Chairman Mao taught us to serve the great public without any private. We should respect the old and cherish the young. I think the traditional way of nurturing life and Confucian thought—the ideas that human nature is basically good, you should respect the old and love the young, be painstakingly moral, think of others, cultivate humility—these are convergent with Chairman Mao's "Great public, no private," "Serve the people," and "Study Lei Feng" slogans of the 1960s. These are all on the same track as Jiang Zemin's policy of the "Three Represents," and [they all boil down to the] "serve the people" idea of Mao Zedong Thought. Traditional beauty and morality should be well continued and developed. People of my age have been rather much influenced by Mao Zedong Thought, and I especially esteem Mao Zedong Thought. "Serve the people"; "Great public no private," "We all drink from the same cup of water"; "Don't be selfish"—these are my mottoes.

In the present commodity economy, I mainly just try to maintain a peaceful heart; I don't do anything bad, and I don't especially focus on doing good. . . . If your own health is good, but you are quite selfish, that's just too narrow-minded. If you're too selfish it's very tiring.

Spiritual health is more important than bodily health. The spirit is the
mainstay (the prop) and matter is the basis; spirit is the number one essential of life. If a person is happy, there will be no illness.

JF Mr. Su relies on a Maoist language and mode of thought to articulate his experience. He mentions the contrast between present-day
comforts and difficulties past, and he talks of serving the people.
These are topics dear to the hearts of many of those we interviewed.
But his interview stands out for the effortless way in which he combines the performance of a public duty with relaxed and enthusiastic
enjoyment of life's other pleasures. At the same time as he talks
freely about indulging his appetites for food without worrying too
much about scientific nutrition, he says that his working life at the
neighborhood committee is pleasingly bland. In fact, he says, "I was
born as a child of bitterness" and "The best thing about my daily life
is its boring routine, its blandness." (It is rather standard to refer to
the difficult collective past as "eating bitterness.")[4] But even as he
notes that his job at the neighborhood committee is not stressful, he
also insists on a close connection between serving the "great public
without any private" and the achievement of personal health and
happiness. This is an impressive way of organizing experience on the
part of a retired skilled worker who could certainly have done something else in his retirement besides volunteer at the neighborhood
committee. Presumably he could have had an even more peaceful
and "bland" life playing mahjong under the trees and watching TV.
Living such a life—and we see many who do—he could still have felt
eternally grateful to have entered a more secure and less demanding phase of life. Instead, he chose to remain an activist and use his
organizational skills in the neighborhood committee office. It is difficult not to be persuaded by Mr. Su's cheerful reminders that public
service, with its attendant requirements of tolerance, humility, and
generosity, can take its place beside other pleasures of everyday life,
such as eating what one likes and "achieving inner peace."

Before retiring, Mr. Su suffered the constraints of work as a
factory electrician, and he implies that his working life was one of

stress and pressure. Surely, running a state-supported trade union in a state-owned enterprise—his former job—had its share of stressful politics. Though he is free from those pressures now, he lives on a small pension and hasn't the wealth to do just anything he pleases; moreover, he apparently transferred the collective orientations of his working life directly into a less demanding collectivism in his neighborhood by volunteering at the neighborhood committee. Not only does he not approve of selfishness, he can't even imagine it, really. In his view, it would be just too exhausting to have to rely on oneself alone to meet any sort of life goal.

I think his little remark, then, "being too selfish is very tiring," opens a window into a generational habitus for a whole cohort in Beijing. Habituated to providing for others while relying on them at the same time, the daily lives of old rank and file Maoists like Mr. Su diverge from the market-oriented path of Beijing's more highly visible entrepreneurs and youth. In fact, the most fatiguing part of "being too selfish" is probably the constant effort to decide what you want and figure out how to get it for yourself. Obviously, Mr. Su has no patience for this kind of competitive and consumerist calculation. In speaking of the "great public no private" world of the past, he resists the economic policies and emergent life forms of the new China by crafting a new life in which the old collectivist structures, cooperative skills, and mundane pleasures are still salient and usable. He has found a way of life in retirement in which his particular skills are still useful in the service of others; one could see this as a desirable, if "bland" life, one that realizes the pleasurable and healthful logic of *yangsheng*.

ZQC Su Jinqing is like other neighborhood activists in his frequent quotation of Mao Zedong. He says he doesn't pay much attention to *yangsheng* himself and hasn't studied any techniques with anyone, but he does often speak of the importance of spiritual happiness, finding one's own happiness, getting exercise, and not being lazy. Actually, "finding happiness" is the most important part of *yangsheng*. In the interviews, many people said they didn't understand or

189

pay special attention to *yangsheng*, but all spoke of the importance of pleasure or happiness.

Another very important point about Mr. Su is that he unifies *yangsheng* and political thought (*zhengzhi sixiang* 政治思想) in a notion of moral character. *Yangsheng* is not undertaken for oneself alone; rather, correct thought must be emphasized, because it tends to more good deeds. Mr. Su uses the word *sixiang* 思想 when he says that a person's thought is important. This term these days means not just philosophical thought or a system of neutral ideas, but morally and ideologically correct thought. This usage of "thought" dates from the era of Maoist ideological hegemony, but this kind of normativity, these disciplines of thought, do not appear to be uncomfortable for him. On the contrary, a certain life in collective consciousness is integral to his cheerful activism. When you do good deeds, you feel happy, he says. When you feel happy, then your health (*shenti* 身体) will be good.

Mr. Su even uses the word "spirit" (so did Mao Zedong): spiritual health is more important than bodily health, spirit is the mainstay, while matter is the foundation. Spirit is the sine qua non of life. There is no illness when a person is in good spirits. He does not distinguish this viewpoint from his moral outlook and his respect for Mao Zedong Thought. In his remarks, he not only quoted the slogans "Serve the people" and "Great public with no private," he also quoted Confucian thought, the traditional ethical virtues of respecting the elderly and cherishing the young, putting the stress on morality, considering the needs of others, and modestly yielding place to others. This way of thought that unifies the nurturance of life, political commitment, and morality together is an important synthesis of *yangsheng* culture. The nurturance of morality is achieved through the elevation of ethical precepts, and it achieves the goal of simultaneous and inseparable spiritual and physical health. Perhaps this viewpoint on *yangsheng* is difficult to grasp from a Western perspective?

The word he uses for "private" (*si* 私) is quite interesting. The oldest way of writing it is 厶. The *Hanfeizi*, a legalist work of the third century B.C.E., interprets it as "*si* is a self-enclosed camp" and also writes that "*si* circles in on itself." The very form of this character suggests that "*si*" is a state of considering only oneself, not thinking of others, a state in which everything takes the self as its center, everything circles around the self. The form of this word is directly counterposed to "*gong*" 公, still used in its ancient form. The *Hanfeizi* explains that "*gong* is the backside of *si*"; this idea is visible in the character itself: An "eight" 八,pronounced *ba* or *bei* (a homonym for "the back") sits atop 厶; thus, *gong* is a counter to *si*; the public is precisely *not* what circles in on itself. The use of the literal word "backside" here might also invoke a dynamic and interactive *yinyang* relationship, since the front of the body is usually classified as *yin* and the back is classified as *yang*; but if the *gong/si* relationship is a *yinyang* one, then already neither word can mean quite what the English words "public" and "private" mean.[5] China's first dictionary, the *Shuowen jiezi* (ca. 121 C.E.) explains it this way: "*si* comes from eight (*ba*)," meaning that *gong* is the reverse (*ba*, or *bei*) of *si*, the opposite of *si*. *Gong*, the attitude of the great public, thinks about others, rather than itself. So when Su Jinqing refers to the Maoist and Confucian ideal of a "great public without any private," his words themselves highlight this contrast.

Although many people speak of a "great public without any private," very few add that "being too selfish is very tiring." This remark on Mr. Su's part actually refers again to the relationship of body and spirit, and at the same time, it includes an ethical element: selfishness of the spirit, the act of severing the natural links inherently relating people to other people, can be a very fatiguing and even anxious process, thus bringing about bad bodily health.

Qu Zhixin is a recently retired rubber factory trade unionist; he was fifty-nine when we interviewed him. On a later visit to his bustling neighborhood committee offices, we found him looking every bit as committed, competent, and cheerful as his interview, extracted below, had made him seem.

I do *yangsheng* for long life and health. I do it so I can do more work and be ready for a future of looking after the grandchildren and relishing the joys of family life [*tianlun zhi le* 天伦之乐]. . . .

What are the specific benefits of *yangsheng*? Many! I eat more, sleep sweetly, and am spiritually fulfilled. [He quotes a proverb:] "The way of *yangsheng* is eating and sleeping, talking and singing, playing ball and taking pictures, writing and painting, writing poetry line by line, playing chess to banish the blues, chatting of heaven, speaking of earth."

I plan to write two books, I thought them out when I was younger, and now I'm all ready to start. Relish eating, exercise, be in a good mood, these are the best *yangsheng*. . . .

I think the human body needs to alternate stillness and movement; on the one hand, you need to move, and on the other hand, you need to be still. Only if you eat well, rest well, and you are happy in your heart will your health [*shenti*] be good.

ZQC Qu Zhixin is someone who, like Su Jinqing, has been much influenced by the thought of Mao Zedong. For example, when there are quarrels in the neighborhood, when people are disgruntled, when people resent being criticized, he quotes Chairman Mao's famous phrase "Eat simple food, and don't let things get you down." He also cites the example of Deng Xiaoping's "three high moments and three low moments" when he mentors others. He says these ways of thinking through problems are always very effective. Perhaps they are, because he himself seems very satisfied with life and very optimistic.

The proverb he quotes is actually a charming description of the *yangsheng* public culture of this part of Beijing. But Mr. Qu links these life-nurturing enjoyments directly to his goal of serving the community. After retirement, he began to work at the neighborhood committee office, hoping to do some good for the residents. This was not for the money: he gave up some jobs that paid more than the small stipend provided by the residents committee. He believes that the goal of *yangsheng* is to serve society, and he connects *yangsheng* organically with society and the nation. He even links his pastimes and hobbies and his skills, such as seal carving, together with society and the national. (He teaches a seal-carving class in the neighborhood committee office. This art is by nature closely linked to national traditions and national culture. The authority of the imperium and the identity of lordly individuals are embodied in carved seals and their red imprints.) *Yangsheng* is thus endowed by Mr. Qu with a very broad meaning. As he put it, everything he does, and especially his study of seal carving, is first and foremost a way of conducting oneself as a human being: "Whenever I see injustice, I immediately want to intervene. Perhaps this is also a great virtue of the common people." This is a clear reference to classical philosophies of human nature. For Mencius, the proof that people are basically good is that no one can remain passive when witnessing another person in danger.

Though his *yangsheng* activities are not elaborate, he seems to have deeply understood the kind of *yangsheng* theory we discussed in Chapter 2. He pointed out that in *yangsheng*, both movement and stillness, activity and rest, must be enjoyed. This is a really important idea, completely consistent with the tradition of Chinese *yangsheng* thought. It's a question of attending to the temporalities of life. Only when movement and rest are woven together—first moving, then being still, eating well, then resting well—can the heart be happy and cheerful and the body sound.

JF Mr. Qu's thoughtful approach to *yangsheng* issues is not surprising. He has been planning on writing two books on *yangsheng* and health. Much of what he says sounds rather prescripted, as if he has been thinking for a long time about how to express his perceptions and ideas in effective language. Moreover, he often spontaneously adopts Maoist language to express his thoughts. Maoist language of this "serve the people" kind has been discredited or rejected by many in Beijing, but it sounds quite sincere coming out of Qu Zhixin's mouth. And some elements of this idiom remain quite natural in the usage of many people, old and young. So it is also fitting for a person who plans to write a book that he actually has a rather broad vision of *yangsheng*, beyond the considerations of his own "optimistic" personality and its relationship to his individual health.

What relationship does he see between "society" and the more individual questions of personality and life regulation? He didn't really specify, but his approach to social issues impressed Lai Lili and

JF when we went to visit him in his neighborhood committee office. Mr. Qu is a true activist, one who works long hours for his community, fluently quotes Chairman Mao, and acts as an instigator of collective organizations. His neighborhood committee, for example, decided to surpass the expectations of the city and the street committees in organizing not just a few, but eight hobbyist and health clubs for residents of their neighborhood. Several times during the interview, he insisted that one should keep one's health in order to serve the community better. In this connection, he also mentioned the contribution of the very old to their social environment; simply by managing to live their own lives at an advanced age, they improve the neighborhood. Basically, then, he begins with the expectation that life involves engagement with and service to the social environment (he didn't talk at all about "nature" in his several interviews), and the nurturance of this sort of service-oriented life demands the kind of regimes that others interested in *yangsheng* often discuss. A life of service is for him the default position.

Cui Xiumin, *age fifty-five, works as the bookkeeper for her neighborhood committee. Unlike the two men discussed above, she does not take a major leadership role in the organization, and at the outset of our interview, she cautioned us that she could not speak for the committee, only for herself. But much of what she said did sound like the views of a person committed to working for the city and the community.*

In the last ten, twenty years, the attitudes of the ordinary people in the Houhai area toward *yangsheng* have changed a lot! Now people have nothing much to worry about, old people have their pension and supplements for the elderly—now that people have no more fear of the "sneak attacks" of unexpected calamity, when they can eat their fill, they think that life is better. These days, things are so much better, aren't they? Society is stable, it's possible to think of one's health, live more actively, appreciate more, so there's more emphasis on *yangsheng* and that sort of thing. . . .

My mother-in-law passed away at age eighty-five in 1992. My mother also died at eighty-five in 1996. Now society is aging;

married couples living on their own in small families can't take care of four old people, their elderly parents, so there will be issues in the future. Our children both have jobs, [which would make it hard for them to care for us in person], so we hope to get a supplement [*yang lao jin* 养老金] and get into an old folks' facility. This reduces the burden on the state, and we could pass a comfortable old age there. I hope the government establishes more old people's homes. In this area, there's one run by our street committee. Last month, our residents' committee arranged for an elderly resident to move to an old folks' home in Chang Ping. For one month, you pay 500 to 600 RMB (U.S. $40 to $50). She's been there over a month. I asked her children—they say she's very well. Before, we sent another one there; he also did very well. My husband and I are quite willing to go into an old folks' home. Our daughter has her own things to worry about, her own family. Living together with family is the best, but if you don't live together, they'll always be running around on errands for us; this sort of thing saps your strength in every way. On the other hand, we thought it through—in the old folks' home, everyone is elderly, you have the same language you can speak; if you want to have fun, you can. If you get sick, there's a doctor there who can treat it. If the government gives us an elderly supplement, I'm very willing to go. The main thing is the elderly supplement account—we could draw from it every month; right now, there is only elderly care insurance. The state is emphasizing the life care of the elderly more; it has begun with elder-care insurance and has promised that later there will be elderly supplements. That way, life could be especially happy [*kaixin* 开心]....

What are the reasons for *yangsheng*? Nowadays, life is very good, very happy and fortunate; people are willing to live a few more years. For the nation, for society, regularly focusing on *yangsheng* and on health protection, it can 1) save the state medical costs; 2) make for less illness for yourself, prevent a lot of suffering; 3) lessen the burden on the family; and 4) going out into the streets, the elderly are especially spirited; they set up [*shuli* 树立] an exemplary image of and for the Chinese people.

JF Cui Xiumin talks like the neighborhood committee worker she is, continuously linking the public good with the personal concerns she and her husband face as aging retirees. Thus, she phrases the challenges faced by her family in terms of a familiar formula derived

195

from modern demographic consciousness: "society is aging; married couples living on their own in small families can't take care of four old people." This is a constant refrain in the news as the consequences of China's one-child policy are becoming more clear: the generation soon to reach middle age will have an especially heavy burden of care for their (more numerous) parents' generation, since they will lack siblings to help support or nurse ailing elderly parents. Unlike many we spoke with, who would probably never consider moving into a nursing home, Cui Xiumin is thinking about it and brings up the topic spontaneously in our interview. This rhetorical choice may reflect persistent anxieties she shares with her husband about what will happen to them as they age, given that they cannot afford to seek expensive medical care should they fall ill. But her tone in reporting their calculations about the future is insistently cheerful. She has gone so far as to figure out that she and her husband will need a government subsidy to afford a nursing home, but having read that such subsidies may soon be forthcoming, she is talking herself into this plan. In doing so, she depicts life in this new-style collective as rather idyllic: "we thought it through—in the old folks' home, everyone is elderly, you have the same language you can speak; if you want to have fun, you can. If you get sick, there's a doctor there who can treat it."

It is interesting that she sees virtues in being around people her own age, especially in terms of being able to speak the same language and enjoy the same activities. The sense of being linguistically and culturally estranged from a younger generation is fairly chronic among Beijing's retirees. They lived most of their lives as workers and cadres in state-owned enterprises and government work units and gained their idioms of self-expression during a period when Maoist language dominated everyday talk. Their children's generation, those under age thirty or so, don't even remember or understand that language. Many Beijingers over fifty have told us that they just can't talk to their children and their children's friends any more. Thus, it seems as if Ms. Cui is imagining an "old folks' home" as a return of some kind: a return to a secure work-unit way of life, a return to a more familiar language, even a return to a prework, prehassle life of "fun."[6]

She also enjoys her current way of life. She is the neighborhood committee leader of a disco dancing group that meets every night at the edge of the lake, and she enjoys walking around the lake and doing *taiji*. Leading the disco dancing group is quite a time commitment on her part, and she does see this activity as a public service to the women in the neighborhood, who—she says—benefit from the exercise and the friendly ties in the group. But she clearly enjoys the dancing group, as well, and the daily exercise she gets must be important in maintaining her obvious good health.

Cui Xiumin is not only healthy, she is an optimist. Perhaps she felt that she should speak to our group (and its foreign scholar) in especially positive terms on behalf of the neighborhood committee, though she began by assuring us that she would speak only as an individual. Her vision of social changes since the beginning of the reform period was rather comprehensive and very positive: because life has gotten both more comfortable and more stable for everyone, she suggested, people now speak more often of achieving longevity (*changshou* 长寿). She says that people in this area are "willing to live a few more years" under these excellent new conditions. And *yangsheng* activities help them to achieve an extension of their years of enjoying a life without the "sneak attacks" of hardship and disruption. Is Ms. Cui suggesting that a few years ago, when times were hard, older people were less interested in long life and good health? Were they perhaps more "willing" to die young, just to escape the daily grind? To conjure an image of an earlier generation of despairing and suicidal elders would certainly be an overinterpretation of Ms. Cui's phrasing, and it would also be historically wrong. But her way of thinking about possible new ways to enjoy old age in an improving central Beijing certainly grounds the pleasures of *yangsheng* in social and economic changes.

Like Zhu Hong and many others, she sees spirited old people doing *yangsheng* in public places as "setting up a good image for China." Is she speaking for the local government here, expressing a concern for the impressions made on foreign visitors to the Houhai area? If so, this would be a view much influenced by sentimental media images of rugged-looking, but rosy-cheeked old people in "traditional" Chinese settings. The culture of tourism is readily available on television and undoubtedly affects the self-consciousness of Beijingers. Or is she referring to a more subtle logic in which models and exemplars—simply by embodying certain virtues themselves—directly serve the collective?

This mention of exemplars reminds us of some long-standing Chinese theories of rulership, which develop the idea of "ruling as an exemplar" and speak of the true lord or sage king as one who cultivates his own virtues, eschewing direct intervention in the social world. A virtuous social order crystallizes around him solely through the power of his example to others. Such a lord can rule through self cultivation (*zixiu* 自修) and "nonaction" (*wuwei* 无为). Needless to say, much has changed in China since these ancient theories of rulership were first advanced, and nationalist and anti-imperialist political movements, as well as a modern, Communist emphasis on creative activism, have intervened historically to make a very different political world. Still, the notion of the model or exemplar has not been entirely abandoned in modern Chinese political practice. What sorts of influence were model soldiers and model workers, for example, actually supposed to have? Presumably, they were at least meant to demonstrate that an effective revolutionary life could actually be successfully embodied. An "actually existing socialism" was inhabited by persuasively actual "new people." In the case of elderly exemplars, then, under today's very differently politicized conditions, an important point is being made about life, longevity, and all the other issues that concern the optimistic Cui Xiumin. Again and again, we see in people's commonsense remarks a slippage between "the individual" and "society"; healthy old folks simply *are* the substance of a healthy society and a sound nation. Their simple existence is their service to the collective and the source of their elder authority; approaching the self-cultivated sovereignty of the sage king, they need do nothing else but live moderately well.

ZQC Cui Xiumin presents herself as a conscientious retired cadre who practices *yangsheng* through dancing, walking around the lake, and *taiji*; she says she is content with recent changes in Beijing and with government policies. She feels that *yangsheng* is good for the state and society. So she seems very relaxed about life and looks forward confidently to a fortunate old age with state support. In her view, *yangsheng* appears to be a kind of "harmony" rather than a form of "resistance."[7] Her understanding of the significance of *yangsheng* is much like that of many others her age, intimately connected to the welfare of society and the state.

The styles of *yangsheng* adopted by Cui Xiumin are like those of many other city dwellers; they don't require any particular place to be performed. But her inclusion of walking around the lake is interesting. This is not a strongly collective form of exercise, though it's done in public. Around Houhai in the early morning, people usually walk alone or with one or two other people.[8] This long, narrow string of lakes is large, and to go all the way around it takes a long time. As early as 4:00 A.M. there are walkers and runners out, and not a few of these like to exercise for as much as five or six hours. Some go around the lake three times. There are several methods of circling the lake: fast walking, jogging, slow walking, backward walking. Cui Xiumin says she likes backward walking. Because normally we walk forward, backward walking serves as a good correction to this, leading to a deeper harmony. There is a *yinyang* logic to this idea: any extreme tendency in one direction should be balanced with its opposing tendency, at least for a while. *Yin* and *yang* continuously correct each other to seek a middle way. It's not surprising to see an ordinary Beijing retiree adopting this philosophically informed way of acting. This is the result of the sedimentation and accumulation in ordinary attitudes of several thousand years of traditional Chinese civilization.

Zhou Xiao is a young mother who works at the same neighborhood committee as Mr. Su. She takes her job in neighborhood family planning work seriously, and unlike Cui Xiumin, she is willing to speak for the committee: at the end of the interview, she offered some prepared comments for us about the city's public health priorities. At the time of our interviews, she had a six-year-old son who would soon be starting school. Her husband worked as a Western-food cook in a big hotel.

I regularly go out to exercise with my son; he weighed nine *jin* seven *liang* (over ten and a half pounds) when he was born, and he's a bit fat, but he's basically fine. I fear him getting fat; he's not very tall, so I always take him to play at the community exercise-machine area. Every evening we go out for an hour of exercise, between 7:00 and 8:00 p.m. . . .

After I gave birth to my son, my blood sugar was high, and my mother has diabetes. I'm not willing to admit to the fact of diabetes. I undertake my own exercise, dieting, and mood [work] to regulate myself, but basically, I don't take medicine. Drugs aren't good for the body; they always include dangers [*shiyao sanfen du* 十要三分毒]. My mother got diabetes when she was forty-two—she was bleeding from around her eyes and so forth. . . . She belongs to the Diabetes Society, and sometimes I go with her to listen to lectures. . . .

I basically live an orderly life. From the time I first became a mother, I felt that a small child should have order, should eat at the same time every day and sleep at the same time every day. If he is orderly, you can be orderly. I feel that order is very important. As for me, going to work every day, of course my life is very structured. I get off work at 5:30, cook dinner at 6:00, go out to walk at 7:00 after eating, and then at 8:00 after coming home I wash up and clean. On the weekend, we watch TV, stay up until 11:00 or 12:00, usually we put the child to bed at around 10:00. Before, when my health was better, I could still do some housework after he had gone to bed, now I just go to bed when he does. . . .

The key thing about *yangsheng* is that it allows you to avoid harming your body with drugs. It definitely elevates the quality of your own life. The herbal medicines and [traditional medical] teachings that have come down to us about *yangsheng* are very useful. Now science is advanced, but I am suspicious of all these cloned plants and animals. Are genetically modified foods good for the human body? I buy old-fashioned foods, but today's foods are not as tasty as those when we were young. Genetically modified foods are no substitute. In our neighborhood, a certain kind of new cucumber was introduced, and while it was growing, you could smell it all over the courtyard. But when you now peel it and eat it, it has no flavor. Things nowadays don't have their original flavor, they're all just a product of chemistry. . . .

Nowadays, few young people do *yangsheng* to protect their health; mostly it is the retired and elderly who come out to exercise. Of the retired residents (forty-five to sixty-five) who come out to exercise, maybe 60 percent organize their own dancing groups and *taiji* sword groups in the morning. As for solitary exercisers, I know an old guy over eighty—every day he gets up just after 3:00 a.m. and takes the first bus to climb Xiang Shan in the Western Hills. He climbs to the top and then comes down, and he's home by around 9:00. He says the air at Xiang Shan is the best for the health. Exercise in the schools is not emphasized a lot, but one sees a few students running on the street. But I don't think the city air is very good.

The most important things about *yangsheng* are: 1) Have an orderly life. 2) Diet. You should eat according to your own situation [*yinshi lidao* 因势利导], according to your own needs. Set up a normal way of eating and a normal way of drinking. Now we can speak of the three great drinks of the world: soy milk, green tea, red wine (4 percent alcohol, more or less). I drink a little of each every day. If I drink soy milk in the morning, then I don't need to drink tea or wine. Every month, when I get my salary, I buy a bottle of red wine, low alcohol content, I buy Fengshou brand, midpriced, thirty to forty RMB per bottle, and keep it in the refrigerator. When I am feeling especially tired before going to bed, and need to go to sleep, I drink a small glass—it helps me sleep peacefully. Soy milk is the cheapest; you get a big bag for one RMB, and it's good for beauty. You have to drink soy milk fresh, though. For diabetes, you should drink cool weak green tea in order not to lose its nutritional value; it has the function of clearing the liver system and brightening vision.

On the relationship between *yangsheng* and society, if your health is good, you have resistance to diseases that come up suddenly; you have the power to halt them. In April [2003], with SARS, part of [our success in managing it] was the solidarity of all the people, part of it was that the health of Beijingers is better than it was in the past. The Olympic bid has made people go out and get more exercise. The level of life has been raised now, day by day, year by year. In a peaceful and settled society, everyone wants to live a few years longer. This is my own viewpoint on the way of *yangsheng*.

ZQC Zhou Xiao differs from many of our interviewees in that she is a young woman, just over thirty years old; as a neighborhood cadre charged with public-health-related duties, she considers herself rather expert on *yangsheng*. Her own main *yangsheng* activities are walking and using the exercise machines in the public park near where she lives. Nowadays in Beijing, many public places have such small exercise facilities. Many elderly people also like to use these body-building machines for their daily exercise. In fact, the machines are designed with the physical needs of elderly people in mind. They are intended to encourage gentle, repetitive exercise; it would be difficult to overdo it on these machines or to injure yourself. Ms. Zhou's main motive for *yangsheng* is for the management of illness, even though she doesn't really admit to being ill. She is, however, trying to avoid taking medicine. Many people in China are like this; they may be ill, but they are not willing either to believe it or to admit it. Perhaps this is a difference with Westerners, who might see this tendency as rather strange by comparison: why wouldn't one admit to being ill? I think this is a kind of "mind over matter" function: by not admitting to illness, one feels one can use the force of spirit to minimize it and overcome it. Many people have this sort of faith in spiritual, psychic power. Ms. Zhou is not only unwilling to take medicines, she is also suspicious of nutritional supplements, first of all because they are too expensive and second because she feels the body does not lack these things. Faced with the specter of her mother's serious illness, she nevertheless tries to avoid medicine per se. In the process, she lives more cheaply and finds satisfaction in the "bland" routine of an orderly life.

JF Zhou Xiao is perhaps the least "socialist" of the four activists whose comments we have gathered here. Yet I think she should still be considered an activist, since she is taking a lot of initiative while still young to insure her own health and that of her son. Zhou Xiao mixed into her comments about herself a number of general remarks about the phenomenon of *yangsheng* in Beijing; I think she felt obliged, as a neighborhood committee staffer, to educate us on the subject, and I appreciated her observations on the subject. This is one reason we have included fairly substantial extracts from her interview. She seems to pride herself on having a rather scientific viewpoint—or perhaps even a social-scientific viewpoint, with her efforts to inform us about types of *yangsheng*—on health issues; this is in keeping with her position as a family-planning cadre, which involves a lot of health education. But it is worth noting that her comments mixed "Western scientific" information with facts drawn from "traditional Chinese medicine": thus, the virtues of green tea could have been expressed in terms of an "antioxidant" function (this nutritional fact is well known in China), but Zhou Xiao prefers to speak of green tea in a Chinese medical vocabulary, saying that it "clears the liver and brightens the vision." This mixture of genres of scientific information, in which Chinese medical knowledge makes as much sense as biomedical facts to an averagely educated person, is a normal and widespread feature of Beijing's public culture of health.[9]

Among our interviewees, Zhou Xiao was perhaps the most focused on the subject of living a stable, well-regulated life. She takes the temporality of daily life quite seriously, it would seem, and seeks to inculcate regular habits in her young son. This is an old idea. The *yangsheng* classic texts often speak of *qiju* (起居 habits of rising and resting) right alongside comments on diet, exercise, and spiritual self-cultivation. This is one classic idea that does not appear difficult to translate: Ben Franklin's maxim "Early to bed and early to rise makes a man healthy, wealthy, and wise" captures the sense of the ancient texts pretty well. (More than one popular work on *yangsheng* in Chinese quotes Franklin on just this point.) It is tempting to analyze this approach to how time should be lived through a logic of *yinyang*: the day has its *yin/yang* cycles, just as the year does, with its seasons. There are plenty of Chinese medical sources that can explain why doing *yang* things at a *yin* time might be less than wholesome. Though Zhou Xiao gave us little indication that she knows anything about classic philosophy, she nevertheless grasps the value of taking charge of one's own life in order to "protect health." (She used this phrase, *baojian*, quite often.) In this particular sense, then, we think of her as an activist, like her boss Mr. Su and the other neighborhood committee workers we met.

"Don't Get Angry"

One genre of popular literature that circulates widely in Beijing is doggerel verse. Even before cell phones allowed many thousands of rhymed homilies and jokes to circulate unbidden from hand to hand, even before the blogo-sphere facilitated the sharing of every apocryphal or sarcastic remark and commentary, instructive verses formed a part of the cultural background of everyday life. In 2010, we found this dense, but inelegant little verse, "Don't Get Angry," on a blog site.[10] We offer it here without commentary, but its resonance with many other elements of this chapter should be clear:

> Life is like a play, so there's cause for us to gather.
>
> Life is hard, so we help each other.
>
> No matter what, let's cherish each other.
>
> Lose your temper over trifles and soon you'll wonder why.
>
> Stay calm when others anger:
>
> When angry *qi* streams out, illness sneaks in—
>
> It is only you who really suffers.
>
> No one benefits from my rage,
>
> It only harms spirit and wastes strength.
>
> Stay close to those around you,
>
> Do not compete.
>
> Let even your children follow this rule.

These four interesting and committed people—Su Jinqing, Qu Zhixin, Cui Xiumin, and Zhou Qiao—all combined a personal practice of some *yangsheng* activity with their lives of service to the people. We thus think of them as activists, and in most of their language—with the possible exception of Zhou Qiao, the youngest—we hear echoes of an older collectivist politics. But their comments included so much that was ordinary, down-to-earth common sense that it is difficult either to separate their public lives from their private activities or to figure them as engaging in any special kind of mobilized action. Rather, they are just the most articulate of our Beijing interviewees on the meaning of *yangsheng* as action.

Don't Get Angry: Zhu Hong, Qu Zhixin, and Zhao Gang

The health benefits of avoiding anger were often mentioned by those we interviewed and visited. Zhu Hong was typical: "You should find your own happiness, and don't go looking for reasons to be sad. Don't work too hard.... Don't get mad. This advice is good for body and health, spiritual enjoyment, elevating mood, and extending life." During a long day Judith Farquhar and Lai Lili spent hiking with Zhu Hong and her friend Chen Zhihong in Beijing's Western Hills, the "don't get angry" refrain kept returning to our conversation. Chen Zhihong was dealing with some serious difficulties at the time and suffering uncomfortable physical symptoms as a result, explaining that she has diabetes and a heart condition, which usually present no problems. But conflicts with her brother over the use of a few courtyard rooms had given her a lot to be upset about on that particular day. Her friend Zhu Hong had one constant piece of advice: don't think about the unpleasant things in your life, don't talk about them, just forget it all and banish anger. Otherwise, anger will get the better of you and make you even more ill. We were impressed that Zhu Hong was so sure of being able to banish anger just by force of will, as it were. We heard echoes of this view of anger in the remarks of other interviewees as well, though, and the advice to avoid anger is a standard element in Chinese doctors' advice to patients.

Qu Zhixin, for example, echoed this viewpoint: "I have a characteristic: first, I am very straightforward, if I have something to say I say it. Then, I don't get angry. If some people gang up on me to criticize me, usually I wouldn't get angry. But if I do get mad, I express it, express it and get it over with, and then I'm just happy to be over it, no big deal." One imagines, when he speaks of people "ganging up on him," that his work in the neighborhood committee still resembles in some way the highly politicized and stressful workplace of several decades ago. Yet he seems to have found a resource in *yangsheng*-style optimism.

JF Like many others we interviewed, Mr. Qu notes that anger is an enemy of health and happiness. He has a rather hydraulic image of anger, one in which angry *qi* rises up in the body and can be emitted or even excreted from it—a literal understanding of the idea of both generating and expressing anger (*shengqi* 生气). Though the term for anger, *shengqi*, is completely conventional, and normal speakers of Chinese don't consciously connect the term with the generation of physiological or cosmic *qi*, Mr. Qu nevertheless seems to experience *shengqi* in a rather literal sense, as a production of *qi*. Here he opens up its meaning to explain his own experience of relatively brief and minor episodes of anger, the only occasional blowing of a gasket in the context of his cheery and optimistic personality. Like others we spoke with, he sees a basic optimism and a happy outlook as essential to health. And like the activist he is, he believes this "happy outlook" (*leguan*) can be cultivated.

Another interviewee presented a similarly literal idea of the *qi* involved in anger, but his personality was not at all like Mr. Qu's. Zhao Gang spoke at length about his personal *yangsheng* routines:

> Exercising all these years, I have come to really understand something [*tihui* 体会]. Just exercising is not enough. You also have to have a healthful mental state [*xinqing* 心情]. If an individual is angry, then his calisthenics exercise will not be good. Because I haven't stopped drinking and smoking, it's especially

important to avoid anger. Everyone fears illness, and all illness comes from anger. If you can evade anger, you evade illness. You can have the luxury [of getting mad] when you're younger, but older people certainly can't get angry. For example, if two people aren't happy, one of them is going to have to be a little more patient, should not ask his/her partner to be patient, but rather should be patient him/herself. You can't plan anger. Actually, my life has been very difficult, but I can be patient. When a person gets angry, the *qi* collects in the *dantian* (丹田) [in the abdomen], and after you get angry, your stomach can swell. You need to think of a way to expel the *qi*, and the method is, lie on the bed and breathe deeply. Inhale deeply through your nose, and exhale lightly through your mouth. . . .

I don't take supplements; the mental state is more important than tonic or bolstering medicines. My physique is good; whatever I want to do, I do. Also, a person can't gain profit at the expense of others. It's necessary to resign oneself to one's fate; fate cannot be changed. The affairs of state, for example the many corrupt officials, we can't control, so there's no point in getting mad. We can't seek wealth or fame. There's a saying: It's useless to want wealth, but wanting a good reputation is useful. If you're a little poor, it's not important, so I'm happy from morning to night, plus, I'm not poor.

JF During the period of our interviews in central Beijing, we came to refer to Mr. Zhao as the "anger management specialist." He constantly emphasized the bad health effects of getting mad, even as he became more heated and insistent in his style of talking with us. Like Mr. Qu, Mr. Zhao has a literal physiological understanding of anger. He sees the experience of anger as a production of *qi* in the wrong way, in the wrong place, causing bloating in the *dantian* in the abdomen. But unlike Qu Zhixin, he doesn't see the prompt and straightforward expression of angry feelings as a solution; he prefers a therapy he can undertake only at home, lying on the bed and controlling his breathing. This is a solitary discipline: Mr. Zhao lives alone, having been divorced twice. Certainly, Mr. Zhao appears to be a loner. Though he has in the past been active in organizing a large calisthenics group, in general, he seems to have a history of difficulties getting along with other people. It did not surprise us when

Anger

The physiological changes brought on by anger are clearly analyzed in Chinese medical writings. Chinese medicine sees human emotions as belonging to seven types, called the "seven emotional states" (qi qing 七情): these are the seven emotional changes of joy, anger, sorrow, thought, grief, apprehension, and fear. These seven kinds of mental state express the various responses of the human body to objective things. Under normal conditions, the seven types of feelings cannot make people ill. But when there are sudden, severe, or protracted emotional stimuli that exceed the scope of the ordinary physiological activities of the human body, they can make the qi mechanisms of the body chaotic and cause the visceral systems, yinyang, and the qi-blood relationship to lose regularity, thus inducing the onset of disease. The "seven emotional states" are one of the main disease-causing factors that produce internal damage, so they are also called the "seven feelings that do inner damage." The way in which the seven feelings cause illness is not the same as the way the other illness factors, such as the "six excesses" (liuyin 六淫), cause illness. The six excesses—wind, cold, heat, moisture, dryness, and fire—are exogenous: they invade from outside the body, entering through the skin or the mouth, and they produce signs of the early stages of developing illness. The seven feelings injure from within, directly affecting the interacting visceral systems, causing the qi mechanisms of the viscera to run counter to their proper order (niluan 逆乱), causing the qi-blood relationship to lose regulation and producing all manner of other disease changes to occur.

In the heritage of Chinese medicine, people's emotional activity has also been divided into five types, called the "five intentions" (wuzhi 五志).[1] These

208

he complained that the calisthenics group has fallen apart now that he no longer takes a leading role in it; this comment, like so much of his other conversation, had a definite griping quality.

Mr. Zhao experiences anger as a physical change affecting his whole body. Even observing him for the time span of an interview, we were able to see how his negative feelings affected his bodily hexis. If anger is understood and lived in this bodily way—rather than as "emotions" whose existence is more psychological than anatomical—it should be possible to treat it, that is, to banish it through the use of some medical substances or therapies. Mr. Zhao has developed his own method of releasing the excess *qi* that anger produces in him. But this is not surprising; most of the Beijingers we talked to believed that they could banish anger by one means or another.

The material from Chinese medicine we have added here, technical and classical as it is, provides a useful knowledge foundation for the commonsense views reported by Zhu Hong, Qu Zhixin, and Zhao Gang. Anger is one of a series of powerful emotions that act almost like fluids in the human body. Perhaps it can be the most violent and the most damaging, but all the emotions have the power to induce symptoms. Zhao Gang was the expert on the subject and at the same time the least successful in managing his emotional physiology. His technique for avoiding or treating anger was the most explicitly bodily. But everyone seems to realize that the problem is hydraulic: flow (of fluids, of emotions, even of the Dao) can be directed, and damage to human life can be avoided or ameliorated. Anger is not an existential problem—it is a matter for the everyday management of the well-nurtured body.

Qi Craftwork: Wu Liyan

For most speakers of modern Chinese language, *qi* is a form of air; in the body, it is a palpable fluid akin to breath. As Zhao Gang said, it can accumulate in the middle of the abdomen, and it can be controlled through disciplined breathing techniques. In this section, we turn to the comments of one interviewee who became very committed to a systematic form of *qigong*, or *qi* work. *Qigong* styles form are joy, anger, thought, grief, and fear. The five intentions correspond to the five visceral systems. *The Yellow Emperor's Inner Canon: Plain Questions* (*juan* 2:5) says: "People have five viscera that transform the five forms of qi to produce joy, anger, thought, grief, and fear." Clearly, emotional activity must take the jing-essence and qi of the visceral systems as its material base. The same chapter of the *Plain Questions* also says that the heart system "with respect to the intentions is joy," the liver system "with respect to the intentions is anger," the spleen system "with respect to the intentions is thought," the lung system "with respect to the intentions is grief," and the kidney system "with respect to the intentions is fear." Alterations in the different emotions (both the "seven feelings" and the "five intentions") have a close relationship with the inner viscera and qi-blood, and each kind of change has a different effect on the different visceral systems. Moreover, changes in the condition of the visceral systems also can influence changes in the emotions, just as the *Plain Questions* (*juan* 17:62) says: "When blood is excessive, there is anger; when it is depleted, there is fear." *The Divine Pivot* (*juan* 2:8) also says, "When liver *qi* is depleted, there is fear; when it is excessive, there is anger. When heart *qi* is depleted, there is melancholy; when it is excessive, there is uncontrolled laughing."

This kind of influence can be divided into two states. The first is direct harm to the viscera: "[excessive] anger harms the liver, joy harms the heart, thought harms the spleen, grief harms the lungs, fear harms the kidneys." (*Plain Questions*, *juan* 2:5). Clinically, the stimulus of the different emotions can be seen to have differential influence on each of the five visceral systems. But this influence is not absolutely exclusive; for example, most emotional stimuli have some effect on the heart. Also, when chronic anger an important part of the *yangsheng* array of practices. Our initial survey included a question about use of and attitudes toward *qigong*: of the 200 respondents to that survey, 54 of them mentioned *qigong*, and 45 professed a positive interest in practices they identified with this term. A sizeable portion of this group (31) seemed to have great faith in *qigong* and felt it was a very good practice. Seven seemed especially enthusiastic, and seven others, for various reasons, had practiced *qigong*, but later given it up. Nine interviewees said they practiced some form of *taiji*, but did not have faith in *qigong*. As we will discuss below, it is possible to have a very broad understanding of *qigong*, so we prefer to translate this term as "*qi* work." With this active and capacious understanding of *qigong* in mind, it is possible to link the concept and its associated practices to the Chinese medical body that exists by virtue of "*qi* transformation."

Our friend Zhu Hong, discussed at the beginning of this chapter, was quite unequivocal about *qi* work: "I don't believe in *qigong*, I think it is useless. My husband with his hemiplegia asked a guy named Wang in Badachu to teach him how to practice *qigong*, but after a month, it still hadn't helped. The *qigong* guy would keep saying, 'Stand up, stand up,' but when my husband tried it, he would just topple over like this." She reeled dangerously, and went on: "This only made everything more difficult! Practicing *qigong* can sometimes lead to bad things; your head explodes, and the person goes mad."

Zhu Hong confidently makes a distinction between *yangsheng* and *qigong*, a distinction that many experts might hesitate to make so unequivocally. She thinks *yangsheng* is good for bodily health, and she engages in activities that involve physical movement, such as mountain climbing, badminton, walking, and dancing. But she is clearly skeptical about the more inward-turning efficacies of *qigong*, believing that *qigong* may sometimes even do harm to the body. Naturally, she may be influenced in these views by the controversy surrounding the practice of *qigong* since the late 1980s. This controversy has been exacerbated by the similarity of Falun Gong techniques to those of *qigong*. But apparently in the 1990s, Zhu Hong did (*younu* 郁怒) harms the liver, liver *qi* begins to run transversely against its proper upward and downward flow and thus often begins to attack the spleen-stomach system, producing the pathological patterns of liver-spleen miscoordination, liver-spleen disharmony, and so forth.

The second kind of physical influence of anger is influence on the *qi* functions of the visceral systems: "In anger, *qi* rises; in joy, *qi* slackens; with melancholy, *qi* vanishes from sight; in fear, *qi* descends; with shock, *qi* becomes chaotic; with thought, *qi* knots up." (*Plain Questions, juan* 11:39). Excessive rage can make liver *qi* run transversely and rush upward, and blood can follow the disordered *qi* and run counter to its proper flow, also rushing upward. Sudden great joy can also make heart *qi* slacken its flow, so that *shen*-spirit can't be stored, and the mind can't focus, even to the point of manifesting patterns such as "*qi*-loss madness." Excessive melancholy and sadness can make the lung system sluggish, leading to a lessening of will and consumptive damage to lung *qi*. If fear and anxiety are excessive, it can destabilize kidney *qi*, such that *qi* is secreted downward, and control of excretion is lost, or if the fear is not resolved, it can harm *qi*-essence and bring about bone and marrow degeneration, premature ejaculation, and other syndromes. If someone is very suddenly shocked, it can disrupt the heartbeat, drive *qi*-spirit from its normal pathways, unsettle thinking, and produce feelings of extreme panic. If thought is in excess, both the *qi*-spirit and the spleen system are harmed, and a pattern of depressed *qi* function can be induced.

1. The Shuowen *jiezi* 说文结字 (Explaining characters) is an early Chinese etymological dictionary, dating from approximately the second century C.E.

not initially oppose *qigong*; in fact, while her husband was alive, they were willing to try a form of *qigong* therapy for his hemiplegia. It is impossible to know what her views of *qigong* were before this experience at a site in the Western Hills. (Note, though, that they did not find this service in downtown Beijing, where control of "cult" activity connected to *qigong* was tighter, beginning in the early 1990s.) But it is not surprising when people with incurable, hard-to-manage chronic illnesses risk official disapproval to find an effective therapy, and various forms of *qigong* appear to offer a special kind of effectiveness. Like Wu Liyan, discussed below, Zhu Hong and her husband didn't have to "believe in" *qigong* to find it attractive as a form of treatment.[11] But with this negative experience of *qigong* in her past, Zhu Hong can now make a kind of slapstick comedy out of this form of *yangsheng* ("the *qigong* guy would keep saying, 'Stand up, stand up,' but when my husband tried it he would just topple over, like this"). Perhaps the main reason Zhu Hong opposes the use of *qigong* is that she and her husband spent money on a *qigong* practitioner to treat his illness, but the treatment was ineffective. This experience no doubt offended her obvious thriftiness, but she also suggested that she has known others for whom *qigong* practice has led to bad results or even insanity.

Wu Liyan, on the other hand, had come to rely heavily on *qigong* in her efforts to manage both her own and her son's chronic illnesses. Over many years, she had found personal ways to deploy and benefit from a wide variety of healing techniques. A retired tailor in her late forties, she gave us a long narrative of her history of encounters with medicine and with *yangsheng* and *qigong* regimes.

Now, [after a long reported history of illness problems and hospitalizations for both herself and her son], I still practice *qigong*. The eye problem I have, when I look at things, I always see a black spot that goes wherever my eyes turn—wherever I look, there's the black spot. Once I went to the hospital for a gynecology checkup and dropped in to ophthalmology. These eyes of mine, the left was 1.5, and the other eye was no good at all. I was stupefied; my right eye could not see clearly even the biggest words on the testing chart. That time when I registered for ophthalmology, the doctor on duty wanted to give me a shot to treat it. The needle he wanted to [put in near my eye] was this long! [gesture: about 10 centimeters], I was very scared, it would hurt a lot! The doctor wanted me to stay in the hospital and get a series of shots; he said what I had was retinitis and that ophthalmology was successful in treating it. I said I wouldn't go into the hospital and wouldn't have shots. If the doctor had been just a tiny bit careless, my eyes would be put out! I kept on going to the park and doing Ma Litang Nurturing *Qigong*. In the park, I got to know a *"gong* buddy" from Guang'an Men Hospital of Chinese Medicine, so I went and saw a Chinese medical ophthalmology doctor there. I did stay in hospital there and had Chinese medical therapy. I had injectable *dangshen* (党参, codonopsis root) compound and also their special [orally administered] herbal formula for eye disorders. After leaving the hospital I would still go have a [*dangshen*] shot every day, without fail, and then I would return home to look after my son. Every day was like this, it was like going to work and coming home. During this period, when I had free time I would go to the park and rigorously practice Ma Litang *Qigong*. I stayed in the hospital six or seven months, then had six or seven months of injections—I didn't miss one shot. And I rigorously practiced *qigong*. The vision in my right eye improved to 1.2. I went to the Beijing Hospital to get a checkup from the original eye doctor, and he didn't believe it: "How did you treat this?" he asked. I said, "Don't think it's strange. I didn't obey your therapy—I have my own way of thinking about this. You doctors, you chat with each other and give people shots at the same time, I was too scared; my eye could be gone with just one shot, and I would be blind forever. So instead I took Chinese medical acupoint injections while eating Chinese medicine, practicing *qigong*, and doing neck massage, all at the same time. I took a shortcut [*jiejing* 捷径] and so cured it."

Later, I also practiced Zhang Hongbao's Chinese Yangsheng Wisdom *Gong*. I feel that no matter what the *gong*, no matter how extravagant its claims, its main goal is to be good for your body. Don't let the disease demon push its way in. This is the most important goal. So I combined Ma Litang Nurturing *Qigong* with other treatments as it suited me, practicing it just because it was effective in driving out disease. The external phenomena of the various *gongs* are not the same, but on the inside, they are the same. How do you get disease? Because your breathing is not good, your nutritional structure is not good, because you have a lot of pressure in your thoughts—only then do you get sick, right? If you didn't have all this pressure in your thoughts, if your heart was very happy, would you get sick?

JF & ZQC Wu Liyan has a different sense of the task of health than Zhu Hong. She impressed all of us as a person with a long and complicated illness history who, at least at this point in her life, was quite obsessed with illness and its treatment. A hypochondriac, perhaps? But she certainly had what sounded like an objective history of pathologies. Her son's early chronic disease, severe myocarditis, had led her to take a long leave from her job to look after him. This part of her story involved a certain amount of cooperation with doctors to enable Ms. Wu to provide good care for her son at home; much of this care involved *yangsheng*-type activities for him—light exercise, careful nutrition, enforced rest, and so on. She emphasized how hard she had worked to manage a very rigorous rehabilitation program for her son, at home, but in concert with the demands of the doctors, at least at first. But she often ignored medical advice to devise therapies of her own. When she herself became ill with uterine endometriosis, ovarian cysts, and uterine tumors, and later with diabetes, high blood pressure, and retinitis, her pattern began to look more like that of the "noncompliant patient" known to American medical sociology. She shopped for doctors, refused care, joined informal support groups in the park, and committed herself to the "alternative healing modality" of *qigong*.

This is a pattern of "shopping for care" that has long been recognized in medical anthropology and is probably found to some degree everywhere there is any sort of plural medical field. Americans who are told about this process in China, however, usually notice that Chinese patients seem not much awed by the authority of doctors and not always inclined to follow instructions issued by an "expert." Wu Liyan no longer trusted doctors, though she did trust her own instincts and capacities, as well as those of her "*gong* buddies." During our interviews, in fact, many people expressed doubts about

215

doctors' advice. Chairman Mao often said, "As for what doctors say, believe half."[12]

Chinese patients—perhaps more than American or other patients—tend to feel that they are the greatest experts on their own bodies. The laboratory results and prognostic speculations of doctors are much less meaningful to them than the changes they themselves experience as they experiment with forms of treatment. Many—perhaps most?—patients will keep looking for a form of care that produces palpable results in relation to their own direct actions. Thus, for example, routinely taking blood pressure medicine to produce a change that does not register in experience is a regime rejected by many Chinese patients. People such as Wu Liyan would rather adopt an exercise, nutritional, or herbal medicine regime that both controls blood pressure and makes one feel more well at the same time. Wu Liyan claimed a superior expert understanding of both her son's rehabilitation needs and her own body's habits. She talked at length about the slow but steady kind of progress she sought, both as she gradually increased the amount of activity her son could take and as she gradually felt her own (postsurgery, postchemotherapy) strength return after she started practicing *qigong*.

Isn't it interesting that she sees her elaborate self-care routines as a "shortcut"? Normally we think of the surgical interventions and quick-acting injections of Western medicine as being the faster route to controlling symptoms. But Wu Liyan seems to think of time devoted to therapy in a different way, more like a patient craftsman. Thus, she feels that biomedical cardiology would have never cured her son, but with her laborious nursing and exercises, she did. She believed that ophthalmology could have ruined her eyesight, so she found a (time-consuming, daily) way to work on her vision without biomedical injections. This felt to her like a "shortcut," or perhaps a more trustworthy route to a surer cure; she would no doubt agree that "health is not a [biomedical] express train."

With this long career of being a professional patient, as it were, Wu Liyan appears to have developed a sense of the dynamic of her body that is much indebted to the logic and experience of *qigong*. In *qigong* practice, it becomes possible to feel the substantial existence of *qi*, to develop and even manipulate fields of tangible force in and around the body. Thus, her notion about not letting "the disease demon push its way in" is not just an invocation of a conventional way of thinking about contracting disease. It implies an experience of a body fortified from within by *qigong* techniques, a body defended against pathology by the systematic generation of positive, wholesome, and personally powerful forms of *qi*. Perhaps a body filled out or charged with healthful *qi*, *qi* transforming in physiologically appropriate ways, is also one that is well defended. But note that this is not a defense that destroys pathogens that have gotten into the body; rather, it is one that does not allow pathological process to begin, because the "disease demon" is kept at bay by a body fully charged with wholesome protective *qi*.

Little wonder that Wu Liyan particularly wanted to follow the advice of a "*gong* buddy" with ties to Chinese medicine. Surely she understood at some level that the Chinese medicine body is constituted by *qi* transformation (in fact, we expect that her friend explained something like this to her), so Chinese herbal medicine was addressing the body she experienced as a *qigong* practitioner. The Western medical body she also acknowledged in practice—her son's heart disease was monitored by EKG, her vision disorder was caused by retinitis—does not seem to contradict or invalidate Chinese medical *qi* transformation or the *qigong* body, but she has evolved in her life a mode of intervention, a personal health activism, that prefers *qi* (craft)work in all its gradualness and tangibility to the direct assaults on invisible organic structures offered by Western medicine.

We saw in Chapter 2 that Zhu Hong was not a credulous or uncritical reader, and here we have reported her slapstick comedy routine making fun of a *qigong* healer who tried to rehabilitate her paralyzed husband. Ms. Zhu did not think much about *qi* and had no patience with self-appointed gurus. Wu Liyan might be seen as more credulous about all manner of medical and health knowledge, but she, too, kept her own counsel in relation to authoritative medical advice. Her labor-intensive "shortcuts" to better health for her son and herself were crafted from her own experience of doing things that worked. She knew that moderate exercise worked for her ill son because he grew stronger as a result; she knew that Ma Litang *Qigong* was healthful because in practicing it she could feel the power of *qi* and feel that she was herself working to configure it positively. This is an expertise in self-care, in nurturing one's own life, that is deeply rooted in the body.

Balancing the Bitter and the Sweet: Professor Song, Zheng Liansheng, Policeman Zhao, and Xu Zhimao

Because most of the people we talked to in Beijing spoke of deriving pleasure from their *yangsheng* practices and achieving happiness through the careful nurturance of life, it would have been easy to conclude from the interviews that few city dwellers have serious problems or that, thanks to *yangsheng*, few suffer. Of course, this would be wrong. We have already discussed the situation of Wu Liyan, with her many chronic ailments and her son's dramatic history of life-threatening illness. There were others we met who were also willing to give us some insight into the problems they faced in their lives. Given the fact that we were undertaking these interviews as complete strangers, of course we had to presume that few of those interviewed would reveal many of their private concerns to us. In some cases, we were able to infer much about the background to what was said on the basis of our local knowledge. In other cases, speakers were only too eager to tell us some of the more troublesome parts of their lives. Here, we select for discussion a few whose difficulties, though they all differ from each other, are not unusual for contemporary Beijingers.

Song Xiuzhen was a semiretired professor, eighty-seven when we met him, who had graduated from the famous Whampoa Military Academy run by the Nationalist Party government between 1924 and 1949. In our interview with him, after sharing a rather elaborate life history—one that had doubtless

included much bitterness—he told us about his health status and systemati-
cally outlined the theory and practice of his own yangsheng *routine.*

When I was age eighty-three, I [began to] suffer from dizziness and harden-ing of the arteries, and I also have high cholesterol. I take Chinese medicine for these conditions and also Western medicine for high blood pressure. When it comes to taking medicine, I like Chinese medicine—it has fewer side effects. Now, at eighty-seven, I have driven out the hardening of the arter-ies, and I'm able to run my own life; my brain is still clear, I walk wherever I like—it's just that I need a hearing aid. . . .

Every day before 7:00 a.m., I turn to *yangsheng.* I do my own system of calisthenics. Every day before getting out of bed, I do self-massage, rubbing the face, ears, and nose, and the *taiyang, hukou, zusanli,* and *tongchuan* acupressure points for fifteen minutes. And I do fifteen minutes the same before going to sleep. I rigorously do this every day. I also do slow *taiji*—this is a kind of exercise that I've worked up from the basis I learned in the army. After getting up, I do head, back, and whole-body stretches: thirty-six front, back, left, and right movements of the head, whole body pushing forward and back eighteen times each. . . .

I pay attention to nutrition and food and drink, having a glass of milk in the morning and an egg. I eat two heads of garlic a day, without fail, some raw onions (my daughter in America says that white onions reduce choles-terol), a dish of soybeans, plus fruit, tomatoes, watermelon, bananas, and so on. I often eat fish, but little meat. I stick to bland food and drink, mainly. I eat breakfast at 7:30, spending about twenty minutes. Then I go out to Houhai to walk, going at least three to four kilometers. I start lunch at 12:30, spending thirty minutes, and for the evening meal (twenty-five minutes) I drink congee, have a steamed whole-grain bun, and a tomato every day for sure. I also take American lecithin every day, and I wear an American hearing aid. . . .

Every day, I do exactly as I please; I'm very happy. I work on writing my essays for publication in the *Whampoa Journal.*

My view of *yangsheng* can be summed up as "Life is exercise." My exer-cise *gong* [*duanlian gong* 锻炼功] is as follows:

219

1. Exercise your thinking [*sixiang* 思想]. This means that you must maintain a correct worldview, view of human life, view of value. A correct worldview and view of human life means that you must serve the people, serve the state, and serve humankind. Individualism is a thing for the capitalist classes. If a person's private mind is too overweaning [that is, thick, *zhong* 重] then he cannot live long. In Beijing alone, we have more than four hundred older people in our Whampoa [alumni] group; their average age is eighty-two, and 70 percent of them can manage their own lives. One could say that this health and longevity is because from our entry into the Whampoa Academy until our graduation, we always received a strict "*yangcheng* education" [*yangcheng jiaoyu* 养成教育, training for civic prominence]. This just means that we underwent a strict political-thought and preparation process that manifested the Whampoa spirit of patriotism, revolution, and continuous progress.

Having a viewpoint on values means that you should also have a spirit of making a contribution. Making a contribution is the most fortunate part of human life. Nowadays, when I remember times past, I have no guilt and no regrets toward the state, the people, or the world. My way of long life has been never to contend for a name or struggle for my own interests. After undergoing so much struggle and so much hardship, my happiest time was [after the reform started in the late 1970s] when I founded the Whampoa Alumni Association and was doing educational administration. Remembering this life, I am very happy and very proud. I didn't only take, I gave.

2. Exercise willpower. This is part of the Whampoa Academy's "training for prominence": [one develops] a will that is "firm and tenacious," and "keeps on carving [refining the self] unflaggingly." While we were at Whampoa, our training was especially harsh, really hard. Willpower must be founded on correct thinking. When we speak of *yangsheng*, thought is the key; without correct thinking, you might as well not even talk about anything else. . . .

3. Exercise [your] talents. This means, bring to fruition your ability to command a thousand troops and ten thousand horses as commander in chief. Talents also need willpower. For example, I practice public speaking and writing articles on education; I have to practice and revise constantly. . . .

4. Exercise [your] body [*shenti*]. The body is not only blood, cells, not only the carnal body—the body includes thought. A human in a vegetative

state has no thought, so I say that for a body to be strong and healthy, it must be guided by thought. First, you must unflaggingly exercise the body, and second, your methods of exercising the body must be appropriate.... When the weather isn't good, I do [*yangsheng*] activities indoors; this is what I mean by appropriate.

ZQC When it is considered together with his *yangsheng* practice, Professor Song's thinking is very valuable. He holds that the most important thing is to have a truthful worldview, life outlook, and value system. He boils these three elements down to a few principles: dedication to service, freedom from selfish desire, and exercise. He considers that dedication to the social good is the greatest happiness of human life; if one is dedicated to serving the nation, the state, and the world, then one need have no guilt and no regrets. This is quite an extraordinary thing to say for a retired Nationalist Party officer who spent twelve years being "politically rectified" through factory work. Most people believe that it was socialism and the worldview and life outlook of the Communist Party that continuously advanced the cause of service to the people, selfless generosity, patriotism, and revolution. But this old alumnus of the Whampoa Academy believes that these principles express the Whampoa [Nationalist Party] spirit.

He said in his interview that he still believes in [scholar-artist] Zheng Banqiao's motto "Treasure confusion" (*nande hutu* 难得糊涂). Minor matters can be muddled and are more generative as muddle. But the military man in him insists that great affairs must be approached with a clear head and correct thinking. He also emphasizes that the way of long life depends on not striving for a great name or personal interests, being tolerant of others and at peace with himself. Make few enemies and many friends, he says.

We must hear these homilies in the context of the personal history of someone who was undoubtedly denounced as a Rightist and for many years prevented from achieving the civic prominence for which he was originally trained. But these important principles of social relations also embody the Chinese tradition of harmony: many people even today in China seek to minimize antagonism, minimize conflict. This also involves minimizing individual private interests. Recall the Daoism of Laozi and Zhuangzi. Laozi said, "The greatest virtue is like water, which does not contend, but effortlessly benefits the myriad things." "Not contending" is certainly not a stressed state of mind; rather, it is a kind of free and easy state, à la Zhuangzi, that has transcended desires for name and profit.[13] This is hard for younger people to understand, but as people reach middle age, they begin to understand this at a deep level. "Not contending" has many advantages in *yangsheng*. If there is no contending, it is possible to maintain an even temperament—nothing can bother you. Thus, minimizing worldly desires is perhaps a broader and deeper way of saying "don't get angry."

Zheng Liansheng worked as an accountant until health problems forced her to retire in her forties. She seemed to think of herself as a chronically ill person who had pulled a life out of hardship through determination and the support of her family.

Every day, I spend about three hours on *yangsheng*, exercising in the park. I get up alone at about 4:00 a.m. and walk twice around the lakeshore, I do health calisthenics, including tapping on acupoints, then I go home and make breakfast for my son. I am also really interested in medicine, and I do self-massage on acupoints according to directions I have read in books. In the evening from 7:30 to 9:30, I am out at the Song Qingling Residence, dancing—there's a teacher there. Four-step, sixteen-step, four-step line dancing, and ballroom dancing. I am one of the organizers. We made ourselves a tape, and every month, each person pays two RMB. Forty to fifty people participate. I don't particularly like to play mahjong or drink, so I decided to do this after talking it over with the neighborhood committee. I feel that dancing is good for giving activity to the lower back and legs, and it's especially good for the heart. It also makes you happy—you can forget your cares—[and it allows me to] give my son a little time and space to study.... Our house is too small. In the evening, I just watch the news a short while; basically, I don't turn on the TV. When we're dancing, we're all very open and free with each other. Every evening, we can dance twelve dances—for each song, we dance twice; there are two [different] dances for every song. It's so enjoyable. *Yangsheng* can make people's mood a lot better; you come to care more for others and others come to care more for you, and your mood is just very happy. For these last four years, I have not broken this exercise routine.

ZQC Zheng Liansheng is a woman of about fifty whose health has not always been very good; she is a good example of someone who particularly benefits from *yangsheng*. Group dancing is currently a rather fashionable *yangsheng* activity in Beijing. I have the impression that it really gained ground after Falun Gong was severely banned in 1999. Usually between 7:30 and 9:30 P.M., alongside wide places in the road, in the space provided by urban plazas, we often see Beijing's city dwellers dancing in organized groups. The dancing styles vary. They include *yangge* line dancing, ballroom dancing, disco, and many kinds of folk dancing. The kind practiced by Zheng Liansheng includes ballroom dancing and disco; she thinks it is good exercise for the back and is especially beneficial for her compromised cardiac function. In addition, it "opens her heart," makes her happy, and helps her forget her troubles. This really is the deeper reason why middle-aged and older people dance, but even many younger people also can't resist the temptation to join in with the infectious joy of dancing groups like this one.

There's another reason to go out of the house to participate in dancing exercise, and that is the limitations of living space. For most of the people who live in the Back Lakes area, their living space is quite small; Zheng Liansheng is no exception. The room she shares with her husband and son is very small and crowded, with barely room for the bed, some cupboards, and the desk and computer where her son does his homework. Especially in the evening, when the child in a family like this wants to study quietly at home, it is common for the adults to go out. Ms. Zheng uses this time to exercise and dance, a custom that kills two birds with one stone. An intelligent arrangement!

JF Zheng Liansheng presented us with an impressive example of the benefits of *yangsheng*. She felt she had vanquished asthma, heart disease, and cervical vertebra disease through the adoption of a very regular and vigorous *yangsheng* routine. When we interviewed her, she was slim, strong looking, and animated, but she said that before she retired she had been depressed and forty pounds heavier. She still complains of menopause symptoms, including insomnia. But she speaks glowingly of how helpful her husband and son have been as she copes with these chronic problems.

She took early retirement from her job as an accountant. Unlike most of the retirees we interviewed, however, she does not view her current situation as free of pressure or entirely preferable to the difficulties of her working life. The family is still struggling to get her son into college, their housing situation is very inadequate, and her husband—now the sole wage earner—works and mostly lives far away, out by the airport.

But these problems only make the usefulness of *yangsheng* practices in her life more clear. She was quite explicit about the social and physical enjoyments she gathered, especially from her dancing group: "When we're dancing, we're all very open and free with each other." This vision of a warm and caring sociality, both in the nuclear family and in the dancing group, reminds us that deliberate life nurturance is often an occasion for forging deep personal ties. I feel this is particularly true in China, where it is conventional to express concern for others through unsolicited health advice and where we often hear long discussions among friends about understanding symptoms, finding good doctors, choosing medicinal foods, preventing infections, and so forth. Thus, even though we had some hints from Zheng Liansheng that she feels vulnerable and anxious in her neighborhood and facing her particular life problems, she also gives us the impression that she knows how to find a community after retirement. And it is through collective *yangsheng* that this group of friends have occasion to take joy in each other. Rather than compensating in the present for past bitterness, Ms. Zheng's dancing and exercise seem to compensate for worries and discomforts she still must face in the present. In *yangsheng*, she has a method for finding her own happiness despite poor housing, health worries, and inadequate income.

Zhao Xinyi is a policeman, aged thirty-four, whose mother is a doctor of Chinese medicine. He is an avid reader of Chinese medical texts and enjoyed consulting with one of Zhang Qicheng's graduate students about some of the more abstruse aspects of medical theory and canonical writing. In various contacts we had with him over several months, we began to see him as having a rather dark view of human nature. Perhaps police work does that to people.

What significance does *yangsheng* have? It lifts up the soul [*xinling* 心灵], and it is traditional Chinese culture. *Yangsheng* is not only for extending the life span of the physical body [*routi* 肉体], making it live one thousand years. Without any reference to correct thought, cultural beliefs, deep understanding of natural life, *yangsheng* would be entirely without significance. Man is a vehicle of culture; if he has a healthier body, he can do better work, he can better realize [*yinzheng* 印证] a kind of spiritual plane and better achieve a kind of cultural reason [*linian* 理念]. *Yangsheng* seeks out a higher culture. . . .

I have learned the most useful *yangsheng* information reading the *Yellow Emperor's Inner Canon*. The *Inner Canon* is a really fine book; it made me understand the balance in life, the balance in the body, and the relationship of mutual generation and mutual control among the visceral systems. The first chapter of the *Inner Canon* . . . tells us that our bodies are made to work just like cars: if you want to use them for the full term of time, then use them well, take care of them, nurture them—only that way can you get a long period of use out of them. If we "make over" [interpret] its language, the human body is just like a car, it's not for using up carelessly.

I didn't read the *Inner Canon* for *yangsheng* purposes; rather, I read books for my work; the reasoning is all held in common. *Yangsheng* and the management of social contradictions are not really very different.[14] In my opinion, the ecological environment, the social environment, and man's physiological environment have no basic differences. The key is the resolution of contradictions, the achievement of "balance." This is like the management of international problems, like talking at the bargaining table; we need to balance out the relations in every respect, compromise the interests, and the thing will be solved. Of course, if things are put in a bad environment, then you need an appropriate process. A person who has smoked for a long time, or been a heavy drinker, if you suddenly make him stop smoking and drinking, very possibly you will soon have problems, because in his body he has formed a need for certain things, he has formed these habits over several decades. If you suddenly cut off the biological entities that are needed in the body, destroying a bodily balance formed over several decades, then you'll have problems. . . .

I think "*yangsheng*" should include a lot of contents. In Buddhism, it is said, "From many causes, only one result." *First*, it certainly has a relationship to [genetic] inheritance. This is the most important: in health, inheritance is primary. *Second*, a normal state of mind is important. In the movie *The White-Haired Girl*, her hair turned white in one night; this indicated that her state of mind was not good, and in her body, some poisons had been produced that interrupted the normal process of producing hair. *Third*, nutritional structure. Man receives energy [*nengliang* 能量] from the outside world every day, so food and drink are very important. I am not a nutrition expert, and in fact I eat some bad things. I recall that in the [ancient divination text] *Guiguzi* (鬼谷子, ca. fourth century B.C.E.) and the early esoteric *Yin Fu Classic* it is said, "Man eats the five grains and the various staples, at once getting their benefits and receiving their harmful elements."[15]

As for my own food, when I see something good, I want to eat it. As I have grown older and my cultural level has deepened, what I like to eat has changed. For example, when I was small, I liked to eat fried foods, and then I liked to eat [more thoroughly] cooked foods. Now I like to eat rather clean and bland things, both because they are better tasting and because I have read some Buddhist and Daoist books. *Fourth*, a good living environment. I think you shouldn't always be changing your environment, including your life environment, your work environment, your psychological environment. It's just like if you're always bending a cable, then it will eventually break. *Fifth*: the influence of culture, one could even say "consciousness," on *yangsheng* is very great. For example, a simpleton doesn't think things through:

someone looks after him and makes his living conditions good, even though he can't live long—the crux of the matter is, he has no cultural thought, no knowledge of "the Way," and he can't manage himself. Man [must] become a vehicle of "the Way"—including knowledge of nature, cultivation of spirit, cultural quality [*suzhi*], and so on. Where culture is different, what people seek by way of diet and housing is also not the same. Why do monks and nuns live a long time? Because they eat vegetables, their state of mind is good; they cultivate interior things. . . . Nowadays, most people just pursue externals; from oxcarts to horse carriages to cars, the outer forms of things have changed, but these are only implements, not basic ways to solve problems. Basic methods still need to come from the very ancient past; we must seek solutions from our past forefathers. It is only because mankind exists that we can speak of *yangsheng*, so we must find solutions in humankind's own self/body [*zishen* 自身].

JF The lengthy remarks of this relatively young policeman presented a fascinating synthesis of sophisticated *yangsheng* philosophy and a practical (if pessimistic) view of Beijing's social conditions. He spoke scathingly, for example, of migrant workers without city residence permits, seeing them as a sort of "social contradiction" in themselves. His relatively recent turn to classical philosophy and medicine may be a kind of escape for him, offering him a more ideal or "lordly" world than the everyday frictions of the city afford.

Officer Zhao's current working life is quite stressful, and it makes unpredictable demands on his time. Under these conditions, he finds it difficult to live a healthy life—that is, a life consistent with the insights he derives from the classical medical literature. Thus, he eats junk food, doesn't keep a regular schedule, and doesn't have time for daily exercise. He does swim several times a week in a big indoor pool near the station where he works. He owns a car, and like many younger male Beijingers, he is quite interested in cars. And as a policeman, he deals all day at work with people whose lives he would hardly call wholesome. In the course of "managing social contradictions," he undoubtedly encounters a number of depressing or maddening situations and a number of people whose lives he might well think of as pretty worthless. In his other remarks, we noted a great reliance on the concept of civilizational development and *suzhi*, or "population quality." For him, a person's health depends quite heavily on his or her cultural level or quality as a person; people who are too low class or "moronic" could never really be healthy. He obviously cultivates his own *suzhi*, at least through reading, even though he really cannot be said to be a practitioner of the arts of *yangsheng*.[16]

It is of course gratifying to see that under the influence of the *Yellow Emperor's Inner Canon*, he tends to think of "the environment" (a very current political and social issue in Beijing) in a broad and cosmic sense. He conflates the ecological environment, the social environment, and the physiological environment. This is an insight he derives from ancient philosophy, and Officer Zhao seems to have no difficulty in seeing the salience of this philosophical holism as he seeks to understand contemporary life. Of course, this could lead to a rather catastrophic vision of the present, since environmental pollution, crime, and disease all seem to be on the increase.

When I visited his family's rooms facing Houhai, Officer Zhao decried the commercial development around the lake and expressed concern about Beijing's acute water shortage; his comments implied a continuing disgust with the "low-*suzhi*" people he encounters on the job, and like other Beijingers, he appears to have been shaken by the SARS episode. No wonder he's pessimistic! But unlike those nostalgic utopians who distrust the amoral capitalist rat race of the present in terms borrowed from Maoism, Officer Zhao seems to root the problems of the present in the basic corruptness of human nature and in the general low "quality" of the population.

His examples and comparisons are particularly fascinating. The notion that the human body is just like a car, for example, will surely startle Americans who have hoped that Chinese medicine and philosophy could take us beyond the literal-minded "mechanical" logic of biomedical visions of the body. Officer Zhao must be speaking as a man who devotes a fair amount of his free time to cleaning, polishing, and adjusting the functions of his car, and he loves automotive metaphors. He surely has an appreciation of the complexity of an

228

internal combustion engine, and he is aware of how carefully its functions must be calibrated. This is to say that he implicitly invokes the kind of tuning up (*tiaohe* 调和) that weekend car mechanics know all about. He could also be thinking of the various fluids that keep a car going: gasoline (and its vapors), lubricating oil, air, and even fire, all of which could be compared to some bodily substance. The metaphor still makes me uncomfortable, since it encourages a vision of the body as discrete, more autonomous from its environment than it really is, and as functioning on the basis of a fixed structure, whereas in Chinese medicine structure always results from the processes that draw focal attention. But I can appreciate Officer Zhao's creativity and intellectual enjoyment in developing the idea.

It is clear from another small example, however, that he has a more processual understanding of the Chinese medical body. In explaining why "a normal state of mind" is an important component in *yangsheng*, he evokes the movie *The White-Haired Girl*. How could the heroine's hair have turned white in one night? Forgetting, perhaps, that this event is a mythic and literary gesture written by an arts collective, Officer Zhao cites the suddenly white hair as proof that when a person's "state of mind is not good," the normal process of producing hair can be interrupted. As I recall the movie version of *The White-Haired Girl*, the actress had quite a lot of hair, and its transformation was quite dramatic. Does Officer Zhao believe that the body continuously produces the hair itself, such that overnight all the black hair could be replaced by white hair? Or does he believe that the color of the hair is continuously being produced, such that the same hair suddenly lost its black color because a bad state of mind had shut down some of the body's productive processes? In either case, with this example, we are well beyond the automobile-like body, with its structural base that supports limited functions. The body of the white-haired girl is a body of ever-transforming *qi*, right down to the ends of her long hair.

ZQC Zhao Xinyi is one of the very few younger people we interviewed at length. This policeman was only a little over thirty. In general, young people don't pay much attention to *yangsheng*, perhaps because their health is generally pretty good and also because they are tied up with work—they don't have much extra time to think about nurturing life. But Officer Zhao is not like this; though he is not especially intent upon engaging in *yangsheng* himself, only going for a swim a couple of times a week, he nevertheless has a rather deep appreciation of *yangsheng*. For example, most people know that swimming is good for you, but they don't really know why. But Zhao articulates a sort of theory: he said that 70 percent of the globe is water, and humans are sprung from water. When people (or, one presumes, the organisms that were their evolutionary ancestors) left the water, they lost an effective kind of *qi*. This is why swimming is good for you, he says. He also counseled moderation in swimming; in fact, he urged moderation in all things; excess is harmful. This is a manifestation of the traditional Chinese "doctrine of the mean." This doctrine argues that we should neither exceed nor fail to meet proper limits. One should rest at the "middle." The middle is not entirely a spatial concept, it is also temporal and processual: in dealing with affairs, we must act for moderation, find a middle way. The "middle" (*zhong* 中) is usually seen in conjunction with "harmony" (*he* 和), if you cleave to the middle, you can bring about harmony. The harmonies of the human body are harmony of form and spirit, harmony of body and nature, and harmony of human life and society—this is the healthy person, the happy person. This is the highest plane at which *yangsheng* aims.

Zhao Xinyi has a rather penetrating grasp of *yangsheng*. He believes that *yangsheng* is not just to keep disease away from the body or to extend life; rather, it is to elevate the soul (*xinling* 心灵) and is inseparable from traditional Chinese culture. He feels that thought and cultural belief are much more important than longevity, pure and simple. Humans are vehicles of culture; if they have healthy bodies, they can work better, they can better confirm a kind of spiritual plane and realize a kind of cultural ideal. This way of thinking is not that of the common people. It should be pointed out that China's traditional intellectuals had this way of thinking, but it is rare for today's youth to think this way, especially if they are not intellectuals. For so many young people in China today, material life is more important than the life of the spirit and the rationality of culture.

Zhao Xinyi realizes that *yangsheng* is not best studied from popular reading materials; rather, it is to an abstruse ancient text that he turns. He also likes to read various Daoist and Buddhist texts. Like so many others we talked with, he connects *yangsheng* with society and politics—in fact, he doesn't see much difference between *yangsheng* and ways of dealing with social contradictions. *Yangsheng* is a way of managing the human physiological environment, which is not fundamentally different from the ecological environment or the social environment. For him, the key is resolving contradictions and achieving the "balance" that eludes him in his everyday life.

__Xu Zhimao__ is a retired worker who recently returned to Beijing after twenty-two years as a "sent-down" factory worker in rural Shaanxi. As she explains, she's got a lot of worries.

My life has been very difficult. At sixteen (in 1958), I went to work as a laborer, was married in 1968, and in 1970, both my husband and I were sent from our homes in Beijing to the Three Gorges area. Both of us were assigned to Factory Number 4390 in Baoji, Shaanxi. At that time I was pregnant, and we moved our household registry to Shaanxi [for the health care]. In 1990, we retired in Shaanxi, receiving 400 RMB per month pension. In 1992, we returned to Beijing, but we couldn't move our household registry back here, so we are here without a proper residence permit. Our daughter is thirty-two, not yet married. Because our registry is not in Beijing, her job is not secure; she can take only temporary jobs. Right now, she's a secretary in an American firm. Our national health insurance is from Shaanxi, so the paperwork for getting medical care is very difficult. Right now, we have my husband, my daughter, my eighty-two-year-old mother, and me living together. But our family has been in Beijing since the late Qing, and we actually own four rooms of courtyard housing. Since we came back from the Three Gorges, though, we've had only two rooms to live in. Our family income is very low—basically, we don't buy anything; we make all our own clothes, even my husband makes his own clothes, and I make my own noodles....

In 1983, I got Meniere's syndrome, had pain in my spine and neck, and often had dizzy spells. Mostly, I take medicine on my own; if I buy some medicine, I prefer to see Chinese-medicine doctors; Western medicines have side effects. Mostly, when I get sick, I prescribe for myself. For example, when I get a cold in the winter, I use tangerine leaves to treat it, or I go to the drugstore and buy [inexpensive Chinese] lung-clearing medicine to take. When my daughter has a cough, I buy pears and fritillary bulb, add a couple of lumps of sugar, and boil them up to give to her to drink, and she gets better when she drinks it. I purposely bought a book on Chinese medicine and pharmacy, and I go according to that when I work out my own treatments....

I started exercising at age forty-four when I contracted Meniere's syndrome. Nowadays, I get up every day at 6:00 and go to Zhong Shan Park to exercise, mainly dancing, folk dancing, fan dancing, and hanky dancing. There are more than twenty of us who gather there. When I hear the music, my mood lifts, and I stop thinking about all these worrying things. I pay three RMB a month to study dancing; we go from 7:00 to 8:30. I don't dance at home. I have participated in a dance group since 1996; before that, I mainly climbed mountains; in Shaanxi I regularly climbed, and played croquet in the afternoon. But when we returned to Beijing, the environment was different, I couldn't go climbing every day, but I do accompany my daughter to climb Coal Hill most evenings....

Everyday life in Beijing is much richer than in Shaanxi. At that time [when we were there], Shaanxi's level of life was twenty years behind Beijing. But for those of us who have no household registry in Beijing, we are like fourth-class citizens. We get together at New Year's and listen to each other's troubles, but still, one must go on getting through life.

JF Xu Zhimao has had a rough life. She and her husband were part of the great "down-to-the-countryside" movement mandated by the government after the initial rebellions of the Cultural Revolution had been put down, in 1967. She retired in 1990 and in 1992 came back to Beijing, but they were not able to shift their household registration back to Beijing, and household registration is quite important in China; health-insurance coverage, for those who have it, is tied to residency status. Thus, although Ms. Xu's family had moved to Beijing, their retiree health coverage was still registered in Shaanxi; this makes for paperwork nightmares. Lacking a household registration might be seen as not terribly important to a retired person, but it is extremely important to a person needing a job or higher education. Ms. Xu's daughter is in this position; her job is not secure, and she can take only temporary positions. Ms. Xu attributes the fact that her thirty-two-year-old daughter is not yet married to the family's lack of a Beijing household registration.

Ms. Xu is not extremely well educated, and she has not systematically studied medicine, but she has read up on Chinese medicine and pharmacy on her own. She not only deals with her own illnesses, she also treats her daughter's illnesses. Her reasons for this approach are several. First, she hasn't much money for going to hospitals for care, and the paperwork is so much trouble. Second, she shares with many others a view of Chinese medicine that is quite widespread, believing that it is without significant dangers or poisons. As a result of this thinking, Xu Zhimao has found her own way of making up medicines and treating illnesses.

We often meet people with only a middle-school education in Beijing who have developed an interest in Chinese medicine and thus seek out books and other published materials on this large and complex subject. In fact, a great deal of publishing and broadcast media programming is oriented toward the "self-study" of technical subjects such as Chinese medicine (see Chapter 2). This is an interesting consequence of the twentieth-century achievement of a very broad-based literacy in China. We can think of this phenomenon of self-study as amateurism or dilettantism and compare it with the inveterate Web browsers in the United States who hunt up information on all their symptoms, sometimes using such information to challenge medical authority. But in China, these habits of information gathering and self-dosing articulate with a very special trust in experience. Xu Zhimao couldn't afford to consult experts, even if she felt a great deal of confidence in their judgment. But she obviously sees nothing wrong with training herself in Chinese medicine and pharmacy and looking after her family's health with her own decoctions, based on what she has learned and personally suffered.

She is not only involved in dosing herself, she also generalizes what she knows about *yangsheng*. She generalizes from what is said about *yangsheng* in newspapers, magazines, and on TV, using her own judgment to compare information on the same or different conditions. In the course of the interviews, we found that Beijingers were often able to articulate some of the basic rationales of *yangsheng*. Ms. Xu is one of these, and she is also an activist who collects materials on *yangsheng* exercise, especially dancing, mountain climbing, and principles of careful diet. Like others, she feels that *yangsheng* has benefits for society and the state, as well as for the individual. It can reduce disease and suffering and lighten the burden of care for the state and the children of the elderly.

Though she has so many personal worries, she does not seem dissatisfied with the current state of society. For example, she does not regret returning to Beijing, her hometown. As she and Judith Farquhar looked at a photo album during a visit to her rooms, she explained that the family had ties to the imperial household (deposed in 1911). An elderly aunt living in Taiwan is the last link to that especially privileged life. Perhaps this family history gives Xu Zhimao a particular sense of entitlement that makes it hard for her to accept the loss of some of her family's living space and the indignities that go with having no Beijing registry. But, she says, "still one must go on getting through life."

People who talk about *yangsheng* often advise a kind of emotional self-control. "Don't get angry," "Eschew selfish desires," "Be tolerant of others," "Seek out happy things," and even "Forget the painful past"—these are pieces of advice that we came to expect in the interviews. Perhaps because they were speaking to non-Beijingers and doing their best to educate us about the topic we had proposed, *yangsheng*, our interlocutors in the West City District felt obliged to present themselves as particularly optimistic. But there are some people—Professor Song, the "old Rightist," and Xu Zhimao, the retired displaced worker lacking a residence permit—whose lives have obviously contained much "bitterness" (*ku* 苦). Their *yangsheng*-informed turn to the optimistic and enjoyable seems particularly touching. Even the willingness of many older *yangsheng* practitioners to forget the past in the interest of present health and pleasures suggests an embodied disposition particular to the history of China and Beijing. Adopting that complex vocabulary of taste so typical of the modern Chinese language, they mix—or perhaps even harmonize—bitter and sweet to make their own quiet contribution to an uncontending urban life.

Conclusion

In this chapter, we have threaded together a number of diverse elements, including commonsense talk taken from interviews, descriptions of ordinary life conditions for some Beijingers, our own interpretations and contextualization of the Beijing field material, and references to both the anthropological and Chinese medical literature. All this has been gathered into a certain order under headings that, we realize, do not add up to an argument or even a list of parallel terms or problems. Rather, these topics signal persistent themes and interests for the Beijingers we interviewed in 2003. They reflect the disorderliness and contradictoriness of common sense, no doubt. But these concerns also impress us as persisting in Beijing conversations for good reasons. In our commentaries above, we have tried to indicate what some of those reasons might be.

But as we have continued to discuss *yangsheng* with friends and acquaintances, including some of those we first got to know through interviews in 2003, these topics have begun to look more and more like expressions of principles that inhere in the practice of the nurtured life. They are not just post-hoc rationalizations or apologetics for a kind of hedonism. Nor are they mere phrases that parrot the propaganda of the Ministry of Health or the medical establishment. Efforts of *yangsheng* practitioners to make an active social contribution, avoid anger, engage in *qi* work and *qi* transformation, and balance or even harmonize the bitter and the sweet arise from a historical embodiment that can never be fully articulated in words.

Reflecting on the whole experience of fieldwork with city dwell-ers who practice *yangsheng*, we have increasingly realized that at the popular level, *yangsheng* is a practice that is very difficult to delimit. This condition has been made clear to us in many casual conversa-tions. An exchange Judith Farquhar had on a bus in 2005 is a good example. An elderly lady spoke to me in English on the bus. In a halting, but careful manner, she said she had been studying English for about a year, in a once-a-week class at a community center near where I was living. After talking for a while, I asked her whether studying English might also be *yangsheng*. She emphatically agreed that it is. First, studying English keeps the brain lively, which is very important for health. It also makes her happy, has helped her make new friends, and also saves money. (This part made me won-der. Surely the class costs money? I think the "saves money" part was thrown in partly because *yangsheng* is always supposed to save money. But I'm sure if I'd had time to ask her she would have had an explanation.) Moreover, exercising the brain, seeking one's own hap-piness, getting out of the house—all these contribute to preventing disease. If you're happy and stay alert, you won't get sick.

In other conversations, members of our team heard women studying crocheting in small groups in Beihai Park argue that this hobby was a form of *yangsheng*, even having the physiological good effect of "enlivening blood." Several others we met in parks told us that "getting out of the house" is a form of *yangsheng* in itself. (At one point, we started asking people what might *not* count as *yangsheng*. Answers varied, but on the whole, those we asked did not consider sitting at home watching TV or going shopping to have much to do with *yangsheng*. Several exasperated wives said to me, "One thing's for sure, *yangsheng* is *not* staying up and playing mahjong all night.") Once one adds the diet and regimen concerns of *yangsheng* to these observations, one can only conclude that for some Beijingers, *yangsheng is* everyday life, it *is* health, it *is* embodiment of sound common sense.

In fact, one of the most general things that can be said about *yangsheng* as a practice is that it should be deliberate. Anyone who seeks to nurture life should be willing to craft the times and spaces of her situation and environment; anyone who seeks to nurture life should be willing to assess the results of his daily activities and adjust his practice accordingly. *Yangsheng* should lead to greater vigor and alertness; it should prevent common diseases such as colds and rheumatism; it should above all make you happy. All of these outcomes can be assessed in person, without the aid of outside expertise.

The deliberateness of *yangsheng* is not an intellectual or moralistic imperative, imposed from above or outside on the passive terrain of the body and the material world by an act of will. *Yangsheng* is not, in other words, a practice that can be ultimately divided into the dualism of body and mind, will and matter. Rather, the common sense reported to us in interviews exists as mental/material fragments, pieces of a mosaic, broken out of a great corpus of embodied, material, spiritual, spatial, and temporal practices. *Yangsheng* common sense adopts the viewpoint of the activist for whom laziness, passivity, and victimization are neither desirable nor necessary. The intentions toward health, pleasure, and calm reported by our Beijing interviewees are propensities that give form to the dispositions of bodies and selves, the routines of families, the sociality of neighbors.[17] Urban spaces and the rhythms of street and park life, too, are given wholesome form by the mundane projects of *yangsheng* activists.[18] Though this sea of small practices is not and probably cannot be articulated, it nevertheless should not be seen as "merely physical" or strictly "behavioral." Nor can *yangsheng* practices be seen as ultimately meaningful only as "spiritual" exercises, though we have often emphasized the importance of *jingshen* above. *Yangsheng* gives wholesome form to life; *yangsheng* extends life toward longevity, toward the nonutopian satisfactions of "moderate well-being" (*xiaokang* 小康), toward more harmonious integration with family, community and—for lack of a better word—nature.

In this most general sense, then, *yangsheng* as it can be witnessed in today's Beijing is an expression, embodiment, and re-creation of some of the oldest philosophical writings in Chinese. The pathways that link a contemporary practitioner of *taiji*, a folk dancer, a choral singing group, or a water calligrapher to the poetic writing of Laozi, to the *Book of Changes*, "The Doctrine of the Mean," or to the *Yellow Emperor's Inner Canon* are not direct or unbroken. There is no single continuous mainstream of a "*yangsheng* tradition." But today's Beijingers, often without really knowing it, are participating in their heritage as speakers of Chinese, as sharers of common sense, and as embodied creatures situated in worlds under construction. Language, common sense, bodily practice, and the architectural spaces of the city are in many respects conservative reservoirs of cultural form. In China, each of these domains serves as a site where distant and deep springs of tradition can sometimes be enjoyed and put to use. Even as resources from the past are built into present lives, however, those same lives expand the reach of philosophy and medical knowledge, extending *yangsheng* into uncharted futures simply by living well, living deliberately, and crafting everyday life.

CHAPTER FOUR

The Meaning of Life

Qi unceasingly moves and changes; this is called "qi transformation." *Qi* transformation produces the ten thousand things and the human body. *Plain Questions (juan* 3:9): "*Qi* comes together so there is form." Every thing (*shiwu* 事物) that has form comes into being from the gathering together (*juhe* 聚合) of the most minuscule *qi*. But the structured existence of things that have form is a relatively temporary state, material forms also accord with *qi* transformation to disperse and lose form, and change is itself a thing that changes.
—Huang Jitang, *Zhongyixue daolun*

Zhang Qicheng opens an informal essay he wrote in 2004 during the course of our postfieldwork discussions on contemporary *yangsheng* practices with the following general definition of *yangsheng*.

> *Yangsheng* is a kind of practical process by which Chinese people approach life [*shengming* 生命], embodying Chinese people's particular life outlook. This Chinese life outlook has certain obvious differences from that of the West. Although Confucian, Daoist, Buddhist, and medical forms of knowledge have certain differences among them—with the differences between Buddhist and the other three being perhaps the greatest—in general these four kinds of understanding can supplement each other. Together, they form the visage of a Chinese philosophy of life and a Chinese culture of life.

The essay is simply entitled "Life." It weaves together quotations from the Chinese metaphysical and medical archive, explores the philosophical riches to be found in terms and phrases, and returns again and again to classic definitions of life (*sheng*), its ingredients, and its patterns. His approach is philological, showing the results of close study of ancient and canonical texts, and his style is didactic. The essay was written, after all, for this book and for coauthorial use, aiming to trace what life has meant in historical China and to provide organized philosophical resources for our joint use in writing about life nurturance. Judith Farquhar, in translating the essay and choosing extracts from it to expand upon, has found its insights forceful beyond a history of ideas or an anthropology of culture.

The essay moves constantly between ultimate patterns of natural emergence and intimate experiences of embodied existence. It invites a reflection on life that is personally consequential, significant in the broadest sense; at the same time, abstract as it is, it nevertheless seems to arise from the experience of everyday life. The somewhat different engagements of both authors with the Chinese literature of *yangsheng* has led into a philosophical terrain where the meaning of life is a serious, but no longer very predictable topic. In this chapter, we seek not only to explore the possible meanings of life, or lives, but also to explore the meaning of meaning. To that end, we hope to allow the voices of the diverse archive cited in Zhang Qicheng's essay to speak alongside and in close relationship to the voices of the writers and practitioners of *yangsheng* who spoke in Chapters 2 and 3.

Though Zhang's essay "Life" is a private communication, its fluid citational style and mode of appreciative engagement with the Chinese metaphysical and medical heritage are typical of a certain kind of scholarly writing on Chinese medicine.[1] Like his colleagues in fields such as *Inner Canon* Studies (*Huangdi neijing yanjiu*), *Classic of Cold Damage* Studies (*Shanghanlun yanjiu*), medical philology (*yiguwen*), and medical schools of thought (*gejia xueshuo*), Zhang here displays his passions as a reader of the Chinese literary tradition and his scholarly sensitivity in paraphrasing ancient language for contemporary use. This kind of writing remobilizes some very old ideas, even suggesting that these ideas, as part of culture, have never been inactive or irrelevant. Though the field of Chinese medicine is one of the few scholarly arenas in the contemporary People's Republic that maintains this deep philological engagement with an East Asian philosophical heritage, writing such as Zhang's is not esoteric. Chinese medicine is a popular as well as a scholarly arena with a vast institutional and discursive presence. Its literature, lore, and clinical practices engage the experience of many different kinds of people in a wide variety of ways. For these reasons, "Life" can be read as an emblematic cultural text.

The concerns of Zhang's essay form the heart of this chapter. In it, he reviews definitions of medical and metaphysical keywords, compiles philosophical remarks about the sources and patterns of life, and turns constantly to the correlative science on which Chinese medicine is based for detailed descriptions of human life processes. We have called this chapter "The Meaning of Life" partly because the essay devotes much attention to defining and characterizing both words for life and life itself.[2] We also thematize "meaning" here because this has been a persistent concern of cultural anthropology (Judith Farquhar's field and Zhang Qicheng's new avocation). The problem of meaning and the allied problem of culture have guided our selection of extracts from the essay for consideration in this chapter. As Zhang signals with his opening paragraph, what follows is, at one level, an interpretation of culture. Indeed, Zhang has been a leader at his university and beyond in developing cultural studies of Chinese medicine and philosophy. In keeping with the American cultural anthropology tradition that has indirectly influenced cultural studies in China, we often consider what words, terms, or rhetorical gestures "mean."

Meaning is not a simple matter of word-to-concept reference, however, and Zhang is not primarily concerned with semantics. Rather, the essay joins forms of saying very closely to forms of being. In the original Chinese, this appears a natural and unforced achievement of scholarship. Meaning is the site where formal thought enters and gives form to everyday life, and vice versa.[3] Thought emerges not simply as a word game, but as a practice inseparable from the tasks of living.

Meaning

It is not only the fields of anthropology, pragmatic philosophy, and sociolinguistics that have addressed questions of meaning as essentially practical. Most readers of classical Chinese philosophy have had to develop some approach of this kind. The writings classed as part of the Confucian tradition are conventionally characterized as secular and materialist, involving "concrete thinking," and are seen as full of chestnuts of mundane advice. (It is no accident that "Confucius says" has become such an everyday cliché.) Daoist writing has also shown a strong bias toward use value. One thinks of remarks like those in *juan* 11 of the *Dao de jing*: "Thirty spokes brought together make a wheel, but the absence at its hub realizes the wheel's usefulness; Clay turned on a wheel is formed into a vessel, but the absence inside it realizes the vessel's usefulness." And we are reminded of the many magical-technical interventions into reality undertaken by Daoist adepts.[1] Increasingly, it has been in the domains of practice and knowledge that Sinologists have found the common ground uniting Confucian and Daoist thought at the metaphysical level.[2] In other words, the "immanental cosmos"[3] presumed by the philosophies of the Zhou and Han periods is a world in which meaning can be derived (and must be actively derived) only from the manifest, the experiential, and the everyday. There is no antediluvian "unmoved mover" to provide a transcendent dimension to the search for meaning. Neither theology nor idealist linguistics really helps; values must emerge from practice.

François Jullien has made this point in a variety of ways in his recent study of the *Zhuangzi, Vital Nourishment*. He explores, for example, a central implication of the bias toward immanence in "Chinese thought." The

Meaning, in other words, presents problems of value that signify not only rhetorically and semiotically, but above all pragmatically.

To speak in English of "the meaning of life" seems to invoke deep and ultimate truths, the sort of thing one reflects on when coming to terms with one's own mortality. The word "meaning" sends us off into spiritual realms, or at least into abstraction; we cross to the ontological other side, the transcendent; from practice to theory; from *parole* to *langue*; from body to mind. Scholarship has offered two main strategies for this journey into the abstract: we can ask existential and theological questions or, more humbly, we can ask semantic and cognitive ones. If we adopted the latter strategy, we could—and the essay certainly does—investigate the denotations and connotations, the agreed-upon conceptual referents, of words for "life." Thus, for example, Zhang lists a number of linked terms, all compounds of the word *sheng*:

> "Life" words in Chinese include the notions of *shengming* 生命, *shengzhang* 生长 (*shengcheng* 生成, *shenghua* 生化), *shenghuo* 生活, and *shengtai* 生态. In the term "*yangsheng*," the word *sheng* mainly refers to *shengming* or life span ["life" plus "fate"]. But it is doubtless easy to see that this "life span" is intimately tied to ideas of generativity *(shengzhang, shengcheng, shenghua)*, living as a process *(shenghuo)*, and the life of nature *(shengtai)*. This word *sheng* embodies the Chinese people's ideas about life *(shengming*, [life-fate]).

This sort of explanation could easily be extended to determine the semantic value of *sheng*, understood as one of a series of linked terms in modern Chinese that define each other in use. *Sheng* corresponds to a richly connotative concept inscribed in the cumulative mental dictionary of our language. But this clarification goes only part of the way to satisfy our interest in meaning.

We could go further by adopting a more philosophical strategy, taking up the meaning of life by teasing out existential values that should concern anyone, Chinese or not, and asking about the ultimate aims of life, the unvarying or transcendent values to which we attach our own life purposes. Such philosophical questions can also "unspoken assumptions that precede all thought" pose a very immediate question: "not what life to choose, which is already very abstract . . . but how to organize, or, rather, 'manage' one's life."[4] "Manage" translates a word (*zhi* 治) that also refers to treating illnesses and governing domains; used in the context of his study, it reminds us that nurturing life is not a "mere" practical necessity; rather, it arises from a metaphysical stance on the world, one that refuses transcendent meanings in favor of an appreciation of the manifold forms of concrete life and a theory of action that presumes a spontaneous Way that is "so of itself" (*ziran* 自然).

1. Nathan Sivin, *Chinese Alchemy, Preliminary Studies* (Cambridge MA: Harvard University Press, 1968).

2. Geoffrey Lloyd and Nathan Sivin, *The Way and the Word: Science and Medicine in Early China and Greece* (New Haven: Yale University Press, 2002); John S. Major, *Heaven and Earth in Early Han Thought: Chapters Three, Four, and Five of the Huainanzi* (Albany: State University of New York Press, 1993); Robin D. S.Yates, *Five Lost Classics: Tao, Huang-Lao, and Yin-Yang in Han China* (New York: Ballantine Books, 1997).

3. The term is from Donald Hall and Roger Ames, *Thinking Through Confucius* (Albany: State University of New York Press, 1987), pp. 12–17.

4. François Jullien, *Vital Nourishment: Departing from Happiness* (New York: Zone Books, 2007), p. 124.

be found in Zhang's essay. As we have remarked elsewhere in these pages, he is particularly interested in questions of personal self-cultivation, and in much of his recent teaching, he acts on the belief that the Chinese philosophical heritage can satisfy the deep personal needs of stressed and alienated moderns.

These two strains of argument about the meaning or value of life—the semantic and the existential—are not clearly separated in Zhang's essay. Though he is trained in philology and has devoted much of his career to close study of difficult, ambiguous ancient texts, his aims go beyond achieving the correct modern paraphrase; he does more than find linkages between contemporaneous vocabularies, other texts, and social contexts. Like many of his colleagues, Zhang orients classical research toward the modern tasks of Chinese medicine, chief among which is relieving suffering through the responsible treatment of bodily disorders. Medicine provides him with a literature that places a high value on life, and insofar as medicine is classically inseparable from philosophy in China, it teaches, at the same time, much about meaning. Zhang constantly returns to the "life" concerns of medicine, such that in his essay, both the existential and the semantic are rendered deeply practical concerns. Chinese medicine helps people, we are often told; it reaches the injuries and dysfunctions of contemporary sufferers with effective remedies. Ultimately, research on the tradition of Chinese medicine justifies itself with reference to this home truth, and many who nurture their own and their communities' lives in Beijing see themselves as life-fostering practical philosophers. The experience of the ancients, correctly understood, sensitively read, and responsibly used, intervenes well in life today. Hence, scholarship; hence, the reading and teaching of philosophy; hence, the nurturance of life.

Though there is a strong emphasis in this chapter on medical knowledge, the power of Chinese thought is not confined to healing the sick body.[4] But bodily life is still a concern when we speak of life's meaning. And as scholars of ancient and modern Chinese medicine and as people who occasionally fall ill, both Farquhar and

Zhang have experienced the efficacy of Chinese medical therapies. Both of us have come to accept almost unthinkingly the fitness to our bodily natures of the field's language, logic, and metaphysics. Depression, indigestion, elation, leg cramps, dry skin, arthritis, jitteriness, and hitting one's stride as a runner, for example, are all well understood as states of physiological "*qi* transformation," to be discussed below. But in his essay "Life," Zhang Qicheng cites medical and metaphysical discourses that have a salience far beyond embodied nature. The writing he invokes and explains makes forays into first principles that ultimately—we will argue—help us to understand the spontaneous patterns in which nature (*ziran*) as a whole and our lives as persons emerge.[5]

Zhang's essay both presumes and articulates the spontaneity and universality of natural emergence, the ceaselessness of certain patterns of cosmic life. His rhetorical style, the mode of influence he seeks, and the metaphysical assumptions he urges on us will become clear in the course of this chapter. But be prepared for a certain difference: Chinese thought does not ask theological questions. The question that Zhang takes to be answered by the texts he discusses is not "Why should I live?" Such a question seeks an external, transcendent source of meaning to which individuals can hitch their own small lives. The uncreated universe of Chinese thought offers little help for such a project. Rather, the implicit question in Zhang's essay is "How can we live well?" And the almost immediate answer is obvious: in accord with the Way.

The question of how to live well we can answer concretely and in detail, drawing on the experience of those who have gone before us, employing methods of knowing the Way that have stood the test of time, cultivating an attentiveness to the state of play to which we must adapt. As was seen in Chapters 2 and 3 of this book, life nurturers in Chinese cities acknowledge that this is the philosophical and practical question they are answering. Relatively unlettered as many of these *yangsheng* adepts are, their experience is nevertheless informed by the linguistic and imaginative orientations toward life—our lives—that Zhang gives us in "Life." His way of reviving classical wisdom asks us to read with our own practical questions at the fore.

In turning here to a fully philosophical language and literature, much of it from the classical period of Chinese thought between 600 B.C.E. and 200 C.E., we are not attempting to collapse all history. Rather, we hope to cast light back on earlier chapters, inviting a deeper appreciation of the civilized, refined, and cultured practice of contemporary *yangsheng*. The metaphysical resources we draw on here are not so much salvaged from a remote and forgotten past as they are drawn from a lively popular discourse to which readers of many sorts turn. Thus far, we have read the daily practices and commonsense attitudes of Beijingers—readers, writers, exercisers, and the rest—as the expressions of practical philosophers. The principles of nurturing life they articulate may at times seem clichéd, ill-expressed, and vague, though their personal efforts to live in close accord with principles of nurturing life are certainly vibrant. But their language and their habits, their tastes and their joys, resonate at a fundamental level with the powers and poetics of the great tradition.

In what follows, then, translated extracts from Zhang Qicheng's essay anchor the chapter. We provide some commentary, mostly written by Farquhar, partly to highlight and explain unfamiliar phrasings and ideas, partly to build links to other parts of this book and to related literature. Both authors have edited the whole. Hoping to serve as companions of reading, rather than authorities on meaning, we have avoided extensive paraphrase and literary interpretation. We have also maintained a challenge to readers in the more "foreign" aspects of the writing. In keeping with Walter Benjamin's advice about translation, we hope the sometimes strange or awkward Englishing of Zhang's text will force readers to slow down, to speculate about possible meanings, to seek links between novel phrasing and forms of experience that could in reading be defamiliarized or reenchanted.[6] Dwell on Zhang's writing and citations. He asks his classical sources to speak not just to speculative thought, but to modern lives.

Culture, Difference, Embodiment

We can begin with a return to the first paragraph of "Life," quoted at the beginning of this chapter. In this very broad opening gesture, Zhang invokes "the visage of a Chinese philosophy of life and a Chinese culture of life." The repetition of "Chinese," and the emphasis on differences in the paragraph—both between Chinese and Western cultures and between various Chinese philosophical traditions—mark this as a comparative project, very fitting for an ethnographic study. The word "culture" (*wenhua* 文化) also invites reflection on a particularly Chinese heritage. By the end of the paragraph, both culture and philosophy have come to stand in for the earlier term "life outlook" (*shengmingguan* 生命观), a word that suggests the view from a situated, embodied position in history. We note that the Chinese life outlook, reflected on as culture, is both different from Euro-American culture and made up of cultural differences (Confucian, Daoist, and other "forms of knowledge"). A comparative approach like that of anthropology can both highlight and helpfully translate these differences for Western readers.

We also note that the Chinese life outlook on *yangsheng* is "embodied." The word is *tixian* (体现), which might be more literally translated as "to make manifest in concrete form." The verb is particularly useful, suggesting that something fairly abstract—culture, or philosophy, or a view—has taken material form, such as, for example, the "practical process" of *yangsheng* nurturance of life. One of ethnography's classic questions is "How is culture (or philosophy, or outlook, or a system of differences) embodied or made manifest in everyday life?" Zhang's essay "Life" provides some answers. By presuming that *yangsheng* activity in contemporary China is a practical process that embodies culture, he both elevates the health regimes of ordinary Beijingers to the status of culture (*wenhua*, also translatable as "civilization") and characterizes such practices as an integral part of the great Chinese tradition.

Grass and Trees

Following the introductory paragraph on culture and *yangsheng*, the essay begins with etymology, a tactic of reading that has special charms in Chinese. Most modern speakers and readers of Chinese are attracted to the idea of the Chinese character as pictograph—people ranging from medical doctors to taxi drivers have explained to Judith Farquhar that Chinese writing is easy to learn because "the word is a picture of the idea." Linguists dispute this popular prejudice. But even they often succumb to the charm of nonarbitrary linguistic representation, especially when they indulge in etymology. Chinese philologists are able, after all, to draw on a historically deep archive of changing written language. Etymology is one way of answering the question "What has 'life' meant in the past?" In the preamble to his long and systematic discussion of past writings about life, Zhang Qicheng provides a brief etymological discussion:

> The modern character *sheng* was written as 生 in oracle bone script; on the top was growing grass and trees and on the bottom was earth. So the root meaning of *sheng* is the growth of plants from the earth, an upward developing process. As the *Shuowen jiezi* says:[7] "Life is forward movement. Like grass and trees growing up out of the earth." Liu Yan, in *The Meaning of the Changes* (*Yi yi* 易意), says: "What comes forth from nothing is life" (*zi wu chu you yue sheng* 自无出有曰生). From a lifeless barren planet to abounding life, this is an epoch-making change; the history of life (*shengming*) begins with this. Hence the praise of the Dao in the *Book of Changes* (*Xi ci chuan* 系辞传): "The great virtue and power (*de* 德) of heaven and earth is called life."

In one short paragraph, Zhang quotes three classical definitions of life, develops the imagery in a three-thousand-year-old word, and places these forms of textuality in the context of planetary life. He does not speak of metaphor. Life *is* plant growth—it has a history grounded in the planet's earliest natural beginnings. The assertion that animal and human life evolved from the first emergence of plants, that "epoch-making change" that occurred on "a barren planet," invokes fundamental processes far beyond the linguistic. The statements from early metaphysical works that Zhang quotes emphasize exactly what it is that our human lives have in common with the life of plants: forward and upward movement, spontaneity (being that comes forth from nothing), the weaving together of heaven's warm sunlight and earth's damp fecundity.

Much is entailed in this simple starting point. (Though it's not so simple. Already, the heteroglossia characteristic of the whole essay is evident, as is the use of complicated concepts such as *de*, "virtue-power," to which we return below.) With this etymology, the original reference of "life" turns attention to forms of generativity, proliferation, and perhaps cultivation. It displays the biases of an agricultural civilization. It does not invite a narrow focus on human consciousness, nor does it encourage the classic Aristotelian division between organic life, *zoë*, and the social life of citizens, *bios*. Though Zhang once in the paragraph uses the term *shengming*, referring to the bounded life of people, the emphasis here is on the richly connotative root of many compounds, *sheng* alone.

Like so many Chinese words, *sheng* can function as noun, verb, adjective, and adverb. Thus, depending on context, speakers use the word to mean "life," "birth," "living," "giving birth," "lively"; "genesis," "generative," and "what is engendered"; and "to produce," "productive," "product," and "productivity." In English, this would seem to be polysemy indeed. In Chinese, *sheng* is a simple natural unity joining process and product in a single form of activity. Its reality is no more or less mysterious than the leafing of trees in the spring or the sprouting of bean seeds in a damp place.[8]

In the classical sources cited in this paragraph and throughout the essay, *sheng* is often used alone to evoke the full dynamism of the single word. But as we noted above, it is also used often as part of a compound to achieve a specific sense of the term. The one used most frequently in the whole essay is *shengming*. This compound modifies the broad living process denoted by *sheng* with the temporal and spatial delimitation denoted by the word *ming*, or fate.[9] The irrepressible generativity of grass and trees is confined, cut, pruned, and narrowed into the rhythms and pathways of the human. Every kind of human growth is a specific kind of action, configured by the original sorting of space and time as dimension emerged from chaos and the void. *Shengming* is perhaps most plausibly translated as "life span" or "a human life." (It would be unusual to refer to the *shengming* of an animal or plant.) Thus, when in his etymological paragraph Zhang says that the history of life (*shengming*) begins with abounding plant life, he suggests that individual, bounded human lives result from a natural history grounded in, but evolving far from, the fundamental and generative marriage of heaven and earth that gave birth to the ten thousand things.

One last point about this dense paragraph: Zhang speaks as a modern when he evokes the beginnings of biological evolution from "a barren planet." But he brings equal relish to the citation of irreducibly nonmodern terms: *de* 德, which I have here conventionally translated as "virtue and power," is only one example. In modern Chinese, *de* most often refers to some form of morality or mentality. But in this quote, "The great virtue and power (*de*) of heaven and earth is called life," it can hardly mean that. Zhang does not explain. He provides no translation of such terms into modern scientific or sociological concepts—rather, his treatment demands that in reading them, we see them as the spontaneous cosmological forces they are.

Life (Shengming) Is a Process

Early in the essay, Zhang refers to the process of life as *shengsheng huahua* (生生化化), a paired doubling of the words for life/to live and change/to change: "Since we take man to be a part of nature, we consider the life activities of humans against the background of the *shengsheng huahua* (生生化化) of the myriad things between heaven and earth." Though this phrase is supplanted later in the essay with other terms for natural generativity, such as *shengsheng zhi qi* (生生之气), or the *qi* of giving birth to life, it nevertheless remains a good phrase to denote transformative and generative natural process. It resonates, for example, with the paragraph below:

Life is a process of "unceasing genesis" [*shengsheng buxi* 生生不息]: the Chinese ancients considered that life is an evolutionary process of becoming [*shengcheng yanhua* 生成演化], uninterrupted birth and more birth [*sheng er you sheng* 生而又生], continuous without cessation. The natural world is vast and unbounded, infinite and without horizon, always in the midst of limitless activity and change. The natural world's unceasing birthing and growing, producing and ripening is called "giving life to life" or "birthing birth" [shengsheng 生生]. With regard to the myriad things [wanwu 万物, literally the ten thousand things], this is called "the virtue/power [de 德] of life giving rise to more life." "The virtue of giving life to life" vested in the myriad things is manifold to the most extreme extent, a life mechanism without limits, transforming in countless ways, without gap and without end. The meaning of the ceaseless becoming of the natural world, its ceaseless creativity, its unending change, is to make of life an unceasing generativity. "Generativity" [shengsheng 生生] is not only the basic mode of being of the natural world, it is also the root of all change; the Book of Changes says: "Generativity is spoken of as the changes" [shengsheng zhi wei yi 生生之谓易]. Among the myriad things of nature, humans are not only the product of "the virtue of giving life to life," they also are most suited to embodying and making use of "the virtue of giving life to life."

This piece of teeming prose falls under the essay's first main heading, "Characteristics of China's Culture of Life," and follows upon a short section that discusses holism. (Heaven and earth, mind and body, and the body's organ systems all ultimately form unitary wholes.) Doubling sheng for the first of many times in the essay to make a verb-object compound—giving life to life, birthing birth, and so on—Zhang figures in the writing itself something of the unbounded process that is natural life. He noted in conversation, as we discussed drafts of this chapter, "We Chinese say qi is continuous, so our writing should not have breaks in it."

A tremendous uncreated generativity underlies much of the physiology and pathology known to Chinese medicine; we have suggested in other chapters that the logic of commonsense lore and much public-health information also relies on this fundamentally processual dynamic. The assumption that "life is a process" of "uninterrupted birth and more birth" is seldom remarked on. It nevertheless lies at the foundation of even some very modern, very global knowledge—when expressed in Chinese.

Vital powers, Zhang points out, are not only ceaseless, but mani-fold: "'the virtue of giving life to life' [is] vested in the myriad things." The things that are creative agents in the *shengsheng* process are not just those predictable few—earth, rain, sunshine—that we might expect from the language and culture of ancient China's "divine farmer" (*Shen Nong*).[10] Rather, all the things of this world—the scope of the ancient term *wanwu*, ten thousand things, is that broad—are active in the genesis of more life forms. The image could suggest booming, buzzing confusion, a natural world of vertiginous and unconstrained shape shifting.[11] But our world is not in fact so cha-otic. Actual shape, or the observable *forms* of change and the myriad things, is a central concern of the early philosophy Zhang discusses.

Qi *and the Sources of Life*

The fundamental metaphysical and cosmological explanations for natural/processual form are cosmogonic; that is, they tell us how the universe happened to emerge in the actual form it did. They also, implicitly, tell us how the world still emerges from chaos, from the void, from Dao, from original *qi*. "Life" continues, summarizing the cosmogonic insights of ancient China:

> Daoists emphasized that the Dao (Nothing) gave birth to the cosmos. For example, Laozi said: "The Dao gives rise [*sheng* 生] to one, one gives rise to two, two gives rise to three, and three gives rise to the myriad things." Zhuangzi ("Heaven and Earth") said: "At the Origin there was Nothing. Nothingness and namelessness. From this arose the One, so there was one, but it was without form. Things [material-ity, *wu* 物] then took hold and were born, and this was called virtue/power [*de* 德]. Even before there was form, there were distinctions, manifold, but not separated out, and these were called fates [*ming* 命]. Out of the flux and motion, things were born, and as things grew, they produced patterns [*sheng li* 生理], and these were called *xing*-forms [or bodies, *xing* 形]. The bodies and forms came to harbor *shen*-vitality [神], each had its own character and limits, and this was called inborn nature" [*xing* 性]. This refers to the idea of the evolutionary process

of natural genius [*tiancai sibian* 天才思辩] in which the cosmos comes from nothing to be something, and the myriad things arise from the Dao.... Han Dynasty "Changes" philosophers argued that these three stages "*qi*, form, substance" existed, but could not yet be separate, so they are called "Chaos" [*hundun* 浑沦]," and they also called this *taiji*, the supreme ultimate. The four stages of cosmogenesis, then, are in fact Nothing (no *qi*, no form, no substance) → *qi* → form → substance. The first is a stage of absence, the next three are stages of presence. This indicates the great wisdom of the ancient thinkers.

This discussion also indicates the variations to be found in early Chinese thought about the origins of life. In the extract above, we have simplified, deleting quotes from other authorities that use different terminologies and that propose different entities as part of the cosmogonic process. But as Zhang points out, there is substantial underlying agreement among these pictures: the universe began in nothingness, which produced one undifferentiated whole, which then generated differences and particular material forms. Few of these cosmogonic accounts mention human beings—the "bodies" in question are *ti* (体), or the substantial forms of many kinds of things, from animals to asterisms, from earthworks to ancient texts. At this metaphysical level, which admits of no proof, humans and their works are things alongside all the other "ten thousand things" that come forth or are born and transformed in cosmogenesis.

All this speculative philosophy about first causes, causes prior to causation itself, may seem quite pointless. Why speculate about events that could never be verified or falsified? Why study cosmic evolutions prior to the production of any evidence that might be legible to paleobotany or geology or even astronomy? One reason is that cosmogony, if it could be understood, would give us insight into the form of change, the patterns of cosmic motion that arose at the beginning and continue to ripple down the passage of time. Chinese cosmogonies are not, it should be recalled, Garden of Eden just-so stories that account for things such as gender difference and the fall of reality away from the ideal. The preclassic origin stories that Zhang cites presume that genesis (not Genesis) continues now, as in the remote past. The stream that connects us to the ultimate sources of life, though it may have swirls and eddies, is unbroken. Cosmic generativity ceaselessly differentiates from the one *qi*, and if it is always possible for any given form to return to the unity of "Chaos" (as the passage below suggests), then cosmogony might hold practical insights about remaining in step with the Dao.

In other words, understanding the ultimate origins of the human form of life helps us to understand the intimate, concrete, and actual situation of (at least) human embodiment. This gradually becomes clear as the passage continues:

> Chinese medicine also emphasizes that evolutions of *qi* produce life. The *Inner Canon* deploys its theory of "*qi* transformation" [*qihua* 气化] to elucidate and establish a complete and unified heaven's Way system of "*qi* transformation." According to the *Inner Canon*, the becomings, transformations, and dying off of the cosmos and its myriad things are all a *qi*-transformation process in which *qi* comes from unitary Chaos [*hun* 混] to be differentiated (into concrete forms), and then returns to the unity of Chaos.

Qi transformation is a medical name for the general process of physiological production and reproduction. Both healthy growth and pathological change are transformations of *qi*.

What could such a statement mean? Even if the utter transformativity of the world is accepted, how does a "theory" or "system" of transformation of *qi* lead to articulate understanding? *Qi* has been notoriously difficult to define or, more to the point, to translate in the Sinological literature. It is now widely accepted practice to simply use the romanized Chinese word *qi* (Pinyin) or *ch'i* (Wade-Giles). The manifold forms of *qi* are often noted, especially by those who attend to the Chinese medical archive. Nathan Sivin's terse discussion is often cited (see below), but perhaps even more indicative of the relationship between originary cosmogonic *qi* and the multiplicity of things is the index of his 1987 book: under the general heading of "*ch'i*" (*qi*) we find the following terms: "*ch'i* sectors,

Qi

A historian and philosopher of Chinese medicine, Huang Jitang, in a late 1980s introduction to Chinese medicine—a book meant for general readers— wrote the following explanation of *qi* transformation, emphasizing the configurative propensities of all *qi* and thus the at once unitary and manifold nature of existence:[1]

Chinese medicine continues to uphold the doctrine that *qi* is of one origin. *Qi* is the original root of the world; heaven and earth and the ten thousand things are all formed from *qi*, and the life of the human body is generated from the movement and development of *qi*. The *Yellow Emperor's Inner Canon: Plain Questions* (*juan* 8:25) says: "Heaven and earth mingle their *qi*, limit its span, and this is called man." "Heaven covers, earth supports; not confined to humans, *qi* fully suffuses the ten thousand things. Humans are born through the *qi* of heaven and earth, and they grow within the patterning of the four seasons." "The human is what takes heaven and earth as its parents and resonates with the four seasons." The human body depends on the natural world for its nurturance and cultivation, in accord with the natural regularities of life. "Living *qi* suffuses the cosmos." In medicine, as we probe the regular changes of human physiology and pathology, we seek to follow the regular changes of heaven and earth and the ten thousand things. The *Plain Questions* (*juan* 1:1) says: "Pattern is found in *yin* and *yang*, harmony is found in craft and number." So it is that we model research in medical questions on the regularities of growth and change in the natural world, in order to better mobilize life nurturance and disease prevention.

Qi unceasingly moves and changes; this is called "*qi* transformation." *Qi* transformation produces the ten thousand things and the human body. *Plain Questions* (*juan* 3:9): "*Qi* comes together so there is form." Every thing (*shiwu* 事物) that has form comes into being from the gathering together (*juhe* 聚合) of the most minuscule *qi*. But the structured existence of things that vitalities, essences, energies, vital energies"; "hurried, tense, liquid, medial *ch'i*"; "heteropathic and orthopathic *ch'i*"; "circulating, constructive, defensive, genetic, primordial, deviant, inborn, divine, elevating, environmental, great, heterogeneous, reinforcing, pestilential, and true *ch'i*." Sivin's book, *Traditional Medicine in Contemporary China*, moreover, is not particularly technical and does not mention a number of other forms of *qi* that are also important to specialists.[12]

Sivin builds on Manfred Porkert's earlier and more extensive discussion of the problem of defining *qi*. Porkert ultimately glosses *qi* as "configurative energy" (because it is both a force and a tendency to take form, or myriad forms), and he also points out that every use of the terms *yin* and *yang* should be read as *yin qi* and *yang qi*. This latter point emphasizes that a great many apparent substantives in philosophical Chinese are actually modifiers for *qi*: *yin*-style *qi*, *yang*-style *qi*, heteropathic or orthopathic *qi*. *Yin* and *yang* become not column headings for two great classes of things, not forces in themselves, but terms for a type of dynamic—qualities, rather than entities.[13]

Let us return to Sivin's economical and suggestive way of explaining *qi*:

> By 350 B.C.E., when philosophy began to be systematic, *ch'i* meant air, breath, vapor, and other pneumatic stuff. It might be congealed or compacted in liquids or solids. *Ch'i* also referred to the balanced and ordered vitalities and energies, partly derived from the air we breathe, that cause physical change and maintain life.
>
> These are not distinct meanings. Before modern times there was no separate conception of energy in Chinese thought. This is not a sign of deficient curiosity, but of a tendency (like that of the Stoics in the West) to think of stuff and its transformations in a unitary way. We might define *ch'i*—or at least sum up its use in Chinese writing about nature by about 350—as simultaneously "what makes things happen in stuff" or "stuff in which things happen."[14]

This careful wording exhibits an appropriate discomfort with defining *qi* as if it were a simple noun or even as a polysemic signifier have form is a relatively temporary state, material forms also accord with *qi* transformation to disperse and lose form, and change is itself a thing that changes. The *Plain Questions* (*juan* 19:68) says: "Ascending and descending, inward and outward movements of *qi* are never without an object (*qi* 器). So the object is the site of living transformation, but when the object disperses, all falls into pieces, and that instance of living transformation ceases." This "object" is something that has material form; it is the site of the living transformations of *qi*. Ascending and descending, inward and outward movements are the manifest form of *qi* transformation. When the object disperses, this is a scattering of the original gathered state of *qi*; its living transformation process is thus ended and transformed into some other form of gathering *qi*. Thus it is said: "The life of things comes from transformation: when things reach an extreme, they can only change; change is volatility itself; both growth and decay arise from the tendency to change." The human body is also an object, also an instance of "*qi* coming together so there is form." In the process of a life (*shengming* 生命), there is unceasing *qi* transformation, unceasing ascending and descending, inward and outward movement. Chinese medicine physiology is the study of this *qi* transformation process of ascending and descending, inward and outward movement in the human body. If the *qi* transformation of the physical body loses regularity, and ascending and descending, inward and outward become disordered, if a stable condition is damaged to the extent that a good equilibrium cannot be maintained, this is the onset of disease. The study of these irregular processes in the human body is Chinese medical pathology.

1. Huang Jitang, "*Qi* Is the Original Root of [Human] Life" (*Qi shi shengmingde benyuan* 气是生命的本原), in Huang Jitang et al. (eds.), *Introduction to Chinese Medicine* (*Zhongyixue daolun* 中医学导论) (Guangzhou: Guangdong Higher Education Press, 1988), pp. 43–44.

that had accumulated a set of distinct meanings or signifieds over the millennia. Here, the "use" of *qi* can be "summed up" for heuristic purposes of translation into English (Sivin's volume on medicine is really a long introduction to a translation of a Chinese textbook) as two aspects of the same process: a happening and its materiality. A material event. Like many of us who have written on Chinese medicine, Sivin needs to find a way of asserting the simultaneous structurality and functionality of *qi*'s mode of being. Its activity and its objectivity are "not distinct meanings"; rather, "stuff and its transformations" are understandable only as part of the unitary process of coming into being that is nature, or the Dao.

Yet some ancient and humble meanings still cling to the word. *Qi* is known, experienced, taken for granted as air, breath, vapor, "pneumatic stuff." Shigehisa Kuriyama, in his discussion of winds in physiology and cosmology, suggests that a preclassical, Shang-period obsession with knowing winds and managing the good and bad things they blow to us was gradually transformed and rendered technical. The concept of *qi* was refined from early knowledge of winds, as systematic metaphysics and medicine developed in the classic period after the fifth or sixth century B.C.E. *Qi* made the forcefulness and materiality of wind more exact and less global. In medicine, the acupuncturist knows she has found the right acupoint when she can palpably "get *qi*" (*deqi* 得气). But this takes an educated touch. The *qigong* adept learns to feel *qi* as a specific resistance in the air or as a kind of effective wind traveling between bodies. This, too, requires experience and skill. Wind, on the other hand, is not only straightforwardly perceptible, it is ubiquitous and unavoidable. For the Chinese ancients, Kuriyama suggests, "wind *was* change." *Qi*, on the other hand, came to have a narrower reference.

But the materiality and perceptibility of moving air, whether thought of as wind or as *qi*, was obvious. It still is. Modern words for gas (*qiti* 气体, *meiqi* 煤气) or air (*kongqi* 空气, *daqi* 大气) require the notion of *qi*; weather is "the *qi* of heaven" (*tianqi* 天气); the bubbles in soft drinks (*qishui* 汽水) are *qi*. Odors are sweet or foul *qi* (*xiangqi* 香气, *chouqi* 臭气). To be arrogant is to display overly proud *qi* (*aoqi* 骄气), perhaps to put on airs (*qipai* 气派). To become angry is to "give rise to" *qi* (*shengqi* 生气), an experience that was once expressed just as concretely in English as "rising bile." None of these uses of *qi* require any explanation to a speaker of modern Chinese. As a result, one suspects that when a Chinese medical doctor speaks of moving *qi* (*yunqi* 运气), bolstering "right" or orthopathic *qi* (*bu zhengqi* 补正气), or "getting" *qi* in acupuncture, even novice patients can draw on a common sense that helps them imagine what is meant by these technical terms. For such readers, Zhang's reference to the most general level of "*qi* transformation" would hold few mysteries.

Zhang's essay does offer a sort of definition of *qi*, however. We are, after all, moderns and must acknowledge the failures of translation of our times, including the gaps in understanding between elderly scholars and much younger students and readers. Definitions must be attempted, some recent language must be appropriated, and terms must be connected to experience:

> Chinese medicine has pointed out . . . that *qi* is not only material, it also has a limitless life force [*shengmingli* 生命力]. It is because the *qi* that makes up the human body is an expression of this life force that man has life. The strength or weakness of the human body's life force, its longevity or the brevity of its life span, rests with the flourishing or weakening, persistence or disappearance of original *qi* [*yuanqi* 元气]. The living process of metabolism is called *qi*-transformation physiology; life phenomena have their origins in the rising and falling, inward and outward movement of *qi* mechanisms, and so forth. This all reflects the fact that *qi* is the basic material composing the human body, as well as the living motive force of the human body.

Here, as in the more detailed explanation provided in the sidebar above, the Chinese medical adoption of the very general cosmological notion of *qi* transformation serves to link the dynamics of *qi* to human physiology and pathology, that is, to human experiences of being embodied as part of a natural process. Our frequent invocation in English of "the environment," with its presumption that bodies and societies are somehow distinct from a surrounding nature, could not survive a serious engagement with *qi*. Wind, breath, the force that drives blood through our veins, gives shape to the developing fetus, adds the twinkle to smiling eyes, produces so many different flowers and fruits—these forms of *qi* are manifold in quality, but unitary in the exuberant transforming of their being.

In his efforts to speak to a modern and even an Anglophone readership, Zhang has found the biomedical idea of metabolism useful in this explanation. But the physiology (*shengli* 生理) and the body he more often refers to are not the hidden processes of biomedical physiology (metabolism, blood pressure, sclerosis, and so on) but the *experienced* signs and symptoms of Chinese medicine. *Qi* transformation is responsible for felt differences in our bodies, from hour to hour, in sickness and in health. Moreover, both the general source and the particular actual forms of *qi* transformation can be understood with reference to the speculative cosmology Zhang has outlined above. His essay thus continues, emphasizing the immanence of coming into being. Any genesis—past, present, or future—is inseparable from cosmic genesis:

> As can be seen from these theories of cosmogony (the birth and transformation of the cosmos), only after there is a cosmos, a heaven and earth, can humans and the myriad things be produced. And humans and the myriad things all have a life span. Man is endowed with the *qi* that generates life [*shengsheng zhi qi* 生生之气] and thus comes into existence; the *Plain Questions* (*juan* 8:25), says: "Humans are born from the *qi* of heaven and earth, and they become human through the seasons of time." "Humans are born on earth, but their fate hangs on heaven; heaven and earth mingle their *qi*, limit its span, and this is called man."[15] Chinese medicine holds that humans are brought forth and made from the *qi* of heaven and earth, and this *qi* is a generative and regenerative *qi*. It is because humans have generative *qi* that they have a life span. The genesis and regenesis of *qi* is unceasing, so life, too, is unceasing. It is after humans have been endowed with the generative *qi* of heaven and earth that they can come into being, and so the generative *qi* of heaven

and earth transforms to become the generative *qi* internal to human bodies, thus deciding the living vicissitudes of a human life.

This passage refuses any division between cosmogony and physiology; the coming into being of the cosmos is not relegated to a remote time of past origins, and human physiology is not cut off from the general natural processes that—still, always—produce everything. But there are two ways in which a specifically human form of life is carved out from the *qi* that generates life, the *qi* of *shengsheng*. Humans become human through the seasons of time, and their span of life is limited in a particularly human way. The term "the seasons" is a resonant way of expressing the qualities of time for humans: our life responds to the vicissitudes of natural time, to the climatic round of the seasons, because the *yinyang* tendencies of warming and cooling, germinating and storing, moving and resting that determined the seasons preceded, cosmogonically, the contingent existence of the myriad things.[16] "Life span" refers to another human relationship to time: "Heaven and earth mingle their *qi*, limit its span, and call it man" (*tiandi he qi ming zhi yue ren* 天地合气命之曰人). We have here translated *ming*, the word for fate or life span, as "limit its span" to connote the notion of cutting that is intrinsic to the term. Particular lives are carved out from the flow; individual physiologies embody in small the great temporalities first put in motion by and as the Dao, arising from originary generative *qi*.

The Spatiality of Qi *Transformation*

Since Manfred Porkert first insisted on the radically functional orientation of the "theoretical foundations" of Chinese medicine, it has been tempting to read the technical concerns of the field as primarily concerned with time. For intellectual historians of the field, the temporal relations of rising and falling, waxing and waning, summarized by the logic of *yin* and *yang*, have provided a systematic framework of medical perception. *Yinyang* understanding reads a functional body, radically different from the structural body known to anatomy, the story goes. The inevitable comparison between "Chinese medicine," where anatomy is classically absent, and "modern biomedicine," founded at least historically on anatomy, demands that the temporal be wholly substituted for the structural: if anatomy is a structural science of bodily space, then *yinyang* analysis is a functional science of temporal change. In what we have written thus far in this chapter, and in Zhang's essay in general, a bias toward the temporal is evident.[17]

But Chinese medicine is a clinical art and was so even in the great age of metaphysical philosophy; it seeks to heal in the world of the myriad *things*, a world full of entities. Practitioners are presented with particular disordered bodies suffering from localized sensations and pains, some of them stubbornly objectlike in their refusal to change for the better. Even though the notion of structure and its allied reliance on the lesion to explain disorder does not help much in a Chinese medical world,[18] we nevertheless need to ask: How is the spatiality of the body understandable to a medicine that presumes the *shengsheng huahua* of ceaseless change and the founding dynamism of *qi*?

The classic texts had a clear understanding of the spatiality of the body.[19] Zhang provides an oft-cited quotation from the clinical classic, part 1 of the *Inner Canon*, the *Plain Questions*:

> "If in and out motion ceases, then the activity of *shen*-vitality is extinguished; if rising and sinking motion ceases, then the basis in *qi* becomes dangerously isolated. So if there is no in and out, there is no site [*ji* 己] for growth and the life course; if there is no rising or sinking, there can be no storage of the results of genesis and growth. Thus, there is no organic thing [*qi* 器] that does not rely on rising/sinking and in/out *qi*-transformation processes. Thus, the discrete body [*qi* 器] is the world of the growth process, if this body disperses, *yin* and *yang* become separated, and the transformations of life cease."[20] Clearly, the life of man begins with *qi* transformation, and if *qi* transformation ceases, then life is over.

Above, we noted that the teeming generativity of things in cosmogonic writings could seem a vertiginous vision of unconstrained shape shifting. The certainties of static materiality appear to be remote from this vision of ceaseless change. Unlike a philosophy that presumes things and that puzzles over change or a Newtonian mechanics that separates objects from processes, the medical insight quoted here derives spatial form from temporal process. In the medical canon Zhang cites, the *Plain Questions*, the general process of *qi* transformation is shown to be a source of material shape; sites and things come into being as a result of up-down and in-out motion. Our translation of *ji* as "site" could be contested, but there's no mistaking the intention of the character *qi* (器, not the same word as the *qi* 气 of breath): The thing or body is the "world" of the growth process, the "stuff in which things happen."[21] And the thing is bodied out in space. As Zhang points out elsewhere in the essay, "*Qi* is not a body, but it is the basis of bodies." At the same time, this dense formula insists that spatial form is a necessary condition for the healthy continuation of *qi* transformation. "If this world disperses...the transformations of life cease." The concept of structure—the abstraction borrowed by Levi-Strauss from geology to inspire a mid-twentieth-century anthropological structuralism—remains remote from this notion of a constantly renewed body of spatial relations. But related words such as "pattern" or "configuration" can refer to a structured spatializing process. *Qi* transformation produces a pattern of upward growth and downward elimination, the filling out of the fragile child's frame, the internalization of food as sustenance, the outward breathing of perspiration. The kidneys are a particular configuration of transformations of *qi*, and their usefulness is reliant on being low in the body, adjacent to the *yin* water of the bladder, the *yin* interiorities of the womb. The lungs, if they are to be the bellows that distribute "energetic breath" up and down in the body, must be higher, but their proximity to the body's main points of entry makes them spatially vulnerable to pathologies from without. The body is a congellation of mundane events that are taking place (or making place) all the time. Dynamic process yields not quite static bodies (*qi* 器), and the things that result from the *qihua* process in turn provide the materiality without which the generative *shengsheng huahua* process would have no basis, no site, no resources.

This relationship between process and product is a kind of *yin-yang* relationship. It is no wonder that classic cosmogony insisted that "one [first] gives rise to two." Oscillation between the two poles of *yang* (everything active, initiating, warming, rapid, and dispersing) and *yin* (everything passive, resultant, cooling, slow, and consolidating) can readily be seen to yield many contingent modes of combination; truly, the "two" of *yin* and *yang* can combine and interact endlessly to generate the myriad things of the world. In Zhang's essay, there is little need either to define the forms of action that are *yin* and *yang* or to justify *yinyang* as a mode of understanding natural (including human) processes. But he does emphasize the relativity of these qualitative poles, especially in his philological discussion of "the *qi-yinyang*–five-phases model": The original idea of *"yin* and *yang"* was the places shaded from the sun's rays and the places upon which the sun shines, respectively.

Thus, these are not really fixed "places," because through the day, the light and shade shift locations. Warming and cooling capacities also move through space and time, following the shifts understandable as a *yinyang* oscillation or cyclicity driven by "heaven." So, even though "later [*yin* and *yang*] came to refer to two mutually contrasting entities, such as the sun and moon, heaven and earth, water and fire, blood and *qi*, *hun*-soul and *po*-soul,[22] male and female, and so on," the two terms were always defined or invoked in relation to each other. Roger Ames, in his efforts to clarify the dynamism of classical Chinese relativism, has distinguished between the dualistic oppositions he associates with a naturalistic Aristotelian cosmology and the polar (*yin* and *yang*) qualities presumed by the logic and language of the Chinese "immanental cosmos." As he argues, a polarity emphasizes the interdependence of terms and cannot allow one term to occlude the other fully; it does not encourage thinking in essences or even strong contrasts.[23]

Zhang continues:

By the time of the Western Zhou (the eleventh to the seventh centuries B.C.E.), *yinyang* had come to mean two formless kinds of "*qi*." Even at the outset, then, *yin* and *yang* had a philosophical meaning, abstract and formless....

Yinyang, from its pure meaning of lighted and shaded objects, came to refer to two kinds of polar, contrasting functional attributes: whatever has the function of propelling, warming, stimulating, dispersing, rising/lifting—this falls into the *yang* category; whatever has the function of slowing and stopping, cooling, restraining, contracting, falling/lowering falls into the *yin* category.

This sounds exactly like Porkert's radically functional account of the theoretical foundations of Chinese medicine.[24] Both authors in their most general remarks about *yin* and *yang* rely on verbal forms that bring us closer to a language of experience: "warming," "contracting," "stimulating"—these are descriptions of everyday bodily life. But they are also medical descriptions, technical notions that insist on—as Zhang continues—the relational and systematic character of dynamic bodies and things:

What "*qi-yinyang*–five phases" represents is a relational reality, belonging to correlative thought.[25] Its special feature is to emphasize the interrelation between one thing [*shiwu* 事物] and another, between one part and another part internal to something; this goes beyond an emphasis on the forms and internal structures of things.[26] For example, *qi* always manifests as the medium through which the myriad things are connected and through which every part of a material body [*wuti* 物体] is interconnected. Between one body and another, and in the inside of each body, everything is charged with *qi*. With the function of *qi*, the myriad things resonate with each other; they melt into each other, thus becoming a unified great whole; and it is thus that each thing can become an internally interrelated whole.

Yinyang is also a kind of relationship, the relations of *yinyang* are: interrootedness, interresponsiveness, mutual waxing and waning, mutual exchanging/responding, mutual constraining, struggle with each other, intertransformability, alternating victory and defeat, and more.

This last characterization of *yinyang* dynamics, emphasizing the contingency of every *yin* or *yang* state on its *yang* or *yin* other, is a rather standard formulation resulting from the intensive philosophical work devoted to Chinese medicine as it was systematized and institutionalized in the twentieth century. The *yinyang* relativism explained here is more than a little indebted to Mao's rendition of dialectics in his philosophical essays "On Practice" and "On Contradiction" and to a particularly twentieth-century Chinese reading of Engels's *Natural Dialectics*. But modern Chinese medical *yinyang* logics are also undeniably indebted to the ancient sources to which textbooks constantly refer.

Also evident in Zhang's discussion of *yin* and *yang*, or the "*qi-yinyang*-five–phases" system, is the "holism" of the Chinese medical body. Every modern introduction to Chinese medicine, both in Chinese and in translation, emphasizes this point. Many treatments of this issue, however, can make the "whole" of the human body seem rather mystical, a matter of faith or—at best—a heuristic allowing counterintuitive clinical strategies. (Treating shoulder pain, for example, by needling a remote site on the calf.) Zhang's discussion, however, roots the manifold relations of all parts of the body to each other in the universality of *qi*. If we accept *qi* as an obvious quotidian reality, it is no surprise that in a system of ceaseless change, as an ongoing process of *shengsheng huahua*, separate parts, relatively far from each other in space, would resonate with each other.[27]

After introducing cosmogony above, we addressed the problem posed by classical metaphysics: If all is change, if everything has its source in the *qi* of *shengsheng huahua*, where does stable form come from, and how can natural processes be predicted and controlled? This is a question of considerable pertinence both for medical action and for understanding and acting on ordinary embodied experience. *Yin* and *yang* show us that phenomena are subject to regular alternations, cycles, and constraints. By understanding how warming tendencies check cold pathologies, how intrinsic to every (*yin*) state is the (*yang*) seed of its eventual transformation, how stable states congeal within mobile activity, and how latent within every thing there is a process of change, we can act wisely in a more or less known world. With medicine (not to mention music, calligraphy, and everyday tactics), we can act to prolong and improve *human* life, to accept and shape the particular form of cutting or fating belonging to our own *shengming*, which is local both in space and time.

Configuring Life

Zhang's essay "Life" adopts other metaphorical language that clarifies the spatiotemporality of *qi* transformation, drawing it from the *Zhuangzi*, the "skeptic" Wang Chong, and, again, from the medical canon:

> In the *Zhuangzi* ("Knowledge Wandered North"), it says: "Human life is a gathering of *qi*; when it gathers, this is life; when it scatters, this is death.... Thus it is said that one *qi* permeates all under heaven." The Eastern Han (25–220 C.E.) philosopher Wang Chong also said, "Heaven and earth mingle *qi* and the myriad things are born from that union" ("Discourses Weighed in the Balance," *Lunheng bianchong* 论衡·辩祟).[28]...
>
> "Heaven is the virtue/power (*de* 德) in me, *qi* is the earth in me, virtue/power flows, and *qi* spreads, and this is life." (*Divine Pivot* [*juan* 2:8]) So, heaven's contribution to human life is "virtue," that is, organic articulation [生机], regularity, and rule [规律]; the contribution of earth to human life is *qi*, and it forms the body's materiality and capacities. The *qi* of heaven and earth makes human life through the "virtue flows, *qi* spreads" style of activity.

The general relationship between the dynamic sources, causes, or raw materials of life and those agencies that accord form and shape to human life is explored over and over in the essay. The point is constantly made that the ongoing configuration of human life—a limiting or fating, rather than a creation ex nihilo—is only a contingent specification of the wider natural process in which "heaven and earth mingle their *qi*, limit its span, and call it man." The texts, in fact, could hardly support any other view.

But in this part of the essay, Zhang finds three rather different philosophical sources for the way in which general natural process becomes human life: the Daoist founder figure Zhuangzi relies on the metaphor of gathering the *qi* that naturally tends to scatter; the Confucian Wang Chong skips directly from the "two" stage of cosmogony (*yinyang* or earth/heaven interaction) to the ten thousand things without concerning himself with a more fine-grained configuring mechanism; and the medical canon introduces *de*, or virtue/power, as the most general delimiting agent.

Considering the last version first, we note that *de* has not remained an important technical term in Chinese medicine. Perhaps the word carries too strong a charge of moralism for moderns, in that its primary modern sense is "morality" or "goodness." A scientizing twentieth-century Chinese medicine does not welcome the (nowadays unavoidable) ambiguity between heaven as a cosmogonic agent (its virtues and powers, or its capacities, reaching far beyond the petty concerns of human society) and a missionary-inflected heaven as a source of moral standards. But as Zhang shows, the meaning of the term in medicine two millennia ago is clear from the context: *de* constrains the general spread of *qi* into a "flow," a particular path or streambed along which the natural forcefulness and mobility of *qi* is directed.

This is not so different from Zhuangzi's view, to which it is juxtaposed. But, as François Jullien has shown particularly forcefully,[29] Zhuangzi is especially brilliant in his ability to speak all at once of the cosmic and the practical, to relate the broadest universal truths to the most mundane personal concerns. His language here of gathering and scattering could not be more down to earth; our hands and feet, backs and bellies, understand these words even better than our visualizing or conceptualizing minds do. *Yangsheng* practitioners in Beijing could easily speak of their daily lives as a process of gathering or making provision against the scattering of things and energies. "Human life is a gathering of *qi*; when it gathers, this is life, when it scatters this is death." Our human efforts to put together a meaningful, wholesome, admirable life are well figured as putting together diverse resources, weaving the natural and cultural materials that come to hand, but that nevertheless constantly escape full management, into a crafted daily life. The dynamism of *qi* helps us understand both the coherence and the contingency, the gatheredness, of our own particular fabric of time and space.

Elsewhere in the essay, there is another redolent phrasing linking cosmogonic *qi* processes to concrete material existence. This is a language of "flowering and fruiting" (*huashi* 华实):

> Chinese medicine also holds that "when the *qi* of heaven and earth is exchanged, the myriad things will flower [*hua*] and fruit [*shi*]." This is to say, without the congress/exchange of the *yang* of the sun and the *yin* of the earth, no life phenomena would be possible. Hence, one of the ruling concepts of the *Inner Canon* is "virtue is the heaven in me, *qi* is the earth in me; virtue flows and *qi* spreads to make life." Here, "virtue flows and *qi* spreads" amounts to the exchange of the *qi* of heaven and earth. Only in this way can things have the ability to be born and transform. The surface of the earth on which we live more or less moderately and evenly receives the sun's influence [太阳能], making a kind of "*yinyang* interweave" or "heaven-earth *qi* exchange" situation, such that under suitable conditions of light, heat, water vapor, atmosphere, and so on, life can change and emerge.

Hua is a word that draws on the fundamental metaphor of the blossoming plant to denote a flourishing or a splendid manifestation; *shi* means "to fruit," certainly, but by extension in modern Chinese, it more often refers to solidity and reality. Both of these widely used words trail their botanic connotations with them in a manner that often goes unremarked, but is nevertheless significant. Any paradox we may feel between the vast generality of a *qi*-driven cosmogony and the particularity and concreteness of the ten thousand things is dissolved in the imagery of flowering and fruiting. The metaphor can be extended. What is the meaning of life for a plant? Does a plant exist to fruit (such that a blossom is a means to that end)? Or does it exist to produce a seed that in turn exists to find conditions in which it can sprout? If the aims of a plant's life are undecidable, what could "death" mean for a plant? Is plant life so different from human life?[30]

Banishing Death

We have seen that Zhuangzi, whose relativism on the subject is legendary, has a powerful formula for understanding the (small) difference between life and death: when *qi* gathers, this is life; when it scatters, this is death. Medicine, addressing as it does the already gathered (but always still-gathering) life of human sufferers, also roots life and death in the mobility of *qi*, but it adopts an evaluative bias toward fostering life:

> *qi* must charge the entire organism and unceasingly flow. It is just as it says in the *Inner Canon*, "*qi* cannot but move; it flows like water; it moves like the endless cycles of sun and moon." The *Introduction to Medicine* [*Yixue rumen, baoyang shuo* 医学入门·保养说] says: "If original *qi* flows, then there is long life; if original *qi* stagnates, there is premature death." This indicates that *qi* is ceaselessly moving in the human body, thereby maintaining the life activities of the human body and advancing health and long life. If *qi* becomes sluggish or stagnant, then there will be many illnesses and untimely death.

Superficially, this text adopts a view of life that somewhat contradicts Zhuangzi's image. Presumably, the gathered body (the living) would be a less mobile or more stagnant situation than the scattering of *qi* that is death. Could a normal form of embodied and fated life be seen as a kind of pathology, then? A stagnation in the Dao? Some Daoists argued as much. But these two imageries can converge on a single understanding of nature and the living body: Bodies, discrete lives, come into being as a result of an ongoing process of gathering. What is gathered is nothing but *qi*, of course. *Qi* transformation, gathered, takes particular forms inflected in a *yinyang* manner: four seasons, eight trigrams, and so on. But the *health* of the configuration depends still on the vigor of *qi* transformation. The task of the medical practitioner is to enable, configure, and re-form that bodily flow. Stagnation could result only from a breakdown in the connection of the body to its dynamic cosmic and natural sources.

We are accustomed to thinking of medicine as concerning itself with life and death, "saving" the former from the latter. Chinese medicine shares biomedicine's bias toward the value of human life, but it adopts, usually inarticulately, a different understanding of death. Zhang Qicheng elaborates this issue first as etymology:

> "Death" [死] is rendered in [archaic] *xiaozhuan* script as 𣨶. On the right is 人 (*ren*, human) and on the left is (*can*), which means "bone fragments." When they are put together, they denote a person with only pieces left, the *hun*-soul and the *po*-soul having departed, such that there is no more spirit—the basic meaning is the cessation of life. The *Liezi* (*Tianrui*) (列子‧天瑞) says: "Death is the end of man." So this is the general term for human death. The *Shuowen jiezi* dictionary defines death as "people's last concern" [*min zhi zu shi ye* 民之卒事也]. The *Book of Rites* (*Quli* 曲礼) also explains: "the common people call it death." Later the meaning of the word "death" basically became set as the end of life [*shengming* 生命].

All this language suggests that death is a situation and a concept of particular interest to human beings. Even Zhang's choice of *shengming* ("life" plus "fate") as his term for "life" in this passage about death connotes the fated lives of humans; plants in their cyclicity do not have an individual *shengming*. Moreover, death is here defined as a mere cessation, or perhaps a final deterritorialization, an end to the delimited (*ming* 命) space and time of a life.[31] Death is perhaps a narrowly self-interested human name for a particular moment in *qi* transformation.

In keeping with his interest as a historian of medicine and the *Book of Changes*, Zhang follows this etymology with a discussion of the epistemological foundations of "knowledge about death." To this end, he quotes from the Confucian heritage, revealing its skepticism about the reach of human scientific knowledge and its "sanguine" and "realist" attitudes toward the inevitability and naturalness of death. But at the end of the essay, he returns to a particularly Daoist way of addressing the meaning of life. This discussion might impress modern readers as particularly philosophical, in that it takes up the question of death in relation to life (a dyad that is notably absent in most of this long essay, though it dominates twentieth-century Euro-American approaches to the meaning of life.)[32] "The Daoist view of life and death is built on a certain understanding of the phenomena of life and death. 'Life' emerges from the Dao and from *qi*. 'Death' returns to the Dao and returns to *qi*. So life, death, and the myriad manifestations [*wanxiang* 万象] of the cosmos are only phenomena [*xianxiang* 现象], all the same in their nature (本质)."

Note that this ontological vision founded on the dynamism and universality of *qi* offers little purchase for distinctions between the living and the inorganic, much less does it encourage deep distinctions between humans and animals or plants. But the Daoists did feel the need to comment on whether there are ontological differences between life and death, the living and the dead. Zhang Qicheng's passage continues:

> If you know the Dao you will embody this understanding and reach a plane of "unity with the Dao," and you can then return to the originary genuine state of life, and you can completely achieve transcendence. With respect to Laozi's understanding of the value of life, he revered and obeyed the spontaneous (*ziran*, what was so of itself), emphasized returning to originary genuine life, opposed living too thickly [生生之厚], holding that "overflowing life is called 'auspicious' [by the conventional] (but it is a great misfortune)," that is, using artificial means to promote one's own growth is a kind of disaster. Zhuangzi holds that "the life of man is a gathering of *qi*; gathered, it can live; scattered, it will die." (*Zhuangzi* [*juan* 22]). Human life and death is the gathering and scattering of *qi*; life is just a temporary existence, so it can't be taken too seriously. "Life is borrowed; when you borrow it you can live [*shengsheng* 生生], but this is dust." (*Zhuangzi* [*juan* 18]). "Life follows on death; death is the beginning of life...since life and death follow each other, what is there to worry about?" (*Zhuangzi* [*juan* 22]) Life is linked to death, death is linked to life; whether any given state is life or death isn't the point. Zhuangzi emphasized "life and death are one," "life and death are the same state," human life and death are about

the same thing, even to the point that he felt that death is a kind of good fortune.

Much could be said both about the Daoist writings cited here and about Zhang Qicheng's purposes in presenting them as he has. But what is interesting for the purposes of this chapter is the fact that in these Daoist sources, an invocation of death does not in itself give contrastive meaning to life. These relativist insights may seem very modern, but this is not the modernity of existentialism or European phenomenology. The logic of "you only live once," existentialist reflections that ask "Why not suicide now?"—these seem foreign to Zhang's appropriations of Laozi and Zhuangzi. Even the theological relativism of "dust to dust" is absent here, despite Zhuangzi's use of the metaphor of dust. He does not refer to the shaping hand of a God who first makes us from dust and then allows our bodies to decompose back into dust. The dust in question for Zhuangzi blows in the winds of *qi* transformation. Perhaps the life he imagined is a cyclonic eddy in the great dusty wind of the Dao, catching up jetsam—broken twigs, dry leaves, insect carcasses, bits of old letters—and spinning it about in a briefly localized body. "Life is just a temporary existence," after all.

These Daoists do not demand that life be either meaningful or meaningless. Rather, these texts—like the many other classic works that Zhang cites in his essay—with an extraordinary economy succeed in placing human life in the stream of natural (or *zirande* 自然的, self-so) process. This natural process, at least for medicine, is *qi* transformation.

We could turn these comments into a classic existential question: Since we have no choice but to exist only as a small part of the great Dao, then why struggle over anything? Why not just go with the flow? However attractive this possibility has been to twentieth-century New Age thinking, we don't think an ideal of foregoing all action ever appealed much to Chinese thinkers themselves. Utter passivity was not, we think, even imagined, even in the classic philosophy of *wuwei* (无为), that antique and untranslatable term that seems to advocate "nonaction." *Wuwei*, rather, is a radical argument against strongly interventionist forms of rulership.[33] But insofar as it presumes involvement in an active and manifold Dao, it cannot suggest stagnation, stoppage, or inactivity. And one key to understanding why is visible in Zhuangzi's remark "the life of man is a gathering of *qi*; gathered, it can live; dispersed, it will die." As we have argued, the image is both palpable and metaphorically powerful; it is a statement of natural fact and a philosophical principle. The natural tendency of *qi* is to scatter, to expand like wind into all available space, but in fact, *qi* gathers into form in at least ten thousand ways (the myriad things, *wanwu*). An understanding of gathered form can usefully distinguish humans from rocks, deliberate actors from swarming bacteria. Certainly, it distinguishes the living from the dead, but it does so without recourse to some "spark" of life present in the first state and absent in the second.[34] In fact, in a universe composed of *qi*, it is impossible to think lifelessness. Life and living (*shengsheng*) precede and underlie the emergence of the myriad things; death names only a return to the scattering that underlies this ceaseless gathering.

Whose hand is doing the gathering, though? There is no convenient creator deity to pitch in and resolve this question—at least, not in Zhang's essay. Not even the inexpressible Dao can help us; Dao seems in these comments to be just as likely to disperse form as to mold it. If life is gathered form, then human life is form gathered by humans (under conditions, of course, that are not of our making, just to insert a reminder from quite another tradition). The intention of this action is presumably pro-life. Certainly, for contemporary purposes, in a society in which the mention of death is not polite, and even the number four, *si* 四, a homonym for death *si* 死, is somewhat tabooed, the gathering required for sustaining a truly human life would seem to be highly valued. Whether this gathered life is literally meaningful is by now not clear. We can in any case insist that the old Orientalist denunciation, "life has no value in the Orient," is downright silly. Clearly, life has too much value in the immensely diverse Chinese archive; there is no life-affirming pole star in the philosophical firmament by which everyone should navigate. But there are many reasons to live well.

So What Is the Meaning of Life?

The problem with the question "What is the meaning of life" is with the question itself. The singularity of the copula "is" and the definite article "the" misleads in the direction of too much ambition. The question makes us suspect that there is something profound "out there" to be discovered. In this chapter, we have pursued meaning in several senses, exploring the metaphorical powers of words and locating embodied and cosmic phenomena within the broad process of reality's coming into being. These have not been separate projects; the world we live in, the world that matters to us, is a nature-culture (to adopt a language from science studies).[35] As the classic cosmogonies and Chinese medicine insist, moreover, the world is irreducibly manifold. Originary *qi* is a kind of theoretical object, but it expresses only as particular forms, and these forms are always undergoing transformation. *Qi* transformation and spontaneous "life upon life, transformation upon transformation" (*shengsheng huahua*) can be neither stopped nor banished in disbelief. The manifest world these processes bestow on us, our everyday life, is named in the classic sources as the ten thousand things. The phrase in cosmogonic context can be turned around: materiality or being emerges only in vast and diverse numbers.

If the insights of classical Chinese cosmogony at its most speculative are appreciated, and if traditional Chinese medicine both in theory and in practice is carefully read, existential and semantic questions about "meaning" become local, momentary, empirical. They become questions about the character, position, and form of some of the myriad things. Even philosophers reading this material find themselves inquiring not into ultimate truths, but into particular items of deep personal concern: the metaphysics of the Way turns attention to those sectors, regions, or collectivities of the myriad things that make up our actual lives. The point of view from which ultimate or ideal meanings could be determined does not really exist; every position from which evaluation could be made is situated among all manner of other things in an immanental cosmos. From any actual point of view, only some things—a lot, but not all—can be evaluated. But we need not imagine locality as an unchanging constraint on perception. Just as the myriad things proceed from an original oneness (itself perhaps preceded by a void) with an irreducible multiplicity and in an inevitably material form, each human life, every *shengming* carved out from the flow, in time can have many meanings perceived from many points of view.

Above, we have reproduced as a sidebar a discussion of natural generativity, *qi* transformation, and Chinese medicine's theoretical foundations by Huang Jitang, a philosopher who taught for years at the Guangzhou University of Chinese Medical Sciences. His sole source in that discussion is the *Plain Questions*, one of the two books of the *Yellow Emperor's Inner Canon*, a source in which there is no shortage of generalizing metaphysical abstraction. But there are other early sources that incorporate an equally powerful understanding of generativity and transformation, the *shengsheng huahua* that has been a continuing theme of this chapter. Turning at last to the manifold specificity of all life forms, then, we think of Zhuangzi, the founding figure of Chinese Daoism, whose "inner and outer chapters" show him as master of the paradoxical story and poet of concrete details:

> The sorts of the myriad things come from the work of the most minute. In the water, the seeds become break vine, but on the shore, they become frog's robe. If they grow on the hillside, they become hill slippers; if hill slippers find good soil, they become crowsfoot. The roots of crowsfoot turn into maggots, and their leaves turn into butterflies. Soon, the butterflies transform and turn into those insects that hatch under the stove: they look like snakes, taking the form of nymphs in molt, and they are called *quduo*. After a thousand days, *quduo* become birds, and are known as dry left-over bones birds. The spit of left-over bones birds becomes *simi* bugs; *simi* are the bugs that eat wine dregs. *Yilu* bugs are born from those wine eaters, *huangkuang* bugs are born

from *jiuyou* bugs, and *maorui* bugs are born from rot grubs. Sheep's groom grass couples with the old bamboo that for a long time has put out no fresh shoots, and this coupling gives birth to green serenity bugs. Serenity bugs give birth to leopards; leopards give birth to horses; horses give birth to humans; humans return to the unfathomable works. The ten thousand things all come out of the works, and all return to the works.[36]

Conclusion

Reproduced below is a conversation—shared over dinner in 2008, in Beijing—about cultural nationalism and the politics of nurturing life in contemporary China.[1] In this exchange, we talk about recent "National Studies" (*guoxue* 国学) valorizations of the Chinese heritage, emphasizing the ways this popular-intellectual movement might be related to *yangsheng* practices. This is not a forced convergence. Some of the materials and interpretations we have included in this book could be seen as contributions to National Studies, though there are many aspects of the movement that neither of us would claim as our own. Just as we cannot applaud every nationalist gesture in National Studies, we also do not agree with each other about every aspect of *yangsheng*, nor do we see contemporary urban culture in Beijing in identical ways. As we did in Chapter 3, then, we have chosen to keep our voices distinct in this last chapter.

Here we offer an account of that conversation as a conclusion to *Ten Thousand Things*. This exchange makes a last effort—last in the book, not last in our conversations with each other—to relate the *yangsheng* world to Chinese history, as well as to the contemporary moment, to classical and popular thought, as well as to our own and our readers' embodied experience.

Especially, we hope that throughout this study, the diversity, historicity, and multiplicity of *yangsheng* embodiment has been visible. Rejecting the universality and singularity of the biological entity referred to as "the body," we have focused on modes of embodiment that are dispersed through everyday practice, material without being merely biological and alive with historically specific habits. Speaking in Chinese, we came to refer to this body as a *zonghe ti* (综合体), a composite or synthesized corpus. This body we link—both in the conversation below and throughout *Ten Thousand Things*—to a rich heritage and a complex contemporary situation; it is, thus, a gathering of forces and forms. We have gathered, translated, and discussed diverse discourses of *yangsheng*—philosophical, medical, public health, popular media, and conversational—that together provide insight on the life of contemporary Beijing bodies. Our method has sought a reflective appreciation of at least ten thousand things about bodies, communities, and forms of life, insisting that the fundamental multiplicity of life cannot be reduced to abstract essences such as "the body," "experience," or an essentialized "Chinese culture."

Some of this critical stance is evident in the dialogue below. Engaging National Studies without fully realizing it, we have also explored the complex living relationships between "tradition," the history of Chinese thought and language, and contemporary everyday lives. In our gathering of materials and commentaries on several Chinese literatures, we showed that modern Chinese common sense is articulate in deeply cultural or traditional ways. We listened for echoes of classical metaphysics in the ordinary talk of *yangsheng* practitioners (Chapter 3). In two chapters of the book (2 and 4), we presented extensive extracts from metaphysical and medical writing—some of it very ancient—showing how classical writing is deployed to modern ends in "traditional" Chinese medicine and the popular public-health literature.

In carving out aspects of *yangsheng* practice, city life, popular culture, everyday habitus, and classical philosophy to present in this book, we have had to find a path through an ever-transforming multitude of things. Much consequently has been neglected. We have allowed our own tastes and fascinations to guide the study, but because there are (at least) two of us, we have here carved out a more capacious way than either of us could have done alone. Finding a way among our commonalities and differences has been a rewarding conversation for us, so it seems appropriate to conclude the book with a dialogue, rather than a summary, a translation, rather than a paraphrase. We have not kept two voices active because we are antagonistic; on the contrary, it has been a continuing pleasure to explore the many ways in which our philosophical and anthropological thinking can make for a more complex harmony in scholarship on China, on the contemporary and its rich past, and on embodied experience. "Harmony" itself is a theme that comes up below; we hope this rather bland noun in English can be heard as a verb when translated from the Chinese; the nominal form loses most of the term's significance in the Chinese context. The authorities we quote, from the last few years or earlier millennia; the interviewees we found so willing to talk with us in West City District streets and parks; the philosophers and other scholars whose insights have inspired us; our own experiences and speculations—all these can be thought of as separate lines of emergence that have become thoroughly tangled, and perhaps harmonized, in this book. The last thing we want to produce, in the end, is a monotone.

We hope that the engagement with life, everyday practice, and the contemporary moment, which has from the beginning kept our project exciting for us, is visible in this dialogue. This is an edited version of a real conversation. We wandered. We indulged personal interests that are more compulsive for us than for our readers. For a time, we forgot concerns about writing *yangsheng* theory and practice and just enjoyed talking about whatever came to mind. But in parallel with the viewpoints explored in the four chapters of this book, we think this conversation touches on some important approaches to anthropology, history, and the meanings of culture and life in today's world.

Heritage, Culture, Utopias, Life: A Mealtime Conversation

JF Can you tell me more about the "National Studies" movement that seems to be so popular right now in Beijing and China? In your writings, you claim an affinity for or participation in this scholarly arena. But I have noticed this movement at the popular level only in the last year or so. National Studies as I read it seems to involve a return to canonical Chinese philosophical and literary works, an advocacy of certain principles of "Chineseness," and a scholarly close reading of some great writing in Chinese. It looks like a return to a sort of philology.[2] How old is this orientation on the Chinese heritage? Where did it come from?

ZQC The "National Studies fever" is comparatively new. It began to appear as a rubric for popular scholarship and publishing in about 2004. The main actors at first, when the term "National Studies" was coined in the early 1990s, were some scholars at Peking University and Tsinghua University,[3] but lately this "fever" is notable for being a movement in society, rather than just in the academy. Yes, it is scholarly and philological, but it urges careful reading on the part of ordinary people, too.

JF Are these "national" or "heritage" studies really so new? I mean, if they were begun by senior scholars at the major universities—who presumably had long been doing research in Chinese sources—what made the "National Studies fever" seem so attractive and innovative, even urgent, beyond the academy?

ZQC Well, of course, the scholarship that was deployed for popular consumption in society under the rubric of National Studies preexisted the popular enthusiasm, but it is all now being remarketed as National Studies. I think the reasons for its popularity run deeper, though. The National Studies fever is very much an expression of the longer-standing nationalist revival [*minzu zhuyi fuxing* 民族主义复兴] throughout China.

JF When do you think the revival of Chinese nationalism really got going, then? It is presently so very obvious in Chinese national public culture, and most particularly it impresses me as a *cultural* nationalism.

ZQC Oh, around the mid-1990s, don't you think?

JF Perhaps it was tied to the Olympic bid that began in the mid-1990s and the later preparation (after 2001) for the 2008 Olympics?

ZQC Undoubtedly. But I think the nationalist revival is also an expression of a deeper malaise: Chinese people are undergoing a crisis of belief—they have nothing to believe in anymore, so they are seeking to rediscover the classical creeds of Chinese culture—Confucian, Buddhist, and Daoist teachings especially—and also turning to other forms of religion.

JF Yes, one could mention Christianity in China and certain cult phenomena, as well.

ZQC Indeed, and I think the growing *yangsheng* fever and a very recent appearance of an enthusiasm or "fever" for Chinese medicine are responses to this crisis of belief, as well.

JF But you know, in American anthropology, we have a lot of suspicion about forms of essentialism and reification that can arise in cultural nationalist movements. Is "Chinese culture" in danger of being oversimplified, reduced to a few abstract essences and presented as a kind of fixed object or oversystematized unity?

ZQC I know what you mean, but I don't think this is as big a problem as you anthropologists make out. Contrast what we do in National Studies with Samuel P. Huntington's approach to "cultures" and their "clashes" in contemporary international relations.[4] Huntington can get away with this vulgar and dangerous approach to civilizations and heritages precisely because he relies on a simplistic black-white dualism that is rather characteristic of Western thought. (Here Zhang Qicheng draws a circle and bisects it vertically, shading one half black and leaving the other white.) The operative word for this kind of dualistic model is "antagonism" [*dou* 斗]. In Chinese thought, on the other hand, our model is the *taijitu* [太极图], the *yin-yang* diagram (which he also draws on Judith Farquhar's index card) in which the two dark and light aspects are joined by a curved line and each has a kernel of the other at its heart. The most summary term for this relationship is "harmony" [*he* 和]. This is a model of thought shared by all the great Chinese traditions, and it makes it difficult to turn culture into a simple fixed object.

JF Well, I am doubtful about the usefulness of any one word or principle to explain or characterize the intellectual habits of whole civilizations over thousands of years. In English, "harmony" sounds like an imposition from above, a kind of arbitrary peace agreement that covers over a great many important differences and reduces the ten thousand things to one. Moreover, the *taijitu* diagram, which is meant to express the inherent dynamism and only ideal symmetry of *yin* and *yang* forces, is too easy to read as some kind of "natural" harmony, not as the ongoing balancing act it tends to be. Of course, I realize that this static image is not how you understand the Chinese term *he*, which classically refers at the very least to the ongoing work of harmonizing distinct strains of activity. Our friend Eric Karchmer worries about the tendency in both languages to overidealize the history of Chinese medicine, calling it "Orientalist," as you know.[5]

But I'm nevertheless interested in your criticism of "Western" dualism. The science-studies scholar Bruno Latour has made a similar argument about modernity, arguing that a dualistic "modern constitution" that distinguishes nature from culture, objects from subjects, and (arguably) "tradition" from "modernity" has formed the modern understanding of history and culture, but has never been a very useful way of actually accounting for the realities of "social-natural" life. So he says "we have never been modern."[6] The simple dualisms of the modern constitution have not explained anything, and what we need is closer attention to the nondualistic mixtures of social-natural and traditional-modern phenomena in worlds of practice.

ZQC Sounds similar to my point about the *yinyang taijitu*; and isn't that what we've been doing in our study, paying close attention to worlds of practice in an effort to see how they embody something like a culture that cannot be separated from the natural? For me—and for our *yangsheng* friends—culture is a refinement from natural resources, not a separate essence.

JF Absolutely. But I'm still curious about National Studies, especially because this scholarly and popular movement actually doesn't seem to concern itself with what contemporary people think or do, and it certainly seems to have no interest in recent Chinese thought, such as the philosophies of revolution or liberalism. Instead, National Studies scholars propose close attention to relatively few canonical works. Why is this movement important? Why should we still study these (mostly) ancient texts?

ZQC This is an important question for contemporaries. It's true that the majority of National Studies writers concentrate on works written during the Warring States Period (475–221 B.C.E.) and the Han Dynasty (206 B.C.E.–220 C.E.). This was a time when there were few outside cultural influences. In the classical period, culture was in a strong sense a local development, so when nationalist scholars search for something that can be claimed by Chinese people as their own heritage, this founding period of our civilization is the best place for them to look.[7] But in my personal view, the greatest value of this research is that it demonstrates, first, that culture has not gotten progressively better or higher through history, and second, that people have not gotten progressively smarter or wiser through history. When we seriously reengage the great ancient works of our civilization, or any civilization, the very existence of cultural progress must be reconsidered.

JF When you talk of seriously reengaging ancient culture, I'm reminded of how my conference papers on *yangsheng* have been received by my anthropologist colleagues in the United States over the last few years. Almost every time I talk, I expect and hope for some engagement with my anthropological theory or method, but what I get instead is tremendous curiosity about how we ourselves should nurture our own lives! As if I knew! This experience might be a testament to the great charm of *yangsheng* philosophy, but it also confirms the historiographic choice we made together a long time ago. Do you remember me mentioning *The Writing of History* by Michel de Certeau? His argument is that conventional modern histories make an other of the past, treating the historical archive and its social contexts as objects of remote contemplation and targets of analysis. I wanted instead to capture the historical as if it were a living organ of modern bodies, incorporated as both limit and resource.

ZQC Yes, and I have always been following the lead of my teachers, Fung Yu-lan and Zhu Bogun, in this highly consequential effort to make past thought live in our present. I fear that this refusal to other the past on the part of Chinese historians of thought has made it more difficult for our work to be taken seriously in the West. We have tended to write ethico-political histories because we know how consequential the writing of history is.

JF Well, in this sense, your thinking may be "postmodern"![8]

ZQC Perhaps it's also ancient. I remain committed to the idea that all the highly diverse traditions of Chinese culture (Daoist, Buddhist, Confucian, and so on) center on two characters, both very important in some of our earliest sources. These are *zhong* 中, centering, and *he* 和, harmony. Both of these concepts make sense only within a metaphysics of *yinyang* and the Dao, and I think this metaphysics is still taken for granted today in arenas such as Chinese medicine, popular practices of fate calculation,[9] life nurturing, and so forth. Centering and harmony are aspects of a Chinese culture that still lives, even though it has been much disrupted in the last century or two. But if ancient reflections on these themes were to really be engaged by moderns, perhaps we could better show each other how to nurture life.

JF In the end, I agree. But I'm interested in the way you used the word "culture" [*wenhua* 文化] just now. In its sense as a word for (Chinese) civilization, it refers to elements in the life of human collectives that are—as Matthew Arnold said when he tried to define "culture"—"the best which has been said and thought in the world."[10] In Arnold's sense, and the usual Chinese sense of *wenhua*, what counts as culture is a relatively small part of all the practices, discourses, values, and material arts of any society.[11] In anthropology, we tend to favor a different usage of the word "culture," first defined by Edward Tylor as a "complex whole" that includes knowledge, belief, art, morals, law, custom, and so forth—all that is social and cultivated, no matter how mundane.[12] In this usage, everything that is somehow specific in a locality would count: not just knowledge and morals, but customs and habits; everything from homemade cloth shoes and hand-knitted long underwear to spending a lifetime learning to be a better calligrapher; even buying a piano (say, in 1980) so your child can learn to play European classical music is a Chinese cultural phenomenon, by the anthropological definition.[13] You could say that the anthropological notion of culture takes "the ten thousand things" of a given form of life quite seriously. Clearly, National Studies scholars are using the first, "high-culture" definition to valorize Chinese civilization (and so are we, especially in Chapter 4!), while ethnographers use the second, "ten thousand things" definition because they care what "a people" (or the "common people," the *laobaixing* 老百姓 so often referred to in modern Chinese speech) do, and they want to perceive the forms of meaning and value that emerge in the collective practice of a group. So of course, in this project, we have long been using the second, Tylorean definition of culture, too.

ZQC I can see that there's a tension between these two senses of the term, but I wonder if they need to be seen as contradictory; perhaps not, when you are doing research on everyday life practices. The two definitions are at least linked by an emphasis on the forms [*xingshi* 形式] discernible in both literature and the arts and in practical activity. Anyway, National Studies scholars argue that at the heart of culture are values [*jiazhi guannian* 价值观念], modes of thought, and norms for behavior. Ultimately, what National Studies scholars do is achieve the goals of life nurturance through mental cultivation and by improving and advancing the ongoing changes in popular everyday life.

JF Why are so many educated Chinese people so devoted to the "high-culture" idea of *wenhua*? There are so many disciplines, especially in the humanities, both here in Beijing and in the United

States and Europe, that take it as their ultimate task to evaluate the goodness or badness (the highness or lowness) of cultural phenomena. So often there is the implicit question, "Is it truly 'art'?" "Is it truly 'literature'?" Why does it seem to be so necessary for cultural researchers to make such judgments?

ZQC Well, there is a lot at stake for Chinese scholars in cultural research; you know this from following philosophical debates in Chinese medicine. Even those of us who study the Chinese classics have to work in a world dominated by Western disciplines, Western models of explanation, Western market forces, Western science. If we didn't find some kind of universal value in our Chinese past and Chinese literature and arts, where would we be? People nowadays feel as if they are cast adrift, our heritage lost or in tatters; we have to try to make a contribution, but we mostly lack the resources and stature to join global culture as full equals.

JF So it sounds as if what's at stake in today's cultural nationalism is something that runs very deep and goes beyond disciplinary training or local definitions of culture, Chineseness, and so forth. If the global dominance of a Eurocentric account of culture and civilization is so inescapable—though both of us know that there's lots of variation among intellectuals on this score—it sounds as if some kind of cultural nationalism is almost not a matter of choice.

ZQC Well, as I said, we are in a crisis of belief, and perhaps most people see nowhere to turn. But National Studies might offer some real hope in this crisis. If a person really accepts the value of the culture explored in the National Studies scholarship—including the health-oriented culture—he would have to subscribe to what I have elsewhere called the "three impossibles" [*sange buhui* 三个不会]: it becomes impossible to be depressed [*buhui yumen* 不会郁闷], impossible to withdraw from the social [*buhui chidai* 不会痴呆], and impossible to kill yourself [*buhui zisha* 不会自杀]. Reading the great classics, one can't avoid the deep lesson of the *yinyang* dynamic of life and experience: the darkest days presage the rise of better times.

288

You have yourself noted the undeniable appeal of much classic philosophy to people who are trying to figure out how to live better. The great books always leave us room for optimism [*leguan* 乐观, "a happy outlook"]. This is one reason I continue to feel that the *yangsheng* phenomenon in all its multiplicity still boils down to finding pleasure in life.

But I don't actually want to sound so entirely optimistic about National Studies. The "fever" is unfortunately deeply rooted in our recent economic development. Everything now comes down to money; there seems to be no value beyond the economic in public discourse. Everybody puts a price tag on everything, and the "successism" [*chenggongxue* 成功学] of economic competition is very disturbing. The fact that National Studies is first and foremost a bonanza for the publishing business is a symptom of this, as are the many elite profit-making schools of National Studies where CEOs go for very high-priced workshops on Chinese heritage.

The fundamental spiritual crisis [*jingshen weiji* 精神危机] that even rich people feel is acutely experienced. It's not just intellectuals or retired people practicing *yangsheng* in the parks who are seeking solutions by turning to Chinese heritage. Successism and the one-note emphasis on money have had the result that people have been made into wild beasts [*ren biancheng yeshou* 人变成野兽]. Perhaps National Studies has the power to turn wild beasts back into human beings [*yeshou biancheng ren* 野兽变成人].[14] But the almost unavoidable commodification of all value is a big national crisis in China.

JF Do you think this phenomenon has anything to do with what I think of as the cultural dilemma of post-utopian ideologies in China? I've been influenced by scholars such as Susan Buck-Morss, who argue that many modern nation-states, especially the United States and the Soviet Union, advanced powerful utopian visions in ways that were very influential in popular culture and national consciousness throughout the twentieth century. I don't think China after the May Fourth Movement was an exception; Chinese popular culture was also strongly utopian for a long time. Now, it is arguably post-utopian. What I mean by this is that a society that most values "moderate well-being" à la Deng Xiaoping Thought, and a society that can accept and even valorize many different degrees of wealth and poverty is no longer utopian; it does not imagine a morally and materially perfect world for a whole society. But isn't there a large gap or vacuum left in the collective desires of those Chinese who were formed by the twentieth-century revolution and the aspirations of the early People's Republic? What can we believe in to fill the vacuum vacated by the hopes for "true communism"? I think this is a way of thinking about your notion of a crisis of belief. There might be a particular feeling of absence or lack that has led people to seek out religion, cults, and various cultural fevers, as well as to become depressed or consider suicide.[15]

ZQC I agree that by now utopian ideals hold the imagination of very few people, and this lack has resulted in the current crisis of belief. Certainly this is one reason for the fevers about National Studies, *yangsheng*, and Chinese medicine. But I really think that this crisis has been a long time coming, with deeper roots than the revolution and the institution of the People's Republic. It has to do with the more than one-hundred-year-long process of the destruction and devastation of traditional culture due to imperialist incursions, dynastic decadence, chronic underdevelopment, decades of armed conflict within our borders, and so forth. In China's several thousand years of history, we *have had* things to believe in, that is, the three great traditions of Confucian, Buddhist, and Daoist teachings. But after the devastations of the last hundred years, these forms of faith are no more; morality [*daode* 道德] has been undermined, and all kinds of ugly things have taken place.

JF But isn't it more than a moral or ideological issue, more than a matter of "belief"? If the underlying situation that has led to the popularity of *yangsheng* in contemporary Beijing is a crisis of *belief* in the narrow sense, we might expect to see mostly ideological phenomena in response; belief is thought of as a psychological or cognitive phenomenon, and its expression is usually thought of as a religious or political or scientific form of faith. But your comments about the "three impossibles" suggest that some form of persuasion or belief is fundamental to everyday experience, social action, life itself. Why do we see in *yangsheng* such a strong bodily, material, and practical response to the crisis?

ZQC Think about what the Beijingers we talked to kept telling us. The aim of *yangsheng* is health, longevity, and above all, pleasure, isn't it? But these enjoyments can't be separated from belief. Vital, spiritual happiness is an intimate experience of the whole body and self. After all, it is the Chinese who say "Spirit and form join as one; mind and body are not two."

You and I have maintained an entertaining disagreement over the last few years about "idealism" versus "materialism." You suspect me of being too idealistic, too concerned with "spiritual" issues in *yangsheng*, and I haven't been very supportive of your efforts to maintain a "materialist" focus on collectives, bodies, things, and spaces. But again and again, we've had to admit to each other that idealism and materialism cannot be separated in any study of China. In Chinese medicine, which is, after all, the cultural foundation we share, "spirit" is a bodily substance, though a particularly volatile one, and "matter" is inseparable from *qi* transformation, and so entirely dynamic. Practitioners of the *yangsheng* arts told us again and again that the highest priorities in the nurturance of life were "spiritual," yet all of them took very concrete routes to the achievement of pleasure, every day, in all sorts of very ordinary, very bodily ways. In the book, we have acknowledged that economic and demographic dilemmas of health care for an aging population are important precipitating factors in the *yangsheng* fever, but we have refused to reduce the phenomenon to the utilities of self-health and physical fitness.

JF Yes, one of our basic commitments has been to the idea that there is always an excess over what can be explained and predicted by the rational models of political economy. Though we have only rarely been able to witness it through our interviews and readings of practices and texts, I do think that one goal of *yangsheng* is to move quietly beyond the "moderate well-being" promised by reform-era modernism. Surely, the pleasure or enjoyment we keep hearing about refers to a surplus, a bonus, an experience of life that cannot be turned to further account. Maybe the ten thousand things of classical metaphysics are—as we say in English—"just one thing after another," a kind of flow, and maybe that continuity, that ongoingness, is a pleasure in itself.

ZQC Indeed. Life nurturance in China today is a form of lived heritage, a continuity, but it's more than that. Embodied, daily, practical, spiritual, multiple, active . . . if we're in the midst of a crisis, *yangsheng* is a powerful response to it. We wrote at the end of Chapter 4 of "gathering" lives and "keeping on" in accord with the generation and transformation of the life-nurturing Dao. Thinking now about "belief," though, maybe we also need to say that *yangsheng* is a form of attachment—not just to Chinese culture, but to the living of life; not just a mental or bodily commitment, but a total participation. No wonder everyone walking, dancing, and singing in the parks, "chatting of heaven, speaking of earth," gathering and harmonizing their lives, talks about enjoyment!

This book has taken a variety of routes into the large and diverse phenomenon that is life nurturing, or *yangsheng*, in contemporary Beijing. It has emphasized the ways in which *yangsheng* activity fills and transforms the space of the city. It has read some of the popular literature that has given shape to an ongoing *yangsheng* movement. It has made acquaintance with the daily lives and values of the postrevolutionary generation that most enthusiastically embraces life nurturance. And it has offered for reflection some of the philosophical resources and challenges that make more lasting sense of *yangsheng* phenomena. Throughout, the aim has been to hear, echoing through the streets and parks of Beijing, the voice of a distinctly modern activism chartered by a protean ancient metaphysics; to read the tastes, pleasures, and disciplines of contemporary urbanites as deliberate and deliberative; and to allow cultured Chinese bodies to resonate with concerns of human embodiment anywhere. The theme has been life, but not life itself—rather, it has been modern life, Chinese life, park life, social and political life, the life of the mind, spirited liveliness, the life of healthy or ailing bodies, family life, lives well nurtured. As the life-nurturing literature keeps telling us, the shapes and currents of the myriad things number ten thousand upon ten thousand: birth upon birth, transformation upon transformation. The meaning of any particular thing—as long as it lasts, and with considerable luck, skill, and determination—is gathered, centered, and harmonized with the Way things go.

Notes

INTRODUCTION

1. "Life itself" and the relationships between life and power in modernity
have been much dwelt upon in several recent literatures to which this study
partly orients itself. Donna Haraway in *Modest_Witness@Second_Millennium.Female
Man©_Meets_Oncomouse*™ (New York: Routledge, 1997) explored the problem
of life itself for bioscience and the politics of feminist science studies. Sociologists, historians, and anthropologists have developed an analytics of biopolitics
and governmentality from Foucault's histories and Collège de France lectures in
the 1970s; see *The Birth of the Clinic: An Archaeology of Medical Perception*, trans.
A. M. Sheridan Smith (New York: Random House, 1973), *The History of Sexuality, Volume I: An Introduction*, trans. Robert Hurley (New York: Random House,
1978), *"Society Must Be Defended": Lectures at the Collège de France, 1975–76*, ed.
Mauro Bertani and Alessandro Fontana, trans. David Macey (New York: Picador,
1997), *Security, Territory, Population: Lectures at the Collège de France, 1977–78*,
ed. Michel Senellart, trans. Graham Burchell (New York: Palgrave Macmillan,
2007), and *The Birth of Biopolitics: Lectures at the Collège de France, 1978–79*, ed.
Michel Senellart, trans. Graham Burchell. (New York: Palgrave Macmillan, 2008).
Philosopher Giorgio Agamben's reflections on sovereignty and life have proven
especially resonant for those researching both medical care and political exclusion
in contemporary settings; see Agamben's *Homo Sacer: Sovereign Power and Bare Life*,
trans. Daniel Heller-Roazen (Stanford: Stanford University Press, 1998) and the
introduction to Thomas Blom Hansen and Finn Stepputat (eds.), *Sovereign Bodies: Citizens, Migrants, and States in the Post-Colonial World* (Princeton: Princeton
University Press, 2005). Sociological theorist Nikolas Rose has been influential
with his ambitious hypotheses on the changing nature of life for moderns within

regimes of biocapital, molecular biology, and a post-Cartesian understanding of the body; see especially *Powers of Freedom: Reframing Political Thought* (New York: Cambridge University Press, 1999) and *The Politics of Life Itself: Biomedicine, Power, and Subjectivity in the Twenty-First Century* (Princeton: Princeton University Press, 2007). Philosopher Roberto Esposito has proposed a vast "immunitary paradigm" of modern politics and life that continues and focuses this Foucauldian tradition of history and sociology of life; see *Bios: Biopolitics and Philosophy* (Minneapolis: University of Minnesota Press, 2008). Anthropologists of science, medicine, and modernities have enriched social thought on life itself with important ethnographies; see, for example, Michael Fischer, *Emergent Forms of Life and the Anthropological Voice* (Durham: Duke University Press, 2003); Sarah Franklin and Margaret Lock (eds.), *Remaking Life and Death: Toward an Anthropology of the Biosciences* (Santa Fe: School of American Research Press, 2003); Susan Greenhalgh, *Just One Child: Science and Policy in Deng's China* (Berkeley: University of California Press, 2008); Sharon Kaufman, *And a Time to Die: How American Hospitals Shape the End of Life* (New York: Scribners, 2005); and Joao Biehl, *Vita: Life in a Zone of Social Abandonment* (Berkeley: University of California Press, 2005). This literature has proven a useful resource for thought to Judith Farquhar as she has explored the nurturance of life in contemporary China, but (apart from Foucault's histories) it is not much known in modern China. Moreover, the situations of life that we two authors witnessed and participated in during our field research propose ways of thinking not especially consistent with the analytics of the biopolitics and governmentality literature. See our "Biopolitical Beijing: Pleasure, Sovereignty, and Self-cultivation in China's Capital," *Cultural Anthropology* 20.3 (August 2005), pp. 303–27, for a preliminary exploration of the usefulness of biopower for understanding contemporary urban Chinese life.

2. Two important encyclopedia articles point out that not even bioscientists are able to agree on a definition of life: Sarah Franklin, s.v. "Life," in *The Encyclopedia of Bioethics*, 3rd ed., vol. 3 (1995; New York: Macmillan Reference, 2004); and Carl Sagan, s.v. "Life," in *The Encyclopedia Britannica*, 15th ed., vols. 10 and 22 (Chicago: Encyclopedia Britannica, 1992). The classical Chinese idea of "giving life to life" or "birthing birth" is not unlike Georges Canguilhem's vitalism, which links a definition of normal life to his concept of normativity: "Man feels in good health...only when he feels more than normal—that is, adapted to the environment and its demands—but normative, capable of following new norms of

life." *The Normal and the Pathological* (1978; New York: Zone Books, 1989), p. 200.

3. The essay from which this quote comes, however, is at times very much like a scholarly summary. See our full discussion in Chapter 4.

4. The word I translate (following generations of sinologists) as "power" and "virtue" is *de* (德); see Arthur Waley, *The Way and Its Power* (New York: Macmillan, 1934). It is used in contemporary Chinese thought to reframe an ethics for the modern age by drawing on a very ancient and complex notion of kingship and virtue.

5. John Dewey, "Self-Realization as the Moral Ideal," in *The Early Works of John Dewey, 1882–1898*, vol. 4 (Carbondale: Southern Illinois University Press, 1971), p. 47. Cited in Patchen Markell, "The Potential and the Actual: Mead, Honneth, and the 'I,'" in Bert van den Brink and David Owen (eds.), *Recognition and Power: Axel Honneth and the Tradition of Critical Social Theory* (New York: Cambridge University Press, 2007).

6. Judith Farquhar has done extensive fieldwork in Chinese medical settings since 1982; see *Knowing Practice: The Clinical Encounter of Chinese Medicine* (Boulder: Westview Press, 1994). Zhang Qicheng comes from a well-known Chinese medical family and has studied the history and philosophy of Chinese medicine throughout his career; we cite his published work often in this book. Throughout this discussion we draw on our familiarity with debates and practices in the professional world of Chinese medicine in China.

7. See, for example, Anonymous, "Comments on the Integration of Chinese and Western Medicine" (*Zhongxiyi jiehe qianlun* 中西医结合浅论), available at http://journal.shouxi.net/qikan/article.php?id=406696 (in Chinese). This comparison between a history of biomedicine rooted in anatomical science of the eighteenth and nineteenth centuries and the changing, but more or less continuous history of medicine in China as a clinical or bedside (*linchuang* 临床) medical art is often made in lectures to students and speeches to foreigners. For polemicists, the ghoulishness and structural authority of anatomy make a nice contrast with "life giving rise to life." They tend to see their own knowledge and skill as fully enmeshed in expressions of life and change.

8. Not everyone in Beijing buys into the health imaginary, especially not in practice. Young entrepreneurial and transnational workers worry about ruining their personal health while being trapped in a social world that is amoral or worse. Many on the edge of economic viability defer healthy lifestyles until they can

begin to get rich along with "everyone else." Schoolchildren become focused on a commodity world that involves more of the logic of conspicuous consumption and recognition by their peers than it does any aim of enjoyment unmediated by consumer goods or any simple good life. Laid-off workers and rural migrants have too many worries to be able to think in terms of crafting a satisfying order in their daily lives. But retirees have the time and the moral/political orientation on the world to fully participate in the imaginary of what Thomas Osborne and Nikolas Rose have called "Hygeia" in "Governing Cities," Working Paper no. 19, Urban Studies Programme, York University, Toronto, 1998.

9. Readers may trace the development and vicissitudes of the goodness of human nature in Chinese philosophy in William Theodore deBary and Irene Bloom (eds.), *Sources of Chinese Tradition*, vol. 1 (New York: Columbia University Press, 1999).

10. We choose to translate *yang* as "nurture," rather than as "cultivate," because of direct references to feeding and growing in the etymology and because of contemporary connotations of the term. Nurturance is provided to all sorts of living creatures, from soldiers to honeybees. Cultivation, *xiu*, is more confined to the human domain; only humans aspire to the lordly virtues. Moreover, nurture is provided to others, so it would be strange to speak of a modern parallel to self-cultivation as "self-nurturance." Food and material support are too important to confine to the individual sphere.

11. For a scholarly discussion in English, see John S. Major, *Heaven and Earth in Early Han Thought: Chapters Three, Four, and Five of the Huainanzi* (Albany: State University of New York Press, 1993).

12. The more common modern usage is not *wanwu*, but *wanshiwanwu* (万事万物), which would be literally translated as "ten thousand matters or affairs and ten thousand objects." This is the main title of the Chinese version of this book. The *wu* of the more classical *wanwu* refers, etymologically, to materiality, and recent materialist thinkers in Chinese have used the term accordingly. See, for example, Wang Min'an, "A Double Materiality" (*Shuangzhong wuzhi* 双重物质), in his *The Factory of Images: How to Look at a Painting (Xingxiang fongchang, Ruhe qukan yifu hua* 形象工厂,如何去看一幅画) (Nanjing: Nanjing University Press, 2009), pp. 31–34.

13. See, for example, Zhang Qicheng on temporality and classic texts: *The Main Stem of the Way of the Changes (Yi dao zhu gan* 易道主干) (Beijing: China Bookstore Press, 1999); *Changes Studies and Chinese Medicine (Yixue yu zhongyi* 易学与中医)

(Beijing: China Bookstore Press, 1999); *The Life-Nurturing Great Way of the Book of Changes* (*Yijing yangsheng da dao* 易经 养生大道) (Nanning: Guangxi Science and Technology Press, 2009) and Judith Farquhar on cultural embodiment: "Multiplicity, Point of View, and Responsibility in Traditional Chinese Medicine," in Angela Zito and Tani Barlow, (eds.), *Body, Subjectivity, and Power in China*. (Chicago: University of Chicago Press, 2004).

14. Judith Farquhar, "The Park Pass: Peopling and Civilizing a New Old Beijing." *Public Culture* 21.3 (Fall 2009), pp. 551–76.

15. As Shigehisa Kuriyama has shown, color in Chinese is more than an objective position along a light spectrum. Even modern terms for color include as referent the desiring relation of the perceiver to the colorful thing. See also Louisa Schein, "The Consumption of Color and the Politics of White Skin in Post-Mao China," *Social Text* 41 (Winter 1994), pp. 141–64. For a discussion of public park life in Beijing, see Farquhar, "The Park Pass."

16. See the *National Geographic* special issue on China (May 2008), "Senior Momentum," n.p. Most of the tourist literature (travel guides and travel magazines, for example) suggests that visits to parks in the early morning to witness *yangsheng* activity is a particularly privileged way to appreciate local culture. We will show in Chapter 2 that the self-health literature published in Chinese for local consumption also takes *yangsheng* to be an important element of heritage.

17. François Jullien, *Vital Nourishment: Departing from Happiness* (New York: Zone Books, 2007).

18. Mei Zhan, *Other-Worldly: Making Chinese Medicine through Transnational Frames* (Durham: Duke University Press, 2009).

19. The term translated as "spiritual" (*jingshen* 精神) in this context refers to both mental and physical aspects of self-cultivation. Spiritual techniques are no doubt experienced as more "mental" and less concrete than jogging or *taiji*, but they are known to increase energy and lift the spirits in a materially palpable way.

20. Three of our Beijing interviewees recited this bit of verse to us when we asked if they knew any proverbs about *yangsheng*.

21. There is a burgeoning anthropology of the everyday to which we here contribute. Key theoretical works and empirical studies include Alice Kaplan and Kristin Ross (eds.), "Everyday Life," *Yale French Studies* 73 (Fall 1987); Michael E. Gardiner and Gregory J. Seigworth (eds.), "Rethinking Everyday Life: And Then Nothing Turns Itself Inside Out," special issue of *Cultural Studies* 18. 2/3 (2004);

Henri Lefebvre, *Critique of Everyday Life, Volume 1: Introduction*, trans. John Moore (1947–1958; London: Verso, 1991); Michel de Certeau, *The Practice of Everyday Life*, trans. Steven F. Rendall (Berkeley: University of California Press, 1984); Ben Highmore, "Introduction: Questioning Everyday Life," in Ben Highmore (ed.), *The Everyday Life Reader* (New York: Routledge, 2002); and Judith Farquhar and Margaret Lock, "Introduction," in Judith Farquhar and Margaret Lock (eds.), *Beyond the Body Proper: Reading the Anthropology of Material Life* (Durham: Duke University Press, 2007).

22. To call Chinese politics "nonmodern" is not to return to a valorization of "tradition." Here we use the term "nonmodern" with reference to Bruno Latour's argument that "we have never been modern" anywhere, in fact. See *We Have Never Been Modern* (Cambridge, MA: Harvard University Press, 1993).

23. See Agamben, *Homo Sacer*, pp. 1 and 8.

24. See Foucault, *The Use of Pleasure* and *The Care of the Self*.

25. See de Certeau, *The Practice of Everyday Life*; Lefebvre, *Critique of Everyday Life*; Andrew Parker (ed.), *Nationalisms and Sexualities* (New York: Routledge, 1992); and Highmore, "Introduction." *The Everyday Life Reader*.

26. Liu Youliang, *Red Flag* (*Hong qi* 红旗) no. 2 (1970), n.p.

27. Judith Farquhar, *Appetites: Food and Sex in Post-Socialist China* (Durham: Duke University Press, 2002); Gang Yue, *The Mouth that Begs: Hunger, Cannibalism, and the Politics of Eating in Modern China* (Durham: Duke University Press, 1999); Liu Kang, *Globalization and Cultural Trends in China* (Honolulu: University of Hawai'i Press, 2004).

28. Farquhar and Zhang, "Biopolitical Beijing."

29. There are helpful guides to finding hospitals, clinics, and doctors published throughout China. They indicate the specialties of doctors and medical institutions and the payment arrangements that are possible.

30. In this insistence on manifold forms of political life, our thinking converges with that of Michael Hardt and Antonio Negri, with their emphasis on the political potential of "the multitude." See *Empire* (Cambridge, MA: Harvard University Press, 2000).

31. Judith Farquhar, "Objects, Processes, and Female Infertility in Chinese Medicine," *Medical Anthropology Quarterly*, n.s., 5.4 (December 1991), pp. 370–99.

32. This discussion is much influenced by the writing of Terry Smith on the question of contemporaneity. See his "Contemporary Art and Contemporaneity,"

Critical Inquiry 32.4 (Summer 2006), pp. 681–707; "Introduction: The Contemporaneity Question" in Terry Smith, Okwui Enwezor, and Nancy Condee, (eds.), *Antinomies of Art and Culture: Modernity, Postmodernity, Contemporaneity* (Durham: Duke University Press, 2008), pp. 1–19; and "The State of Art History: Contemporary Art," *Art Bulletin* 92.4 (December 2010), pp. 266–83.

33. For a history of the People's Republic of China that does not deny its contemporaneity, see Maurice Meisner, *Mao's China and After: A History of the People's Republic* (New York: Free Press, 1986).

34. Bruno Latour calls this ideological and practical disciplining project "the modern constitution." See *We Have Never Been Modern*. See also Susan Buck-Morss, *Dreamworld and Catastrophe: The Passing of Mass Utopia in East and West* (Cambridge, MA: MIT Press, 2000).

35. See the Conclusion for Qicheng Zhang's critique of modernity.

36. Kang, *Globalization and Cultural Trends in China*); John Osburg, "Engendering Wealth: China's New Rich and the Rise of an Elite Masculinity," Ph.D. diss., University of Chicago, 2008.

37. The "traditional" comforts we list here were no doubt enjoyed, desired, and hoped for before liberation in 1949, but things like this became and remained tacitly central to a Chinese socialist imaginary early in the Communist era. The basic creature comforts were the sine qua non of egalitarian socialist provision.

38. Geremie Barmé, *Shades of Mao: The Posthumous Cult of the Great Leader* (Armonk: M. E. Sharpe, 1996); Michael Dutton (ed.), *Streetlife China* (Cambridge: Cambridge University Press, 1998).

39. Su Xiaokang and Luxiang Wang (eds.), *He shang* 河殇, introduced, translated, and annotated as *Deathsong of the River: A Reader's Guide to the Chinese TV Series Heshang* by Richard W. Bodmann and Pin P. Wan (Ithaca: East Asia Program, Cornell University, 1991).

40. Jing Wang, *High Culture Fever: Politics, Aesthetics, and Ideology in Deng's China* (Berkeley: University of California Press, 1996).

41. David A. Palmer, *Qigong Fever: Body, Science, and Utopia in China* (New York: Columbia University Press, 2007).

42. Farquhar, *Appetites.*

43. The popular culture of claiming the city of Beijing by and for its residents—briefly, at least, legal and undocumented alike—characteristic of the Olympic era, from 2001 to 2008, was attested to by numerous journalistic observers.

44. With this use of "coevalness," we invoke Johannes Fabian's influential critique of the classic anthropological chronotope of "the primitive" in his *Time and the Other: How Anthropology Makes Its Object* (New York: Columbia University Press, 1983).

45. Eric Hobsbawm and Terence Ranger (eds.), *The Invention of Tradition* (1983; New York: Cambridge University Press, 1992); for a China studies engagement with the problem, see Ralph Litzinger, *Other Chinas: The Yao and the Politics of National Belonging* (Durham: Duke University Press, 2000).

46. A number of book titles reflect this "wisdom" project explicitly. Examples are *The Wisdom of Not Getting Sick* (*Bushengbingde zhihui* 不生病的智慧), 3 vols. (Nanjing: Jiangsu Literature and Art Publishing House, 2007–2008), Qu Limin, *The Yangsheng Wisdom of the Yellow Emperor's Inner Canon* (*Huangdi neijing yangsheng zhihui* 皇帝内径养生智慧), 2 vols. (Xiamen: Lujiang Press, 2007, 2008), and Zhang Qicheng and Qu Limin, *The Wisdom of Chinese Yang-sheng* (*Zhonghua yangsheng zhihui* 中华养生智慧) (Beijing: Huaxia Press, 2005).

47. "The Four Olds" against which Red Guards hurled invective (and other things) during the first couple of years of the Cultural Revolution were "old customs, old culture, old habits, old ideas." A nice—if somewhat redundant—summary of an anthropological notion of culture.

48. An even more recent phenomenon than that of *He shang* is the often-noted "post-80" generation; these are Chinese people born after 1980, thus growing up in the depoliticized economic and cultural era of "socialism with Chinese characteristics." Older people often speak of these compatriots as "without culture." And in our own conversations with college students and people in their twenties, we find that in speaking of Chinese cultural and historical issues, they tend to cite fragmentary lore garnered from their parents and grandparents, rather than any formal educational resources. In the Conclusion we discuss the recent popular National Studies (*guoxue* 国学) movement that pointedly tries to address this kind of cultural lack.

49. Michel de Certeau, *The Writing of History* (New York: Columbia University Press, 1988).

50. Recent histories of Chinese medicine have much altered and nuanced our sense of "the tradition." Chief among these is Volker Scheid, *Currents of Tradition in Chinese Medicine 1626–2006* (Seattle: Eastland Press, 2007). But see also Hsiang-lin (Sean) Lei, "When Chinese Medicine Encountered the State: 1910–949," Ph.D.

diss., University of Chicago, 1999; Charlotte Furth, Judith T. Zeitlin, and Ping-chen Hsiung (eds.), *Thinking With Cases: Specialist Knowledge in Chinese Cultural History* (Honolulu: University of Hawai'i Press, 2007) especially part 2; and Asaf Goldschmidt, *The Evolution of Chinese Medicine, Song Dynasty 960–1200* (London: Routledge, 2009). Useful recent Chinese histories include Deng Tietao and Cheng Zhifan (eds.), *A General History of Medicine in China* (*Zhongguo yixue tongshi* 中国医学通史), 4 vols. (Beijing: Peoples Medical Press, 2000); Li Jingwei and Yan Liang, *The Eastern Spread of Western Learning and China's Early Modern History of Medical Thought* (*Xixue dongjian yu zhongguo jindai yixue sichao* 西学东建与中国近代医学思潮) (Wuhan: Hubei Science and Technology Press, 1990); Yang Nianqun, *Remaking Patients* (*Zai zao bing-ren* 再造病人) (Beijing: Renmin University Press, 2005); and Zhao Hongjun, *The Era of the Inner Canon* (*Neijing shidai* 内径时代) (Hebei: China Integrated Research Association, 1985).

51. George Marcus and Michael M. J. Fischer, *Anthropology as Cultural Critique: An Experimental Moment in the Human Sciences* (Chicago: University of Chicago Press, 1986).

52. Some examples are David Hall and Roger Ames, especially *Thinking Through Confucius* (Albany: State University of New York Press, 1987); François Jullien, especially *The Propensity of Things: Toward a History of Efficacy in China* (New York: Zone Books, 1995) and *Vital Nourishment*; Shigehisa Kuriyama, *The Expressiveness of the Body and the Divergence of Greek and Chinese Medicine* (New York: Zone Books, 1999); and Geoffrey Lloyd and Nathan Sivin, *The Way and the Word: Science and Medicine in Early China and Greece* (New Haven: Yale University Press, 2002).

53. See, for example, Major, *Heaven and Earth in Early Han Thought*, and Joseph Needham, *Science and Civilisation in China, Volume II: History of Scientific Thought* (Cambridge: Cambridge University Press, 1954).

54. Dipesh Chakrabarty, "Afterword: Revisiting the Tradition/Modernity Binary," in Stephen Vlastos (ed.), *Mirror of Modernity: Invented Traditions of Modern Japan* (Berkeley: University of California Press, 1998), p. 295.

55. Karl Marx, *The German Ideology*, excerpted in Robert C. Tucker (ed.), *The Marx Engels Reader* (1972; New York: Norton, 1978), p. 89.

56. Anna L. Tsing, *Friction: An Ethnography of Global Connection* (Princeton: Princeton University Press, 2005).

57. Qu Limin, *The Yangsheng Wisdom of the Yellow Emperor's Inner Canon*, vol. 1, p. 157.

CHAPTER ONE: CITY LIFE

1. For a discussion of the genealogy of the modern notion of urban community see Duanfang Lu, *Remaking Chinese Urban Form: Modernity, Scarcity, and Space, 1949–2005* (London: Routledge, 2006).

2. Like the other parts of this book, this chapter is coauthored in a particular way. It was mostly drafted by Judith Farquhar, then revised and approved by Zhang Qicheng, then revised and approved again by both. Comments about the life of the city that we share are usually claimed by the use of "us" or "we," but experiences not shared are identified individually, and we refer to ourselves individually, sometimes in the third person. We pin down our observations on the sorts of things people talk about and emphasize as important as best we can with literature or other media citations, and we try to identify speakers of common-sense ideas as to class and generation; both of us consider the films of Ning Ying, on which we draw here, to be a form of insightful social analysis and ethical-political reflection, so in a way we take her (without her permission) as a coauthor. But some of what we consider important here is a kind of floating lore that anyone who chats with anyone in Beijing can pick up. The collaborative part of this chapter is especially strong in reporting these everyday elements of the culture of this city, lived in at this time.

3. Judith Farquhar has elaborated on the notions of peopling and civilizing in modern Beijing spatial practice in "The Park Pass: Peopling and Civilizing a New Old Beijing." *Public Culture* 21.3 (Fall 2009), pp. 551–76.

4. Judith Farquhar has elsewhere explained how one can read realist genres such as Ning Ying's feature films and a number of other modern Chinese fictional genres as cultural documents. While fiction cannot be seen as a transparent window on empirical realities, nevertheless, when it is read as a rhetorical claim on readers' historically formed assumptions about the world, it can serve ethnographic and theoretical projects very well. See *Appetites: Food and Sex in Post-Socialist China* (Durham: Duke University Press, 2002), pp. 17–25.

5. Ning Ying's "Beijing Trilogy" includes the films *[Looking] For Fun (Zhao le* 找乐), *Police Story (Minjingde gushi* 民警的故事), and *I Love Beijing (Xiari nuan yangyang* 夏日暖洋洋, a title better translated as *Prickly Heat*). I discuss the first and third in this chapter. The second, which traces several days in the life of Beijing's lowest level of civil policemen, offers an intimate look at the frustrations of everyday life for those who take a certain responsibility for supporting and regulating city life.

6. Zhang Qicheng earned his Ph.D. in philosophy at Beijing University, then moved across town to build programs in cultural studies of Chinese medicine at the Beijing University of Chinese Medicine. While remaining in Beijing for his teaching schedule, he now also travels a great deal, both in China and internationally, which gives him a comparative viewpoint on the developing city. Judith Farquhar first turned her research attention to Beijing in 1990 for a year of research at teaching and clinical institutions of Chinese medicine (at the Beijing University of Chinese Medicine, at the China Academy of Chinese Medicine, and at the China-Japan Friendship Hospital). Since then, she has stayed in Beijing almost annually for periods ranging between seven months (in 1997 and 2001) and just a few days. Our intensive field research on *yangsheng* took place over five months in the summer and fall of 2003, when the whole group was continuously resident in Beijing.

7. Marc Augé, *Non-Places: Introduction to an Anthropology of Super-Modernity* (London: Verso, 1995). Wang Min'an amusingly points out that very few urbanites collect a broad view of the city as a whole; perhaps only taxi drivers, sex workers, and boys on bicycles approach this comprehensive view in Beijing. See "Prostitutes and Bicycles: Experience of the City" (*Chengshi jingyan: Jinü he zixingche* 城市经验：妓女和自行车) in his *Body, Space, and Postmodernity* (*Shenti, kongjian yu houxiandaixing* 身体，空间与后现代性, Nanjing: Jiangsu People's Press, 2006), pp. 125–36. Certainly ethnographers, even when they work in groups, cannot attempt it.

8. *Laobaixing* is the most usual term in modern Chinese for the common people, and as such it is very complex. Literally, it means "old hundred names," referring to the relatively small set of Chinese surnames in regular use. Thus it certainly refers to a Chinese rather than to a global populace. The multiplicity of the hundred is, significantly, not a reference to class or occupational differences, nor does it refer to differences of wealth, but it certainly evokes a heterogeneous people with diverse identifications and loyalties (implicitly along family lines). The *laobaixing* are also a perennial other in relation to power holders, elites, and visitors. Their life, their needs, and their happiness are often mentioned as what is at stake in modern governance and—for our purposes—urban development. See Thomas Osborne and Nikolas Rose, "Governing Cities," Working Paper no. 19 (Toronto: Urban Studies Programme, York University, 1998), pp. 11–12, on the question of the happiness of the people as a target of governing.

9. Osborne and Rose characterize urban studies of the kind we here undertake as the work of "celebrants" who provide a "personalist anthropology of the city."

"Governing Cities" (Working Paper), p. 27. Thinking of Benjamin, Baudelaire, and de Certeau, perhaps, their remarks are part of an interesting discussion of the city as a site of often "transgressive" pleasure. Though in the early twentieth century, European cities that inspired this image were quite different from (still arguably stuffy and overdisciplined) postsocialist Beijing, we, too, make urban pleasures an issue in what follows. In fact, Osborne and Rose's discussion makes it difficult to distinguish *transgression* as a problem for policing from *excess* as a form of private and compliant creativity. It is in this ambiguous space that we place our "celebration" of everyday life at street level in Beijing. On the notion of "the people," see Li Hsiao-t'i on the China-specific history of the people and the masses in twentieth-century folklore movements: "Making a Name and a Culture for the Masses in Modern China," *Positions* 9.1 (Spring 2001), pp. 29–68.

10. Meng Yue, *Shanghai and the Edges of Empire* (Minneapolis: University of Minnesota Press, 2006).

11. In speaking of making urban places, I draw especially on Stephan Feuchtwang's survey of space and place in anthropology in his introduction to *Making Place: State Projects, Globalisation, and Local Responses* (London: University College London Press, 2004), pp. 3–30. He develops the argument that historically there are always multiple overlapping places and that "space" is an abstraction arising from particular modern histories.

12. The cities I mention here by way of example do not have much more hospitable climates than Beijing, but the relatively greater indoor orientation of their public life is still notable.

13. Thomas Blom Hansen and Oskar Verkaaik, "Urban Charisma: On Everyday Mythologies in the City," *Critique of Anthropology* 29. 1 (March 2009), pp. 5–26.

14. Meng Yue glosses the term *renao* as "noisy, busy, chaotic, full of life." *Shanghai and the Edges of Empire*, p. 243, n. 24. See also Julie Y. Chu, "The Attraction of Numbers: Accounting for Ritual Expenditures in Fuzhou, China," *Anthropological Theory* 10.1–2 (March 2010), pp. 132–42. *Renao* is enjoyable, a sought-out feature of life in particular times and places; the term is constantly in use in modern Chinese. It might be simpler to define *renao* as the essence of the East Asian urban, in that the compound adds a word for heat or intensity (*re*) to a word for noise or commotion (*nao*). The written form of the latter word, moreover, presents a self-evident etymology: a city inside gates. There has been some recent concern in cultural studies with street life in East Asia; perhaps the first prominent

mention of the concept is embodied in Michael Dutton's *Streetlife China* (New York: Columbia University Press, 1998), but there are also a number of interesting studies of particular forms of urbanity in East Asia that engage qualities of street life. See, for example, Won Bae Kim, Mike Douglass, Sang-Chuel Choe, and Kong Chong Ho (eds.), *Culture and the City in East Asia* (Oxford: Clarendon Press, 1997); Nancy Chen, *Breathing Spaces: Qigong, Psychiatry, and Healing in China* (New York: Columbia University Press, 2003); articles by Piper Rae Gaubatz, Vivienne Shue, Shaoguang Wang, and Nancy Chen in Deborah S. Davis, Richard Kraus, Barry Naughton, and Elizabeth J. Perry (eds.), *Urban Spaces in Contemporary China: The Potential for Autonomy and Community in Post-Mao China* (Cambridge: Cambridge University Press and Woodrow Wilson Center Press, 1995); Fulong Wu (ed.), *Globalization and the Chinese City* (London: Routledge, 2006); Anne-Marie Broudehoux, *The Making and Selling of Post-Mao Beijing* (London: Routledge, 2004); articles by Florence Graezer, Graham Johnson, and Elizabeth Lominska Johnson in Feuchtwang (ed.), *Making Place*; Li Zhang, *Strangers in the City: Reconfigurations of Space, Power, and Social Networks within China's Floating Population* (Stanford: Stanford University Press, 2001); and Nancy Chen, Constance D. Clark, Suzanne Z. Gottschang, and Lyn Jeffery (eds.), *China Urban: Ethnographies of Contemporary Culture* (Durham: Duke University Press, 2001).

15. Yue, *Shanghai and the Edges of Empire*, p. 65. Yue's book has provided much inspiration for this and other chapters, but here her nuanced history serves mainly to illustrate the differences between a young Shanghai and a millennial, Olympic Beijing. For the notion of "unproductive festivity," see Henri Lefebvre, *Writings on Cities*, trans. Eleonore Kofman and Elizabeth Lebas (1968; Cambridge, MA: Blackwell, 1996), p. 66, and below.

16. Yue, *Shanghai and the Edges of Empire*, pp. xi, xxv, 65.

17. See Kang Liu, *Globalization and Cultural Trends in China* (Honolulu: University of Hawai'i Press, 2004) on the "revolutionary legacy"; and Lu, *Remaking Chinese Urban Form*, especially ch. 3, pp. 47–79.

18. "Governing Cities" (Working Paper), p. 1.

19. David Palmer's history of a closely related "fever" for qigong throughout China in the 1990s shows in detail how the life-nurturing (and *qi*-deploying) arts were imagined as a contribution to the evolutionary development of human beings in general, led by Chinese adepts and visionaries. See *Qigong Fever: Body, Science and Utopia in China* (New York: Columbia University Press, 2007).

20. Lefebvre, *Writings on Cities*, p. 101.

21. Beijing is chronically dusty, and the city has only slowly become willing to use scarce water to hose down sidewalks, walls, and plaza pavers. But every mall and hotel, every new performance space and gallery, employs armies of cleaners who patiently mop and wipe chrome, glass, and marble surfaces all day, every day. There seems to be a great commitment to high gloss.

22. Lefebvre *Writings on Cities*, p. 191. Many in Beijing have noted the "violent ways in which the 'bulldozer realizes plans'." This was clear in a series of artworks by Zhang Dali documenting the ubiquity of "Demolish" (*chai* 拆) signs spray-painted on doomed buildings in the city of the early 2000s.

23. Walter Benjamin, "Paris, the Capital of the Nineteenth Century (Exposé of 1935)," in *The Arcades Project*, trans. Howard Eiland and Kevin McLaughlin (Cambridge, MA: The Belknap Press of Harvard University Press, 1999), p. 12.

24. Lewis Mumford *The City in History: Its Origins, Its Transformations, and Its Prospects* (New York: Harcourt, Brace, Jovanovich, 1961), p. 387, quoted in James Scott, *Seeing Like a State: How Certain Schemes to Improve the Human Condition Have Failed* (New Haven: Yale University Press, 1998), p. 56.

25. This kind of housing, once dominated by one-story courtyard compounds, is known as *pingfang*, or horizontal, housing. The so-called *pingfang* neighborhoods that remain, mostly inside the Second Ring Road, are now mixtures of dilapidated and overcrowded courtyards, renovated single-family courtyards, and apartment or office buildings three to six stories high. On the razing and reconstruction of the Qianmen neighborhood, see Kelly Layton, "Qianmen, Gateway to a Beijing Heritage," *China Heritage Quarterly* no. 12 (December 2007), available in the archive at http://www.chinaheritagequarterly.org

26. The film analyzed elsewhere in these pages, *For Fun*, is set in the Qianmen neighborhood. A long tracking shot along Qianmen Street at the beginning, filmed in the early 1990s and accompanied by music from Kurt Weil's *Threepenny Opera*, is a clear homage to the particular urban quality of this now-demolished neighborhood of Beijing.

27. Lefebvre, *Writings on Cities*, p. 66.

28. Robin Visser, in *Cities Surround the Countryside: Urban Aesthetics in Post-Socialist China* (Durham: Duke University Press, 2010) surveys recent discussions of Chinese urban form, analyzing the efforts of planners, journalists, social scientists, and cultural commentators, writing in both Chinese and English, to capture

and respond to the city's "urban essence." Visser's thorough and thoughtful account both offers historical context for the present study of *yangsheng* practices in Beijing and captures, in analyses of art, literature, and popular culture, some of the less obvious anxieties afflicting Chinese city dwellers at the millennium.

29. Paul Rabinow, *Marking Time: On the Anthropology of the Contemporary* (Princeton: Princeton University Press, 2008), pp. 2–3.

30. Lu, *Remaking Chinese Urban Form*, p. 142.

31. I take this use of the term "spacetime" from Nancy Munn's recent work on the evolution of city form in New York, and from her ethnographic thematizing of spacetime in *The Fame of Gawa: A Symbolic Study of Value Transformation in a Massim (Papua New Guinea) Society* (1986; Durham: Duke University Press, 1992).

32. The state-led civility, or *wenming*, campaigns have been noted by other anthropologists. See Ann Anagnost, *National Past-Times: Narrative, Representation, and Power in Modern China* (Durham: Duke University Press, 1997), ch. 3.

33. Many urban work units (*danwei*) once required morning calisthenics of all workers, and the counted-out sequence of exercises was broadcast over the *danwei* public-address system. Nowadays, except for some schools, this compulsory morning routine is a thing of the past, though many voluntarily engage in this kind of group exercise.

34. Though there is national legislation, mandated retirement age actually varies a great deal, depending on industry, location, privatization initiatives, and personal circumstances. Overall, though, age of retirement is low in China compared with the United States; pensions are quite low, too.

35. See Judith Farquhar and Qicheng Zhang, "Biopolitical Beijing: Pleasure, Sovereignty, and Self-Cultivation in China's Capital," *Cultural Anthropology* 20.3 (August 2005), pp. 303–27. The paper concludes with a spatial description of *taiji* practice.

36. Liu, *Globalization and Cultural Trends in China*, pp. 86–91.

37. "Inside China," *Life* 70.15 (April 30, 1971), pp. 22–52.

38. Osborne and Rose, "Governing Cities (Working Paper)," p. 2.

39. The history of modern Beijing, to which we can only partly allude here, is not unique. In a survey of urban modernisms by Thomas Osborne and Nikolas Rose, one can see many international movements of planning, economic development, and the imagination of modern space that have been well instantiated in Beijing's rapid expansion and modernization over the last half century. See

"Governing Cities: Notes on the Spatialization of Virtue," *Environment and Planning D: Society and Space* 17.6 (1999), pp. 737–60.

40. Lu, *Remaking Chinese Urban Form*, p. 127.

41. For an excellent historical and ethnographic study of *yangge* dancing and its associated social organizations in the Beijing area, see Florence Graezer, "Breathing New Life into Beijing Culture: New 'Traditional' Public Spaces and the Chaoyang Neighborhood *Yangge* Associations," in Feuchtwang (ed.)., *Making Place*.

42. *Ibid.*, pp. 61–78 and 3–30.

43. "It's Time to Bring Out the Dancing Shoes," *China Daily*, August 2, 1004, available at http://www.chinadaily.com.cn/english/doc/2004-08/03/content_357306.htm. This article makes it clear that some younger people consider the open vulgarity of *yangge* to be an embarrassment, compared with the cosmopolitan elegance of ballroom dancing.

44. Tracey Rosen, "Coming of Age on the World Stage: Beijing's Candidature for the 2008 Olympic Games," M.A. Thesis, University of Chicago Department of Anthropology, 2004. This extensive discussion considers a great many nationalist and other ideological aspects of the city's preparation for the Olympics.

45. *People's Daily* English-language edition, February 19, 2001, cited in C.R. Pramod, "The 'Spectacle' of the Beijing Olympics and the Dynamics of State–Society Relationship in PRC," *China Report* 44.2 (May 2008) p. 123.

46. See Yunxiang Yan, "McDonald's in Beijing: The Localization of Americana," in James L. Watson (ed.), *Golden Arches East: McDonald's in East Asia* (Stanford: Stanford University Press, 1997), pp. 39–76.

47. Internet cafés reached their peak at the turn of the century, popping up in every neighborhood and often running twenty-four hours a day. But after a disastrous and fatal fire in an internet café in 2002, most of these businesses closed. The setback in Web access was temporary. During this period, more people gained Internet access in their workplaces, and in the last five or ten years, many families have purchased home computers. We found or heard about desktop PCs in a number of the otherwise humble homes of our interviewees; investment in a computer was justified as being good for the children's schoolwork. Moreover, nowadays, a host of neighborhood copy shops make their two or three PCs available to customers who pay for time when the machines are not otherwise occupied composing business cards, downloading documents for printing, and Photoshopping passport photos.

48. This is the third film of Ning Ying's "Beijing Trilogy" and the only one made after 1997. See our discussion below. *I Love Beijing* is arguably the most pessimistic of the three films.

49. In our 2003 field research, we included in the questionnaire for a preliminary survey of 200 residents of West City District a question about daily hassles (*mafan* 麻烦). Many respondents were unwilling to say what, if any, *mafan* they had to deal with, but problems that were mentioned included worry about family members' employment situations, annoyances with bus transportation, overcrowded domestic spaces, and expensive and inaccessible medical care.

50. By the end of 2007, Beijingers in *hutong* areas inside the second ring road were enjoying—and paying for—newly installed electricity services and the electric heaters they had recently been required to install in place of coal-burning braziers. Friends who live in parts of courtyard houses tell us this electrification provides much more comfort.

51. See Jinxia Dong, "Women, Nationalism, and the Beijing Olympics: Preparing for Glory," *The International Journal of the History of Sport* 22.4 (July 2005), pp. 530–44.

52. For commentary on urban problems from a central government perspective, see the volume edited by the Sociocultural Unit of the Ministry of Culture and the Chinese Mass Culture Society, *Mass Culture (Lun chengshi qunzhong wenhua* 论城市群众文化) (Beijing: Zhongguo Wuzi Chubanshe 中国物资出版社, 1998); for a rich discussion of debates in the architecture and planning communities, see Robin Visser, *Cities Surround the Countryside*, ch. 2. Liu summarizes important debates on social problems in *Globalization and Cultural Trends in China*, especially in ch. 2. A volume edited by Chaohua Wang, *One China, Many Paths* (London: Verso, 2003) translates a selection of critical essays. Representative writing on social problems published in Chinese includes: Lu Xueyi *On the Three Rural Problems: Research on Contemporary China's Agriculture, Villages, and Peasants (San nong lun: Dangdai zhongguo nongye, nongcun, nongming yanjiu* 三农论: 当代中国农业、农村、农民研究) (Beijing: Social Sciences Literature Press, 2002); Wen Tiejun, *The Three Rural Problems and the Millennial Shift (San nong wenti yu shiji fansi* 三农问题与世纪反思) (Beijing: Sanlian Press, 2005); Li Qiang, *China's Class Divide in the Transitional Era (Zhuanxing shiqide zhongguo shehui fenceng jiegou* 转型时期的中国社会分层结构) (Harbin: Heilongjiang People's Press, 2002); Huang Ping, "The Baseline that Health and Development Can't Surmount: A Report of a Health Survey

in Diqing and Tibet" (*Jiankang,fazhan buneng tupode dixian—diqing zangqu yiliao kaucha baogao* 健康，发展不能突破的底线—迪庆藏区医疗考察报告), in Huang Ping (ed.), *Experience of the West: Investigation and Critical Thought on the Rural West (Xibu jingyan: Dui xibu nongcunde diaocha yu sisuo* 西部经验：对西部农村的调查与思索) (Beijing: Social Science Literatures Press, 2006).

53. Davis et al. (eds.), *Urban Spaces in Contemporary China*.

54. See Visser, *Cities Surround the Countryside*, especially chs. 1 and 2, for the historical situation of a Chinese urban aesthetic.

55. Lu, *Remaking Chinese Urban Form*.

56. See Li Hsiao-t'i, "Making a Name and a Culture for the Masses in Modern China."

57. For a critical analysis of the play of class politics at key moments during the Cultural Revolution (1966–1968), see Yi-ching Wu, "The Other Cultural Revolution: The Politics and Practice of Class in the Chinese Cultural Revolution," Ph.D. dissertation, University of Chicago, 2007. Urban administrative control and surveillance are depicted in detail (and their ultimate failure and banality are analyzed) in Ning Ying's second "Beijing Trilogy" film, *On the Beat (Minjing gushi* 民警故事). We derive the notion of a population politics, or a distribution of powers involved in the disposition of groups in social space, from the work of Foucault, especially *Discipline and Punish* and *The History of Sexuality*. Theorists of modern sovereignty (for example, Giorgio Agamben) and medical anthropologists and sociologists who deploy the notion of biopower (Sharon Kaufmann, Margaret Lock, Nikolas Rose, Kim Fortun, and many others) have added much to our understanding of how people engage the political simply by disposing their lives in the city.

58. Maurice Meisner, *Mao's China and After: A History of the People's Republic* (New York: Free Press, 1999).

59. Visser, *Cities Surround the Countryside*, pp. 27–128.

60. Michel de Certeau's classic essay "Walking in the City" explores this tension between the city seen from a distance and the city experienced, or walked, at many levels. In Steven F. Rendall, trans., *The Practice of Everyday Life* (Berkeley: University of California Press, 1984), pp. 99–110.

61. Shaoguang Wang, "The Politics of Private Time: Changing Leisure Patterns in Urban China," in Davis et al., (eds.), *Urban Spaces*, pp. 149–72.

62. Duanfang Lu notes cases of struggle over the uses of former community

halls in the privatizing work unit she studied in Beijing. Lu, *Remaking Chinese Urban Form*, pp. 148–49.

63. See the Conclusion below, where we discuss debates about memory and civilization in a different, but, we think, linked social sphere, in the form of the National Studies movement.

64. For reasons that we hope are clear, we both recognize the aptness of and seek to go beyond arguments about representations of tradition advanced by Jean Baudrillard and Guy deBord. See Jean Baudrillard, *Simulacra and Simulation*, trans. Sheila Faria Glaser (Ann Arbor: University of Michigan Press, 1995); and Guy deBord, *Society of the Spectacle* (Detroit: Black and Red, 1977).

65. Lu, *Remaking Chinese Urban Form*, p. 126, citing Sigmund Freud, *Moses and Monotheism*, trans. Katherine Jones (1936; New York: Vintage Books, 1967), p. 85.

66. To accept Freud's own formulation here is even more problematic when we consider the various unexamined ways in which the word "tradition" has been used in history and sociology. Some of these are highlighted by Eric Hobsbawm and Terence Ranger in the introduction to their edited volume, *The Invention of Tradition* (Cambridge: Cambridge University Press, 1983).

67. James Hevia, *English Lessons: The Pedagogy of Imperialism in Nineteenth Century China* (Durham: Duke University Press, 2003).

68. For recent developments in this debate, see the *China Heritage Quarterly* no. 12 (December 2007), available in the archive at http://www.chinaheritage-quarterly.org.

69. Lu, *Remaking Chinese Urban Form*, pp. 124–42.

CHAPTER TWO: HOW TO LIVE

1. By far the most common question asked by Chinese people when first intro-duced to a foreigner is "Are you accustomed yet?" (*xiguanle ma?*) Everyone seems to take it for granted that a place far from one's native home will take some getting used to, and no assurances that Beijing is quite a comfortable place and Chinese food naturally easy to live on will persuade Beijingers that adjustment presents no difficulties.

2. Zhongli Baren, *Finding Yourself Is Better than Finding a Doctor* (*Qiuyi buru qiuji* 求医不如求己) (Sanhe, Jiangsu: Jiangsu Wenyi Chubanshe, 2007); Li Dexin and Wang Zhaocheng (eds.), *The Family Yangsheng Canon* (*Jiating yangsheng bao-dian* 家庭养生宝典) (Liaoning, Shenyang: Liaoning Kexue Jishu Chubanshe, 2001);

Liu Hongzhang and Liu Bo (eds.), *Illness Is Self-Created* (*Bing shi zijia sheng* 病是自家生) (Beijing: Zhongguo Youyi Chuban Gongsi, 2006); Wei Junwen and Wei Guojian (eds.), *A Healthy Maturity Depends on You* (*Jiankang changshou kao ziji* 健康长寿靠自己) (Beijing: Hualing Chubanshe, 2003).

3. See recent issues of *The Lancet* for articles on health-system reform in China. Examples are: Hong Wang, "China's Fragmented Health System," *The Lancet* 366.9493 (October 8, 2005), pp. 1257–58; Adrian C. Sleigh, "Health-System Reforms to Control Tuberculosis in China," *The Lancet* 369.9562 (February 24, 2007), pp. 627–27; Shenglan Tang, et al., "Tackling the Challenges to Health Equity in China," *The Lancet* 372.9648 (October 25, 2008), pp. 1493–1501.

4. This chronic complaint about the difficulty of finding decent and dignified medical care was perhaps the stimulus for a minor subgenre of the self-health literature: "finding a doctor" handbooks. These guides to a city's or region's hospitals, clinics, specialties, and individual doctors listed practical information that helped people figure out where their costs might be most reimbursable and where they might find the most appropriate medical specialty for their complaint. Such guides began to appear in the 1980s, and new editions still frequently replace older ones on bookstore shelves.

5. Note that this development is completely consistent with many scholars' discussions of the "risk society" as an aspect of neoliberal governmentality, the biopolitical imperatives expressed by advanced and privatized medical techniques, Kaushik Sunder Rajan's notion of "patients in waiting"(Sunder Rajan, *Biocapital: The Constitution of Postgenomic Life*, [Durham: Duke University Press, 2006]), and the way that self-help literature world wide promotes a pervasive sense of vulnerability, dangerous ignorance, and helplessness. See Sabine Maasen, Barbara Sutter, and Stephanie Duttweiler, "Self-Help: The Making of Neosocial Selves in Neoliberal Society," in Sabine Maasen and Barbara Sutter (eds.), *On Willing Selves: Neoliberal Politics vis-à-vis the Neuroscientific Challenge* (New York: Palgrave Macmillan, 2007), pp. 26–49; and Brian Massumi (ed.), *The Politics of Everyday Fear* (Minneapolis: University of Minnesota Press, 1993). We see something else, or something more, going on in the *yangsheng* literature discussed here, but we do not wish to see China's complex health scene as exempt from these global developments in biomedical technics and public health privatization.

6. In this context, "at risk" really refers to a state of being seen as in danger of falling ill from some specified disease or being a member of a population some

members of which will—according to experts—certainly fall ill of that disease. The self-health literature in China is loaded with "risk" predictions based on epidemiological and actuarial studies done all over the world. Like public-health journalism everywhere, the rhetoric makes little distinction between individual fates and population regularities. Consumers of media public health are encouraged to see their own individual life as tending toward heart disease or breast cancer, even if only a middling percentage of their demographic group is likely to develop these conditions. Nikolas S. Rose, *The Politics of Life Itself: Biomedicine, Power, and Subjectivity in the Twenty-First Century* (Princeton: Princeton University Press, 2001); Mitchell Dean, "Risk, Calculable and Incalculable," in Deborah Lupton (ed.), *Risk and Sociocultural Theory: New Directions and Perspectives* (Cambridge: Cambridge University Press, 1999), pp. 131–59.

7. See Ruth Rogaski, *Hygienic Modernity: Meanings of Health and Modernity in Treaty-Port China* (Berkeley: University of California Press, 2004) for information programs of the Ministry of Health before 1949.

8. Jin Dapeng and Guan Chunfang (eds.), *Get on the Health Express* (*Dengshang jiankang kuaiche*等上健康快车) (Beijing: Beijing Publishers, 2003), p. 2.

9. Chinese medicine has adapted the ancient logic of *zheng*-right *qi* and *xie*-evil *qi* to twentieth-century immune-system discourse, but the logic of these sciences remains somewhat distinct, in that experience plays a more important role in the maintenance of immunity for Chinese medicine than for biomedicine. See Roberto Esposito, *Bios: Biopolitics and Philosophy* (Minneapolis: University of Minnesota Press, 2008) for his argument that places a logic of immunity as central to modern biopower. The history of recent Asia-centered epidemics provides spectacular illustrations of his vision of biopolitics.

10. By contrast, Judith Farquhar has explored the experiential quality of Chinese herbal medicines in "Eating Chinese Medicine," *Cultural Anthropology* 9.4 (November 1994), pp. 471–97 (Chinese translation in *Chayi* [Differences] no. 1 [2005]) and in ch. 1 of *Appetites: Food and Sex in Postsocialist China* (Durham: Duke University Press, 2002).

11. Though these observations about use were mostly made in 2003 and 2004, we don't expect much difference in patterns of book usage since then. What has changed is the greater popularity of television shows about health in 2007 and 2008, but the content of these shows is reflected in the expanding book market, as we have argued.

12. Hong Zhaoguang, leader of the *Get on the Health Express* group, attaches a slogan to this effect to his photo on an early edition in the series: "Be a good citizen of the moderate well-being society; live happily and healthily for 100 years." Jin and Guan, (eds.), *Get On the Health Express*.

13. Judith Farquhar has written on this question of readership from several points of view in three articles: "How to Live: Reading China's Popular Health Media," in Kai Khiun Liew (ed.), *Liberalizing, Feminizing, and Popularizing Health Communications in Asia* (Surrey, UK: Ashgate, 2010); "Sketching the Dao: Chinese Medicine in Modern Cartoons," in Vivienne Lo (ed.), *Globalising Chinese Medicine: A Visual History* (Beijing: Renmin Weisheng Chubanshe, forthcoming); and "For Your Reading Pleasure: Popular Health Advice and the Anthropology of Everyday Life in 1990s Beijing," *Positions* 9.1 (Spring 2001), pp. 105–30. See also John Clarke, Janet Norman, and Louise Westmarland, "Creating Citizen-Consumers?: Public Service Reform and (Un)willing Selves," in Maasen et al. (eds.), *On Willing Selves*, pp. 125–45.

14. Zhang Qicheng, *The Great Way of Yangsheng: Zhang Qicheng Lectures on the Yellow Emperor's Inner Canon* (*Zhang Qicheng jiangdu Huangdi neijing yangsheng da dao* 张其成讲读黄帝内经养生大道 (Nanning: Guangxi Science and Technology Press, 2008), p. 1.

15. *Ibid.*, p. 4.

16. Qu Limin, *The Yangsheng Wisdom of the Yellow Emperor's Inner Canon* (*Huangdi neijing yangsheng zhihui* 皇帝内经养生智慧) (Xiamen: Lujiang Press, 2007), p. 3.

17. *Ibid.*, pp. 4–5, ellipsis in the original.

18. The phrase *changshou* actually incorporates a doubling of the notion of longevity; literally translated, it would be "lengthy long life" or a long longevity.

19. Quoted, for example, in Zhang, *Zhang Qicheng Lectures on the Yellow Emperor's Inner Classic* p. 19.

20. *Ibid.*

21. Zhang explains in his commentary, *ibid.*, p. 22, that the fullness in question involves stores of germinal essence. Though at one level this *jing*-essence is male semen, which is subject to either excessive expenditure or wise husbanding, at another level, in both Chinese medicine and the classical bedchamber arts, germinal essence is a physiological necessity for both genders. The fullness in question is a complicated matter of managing a relationship between nourishment and expenditure of life forces in general. Like the other aspects of *yangsheng* discussed here,

achieving and maintaining the proper fullness is significantly a matter of timing.

22. *Yellow Emperor's Inner Canon: Plain Questions* 1:1. See, for example, Qu , *The Yangsheng Wisdom of the Yellow Emperor's Inner Canon*, pp. 67–88.

23. Farquhar, *Appetites*, ch. 3.

24. This puzzling remark about dragons is discussed above, at the end of the Introduction.

25. Qu, *The Yangsheng Wisdom of the Yellow Emperor's Inner Canon*, pp. 157–58.

26. *Ibid.*, p. 25

27. *Ziran* (自然)is usually translated as "natural" for modern Chinese usage, and the English noun "nature" (as in "Mother Nature") is translated into Chinese as "the great self-so" (*da ziran* 大自然). However, the compound *ziran* is old and embodies only one modern sense of the natural: it refers to those events or emergences that happen by themselves, spontaneously, not uncaused, but not specifically intended by anyone or under anyone's control. Hence the frequently seen Sinological phrases, "the self-so," or what is "so of itself."

28. *Wuwei* is impossible to translate without a lengthy explanation of the classical philosophical environment in which it first figured as a key term. Stemming from the cosmopolitical theories of cosmogony and lordship of the Warring States Period (or earlier), the notion of lordly nonaction tends to refer to a refusal to intervene in the *ziran*, or spontaneous, propensities of the Way. Lordship of this kind involves personal self-cultivation and political quietism on the part of the sovereign; the combination of ethical perfection and governmental laissez-faire allows the well-run domain to accord with the great Dao and ensure that everyone lives well. *Wuwei* is sometimes spoken of as "ruling as an exemplar." Around such a nonactive king, an ethical social order will naturally shape itself.

29. In the context of the lecture discussed here, *he* 和 might be more exactly translated as "calibrating" or "titrating," or even as "intercalating" *yin* and *yang*. All these words are overly technical, however. They neither capture the original musical or culinary reference of the term nor the commonsense notion of harmonizing the nested antinomies of *yin* and *yang* in experience. The Chinese word is a perfectly ordinary one, in everyday use, but, as Zhang's discussion of *yin* and *yang* in the second lecture allows us to see, unlike the English word "harmony," it does not connote a monotone state of stable homogeneity or any banishing of differences, contrasts, or even antagonisms. Rather than a sustained and unified musical chord, the image is one of evolving or unfolding contrasts that can be

balanced relative to each other.

30. Zhang Qicheng, *The Great Way of Yangsheng*, p. 20. Subsequent citations will appear in the text.

31. See also Zhang Yanhua, *Transforming Emotions with Chinese Medicine: An Ethnographic Account from Contemporary China* (Albany: State University of New York Press, 2007).

32. Zhang Hude et al. (eds.), *The Complete Book of "The Yellow Emperor's Inner Canon" Yangsheng: The Yangsheng of the Four Time Periods* (*Huangdi neijing yangsheng quanshu* 皇帝内径 养生全书), 10 vols. (Beijing: Light Industry Press).

33. *Ibid*, pp. 187–88.

34. Qu, *The Yangsheng Wisdom of the Yellow Emperor's Inner Canon*, p. 25.

35. Zhang Hude, et al. (eds.), *The Complete Book of "The Yellow Emperor's Inner Canon" Yangsheng*, pp. 159–60.

36. Zhang Qicheng, *The Great Way of Yangsheng*, p. 173.

37. Zhang Qicheng and Qu Limin, *The Wisdom of Chinese Life Nurturance* (*Zhonghua yangsheng zhihui* 中华养生智慧) (Beijing: Huaxia Press, 2005).

CHAPTER THREE: DAILY LIFE

1. Common sense is most classically thematized by Antonio Gramsci as part of his exploration of the reach of hegemony into everyday life and consciousness. We are especially indebted to his manner of seeing "philosophy" as forceful in practice, as embedded in language, and as offering valid forms of thought far beyond the academic and scholarly context. See *Selections from the Prison Notebooks of Antonio Gramsci*, ed. and trans. Quintin Hoare and Geoffrey N. Smith (New York: International Publishers, 1971). A somewhat neglected and very suggestive anthropological treatment of common sense can be found in Clifford Geertz, "Common Sense as a Cultural System," in *Local Knowledge: Further Essays in Interpretive Anthropology* (New York: Basic Books, 1983), pp. 73–93.

2. Zhang and Farquhar were both present for almost all of these interviews. At various times, (then) graduate students Lai Lili and Qiu Hao were also present, and on a few occasions, Dr. Qu Limin joined us, as well. Sometimes an interviewee would bring a friend or family member along, so these interviews often became convivial focus groups. They were all audio recorded, and transcripts were made from the recordings. It is noteworthy that despite the gathering of academic and Chinese medical expertise at these interviews, the very diverse Beijingers we

spoke with positioned themselves as our teachers. They were conveying to us their hard-won expertise about how to live, and they considered themselves good critics of doctors, formal medical knowledge, and public-health information.

3. For some of the most dimensional anthropological research on aging, see, for example, Lawrence Cohen, *No Aging in India: Alzheimer's, the Bad Family, and Other Modern Things* (Berkeley: University of California Press, 1998); Sarah Lamb, *Aging, Gender, and Body in North India* (Berkeley: University of California Press, 2000); Margaret Lock, *Encounters with Aging: Mythologies of Menopause in Japan and North America* (Berkeley: University of California Press, 1993); and Barbara Myerhoff, *Number Our Days* (New York: Dutton, 1978).

4. See Ann Anagnost, *National Past-Times: Narrative, Representation, and Power in Modern China* (Durham: Duke University Press 1997) pp. 17–44; and Judith Farquhar, *Appetites: Food and Sex in Postsocialist China* (Durham: Duke University Press, 2002) pp. 79–119.

5. In the late 1990s, a popular fever for the notion of privacy erupted with a book by An Dun, *Absolute Privacy: The Emotional Stories of Contemporary Chinese People (Juedui Yinsi: Dangdai Zhongguo qinggan koushu shilu* 绝对隐私:当代中国人情感口述实录) (Shanghai: New World Press 1998). Since 2005 or so, there appears to have been much less interest in the keyword "absolute privacy," but popular psychology, with its emphasis on personal interiority, continues to gain currency.

6. See Michael Dutton, *Streetlife China* (Cambridge: Cambridge University Press, 1998), pp. 42–61; Gail Henderson and Myron S. Cohen, *The Chinese Hospital: A Socialist Work Unit* (New Haven: Yale University Press, 1984); Xiaobo Lü and Elizabeth Perry (eds.), *Danwei: The Changing Chinese Workplace in Comparative Perspective* (Armonk: M. E. Sharpe, 1997).

7. For a more detailed discussion of *yangsheng* and its politics of compliance and participation, see our coauthored article "Biopolitical Beijing: Pleasure, Sovereignty, and Self-Cultivation in China's Capital." *Cultural Anthropology* 20.3 (August 2005), pp. 303–27.

8. The relative individualism of deliberate walking as a yangsheng practice is even more clear in some other parks. In Tuanjiehu Park, for example, where there is a smaller lake with a good path right around it, early mornings see an unbroken line of walkers, each a few feet ahead and behind the next. The line keeps a vigorous pace, and walkers seldom chat or loiter on the side until their walking is done. Then there are plenty of places to meet and greet walking and other early morning

pleasure-seeking friends.

9. Judith Farquhar, "For Your Reading Pleasure: Popular Health Advice and the Anthropology of Everyday Life in 1990s Beijing," *Positions* 9.1 (Spring 2001), pp. 105 30.

10. See http://www.nipic.com/show/2/52/4db6ab0c8db464df.html.

11. The *Shuowen jiezi* 说文结字 (Explaining characters) is an early Chinese etymological dictionary, dating from approximately the second Century C.E.

11. For a discussion of how belief has been problematized in medical anthropology, see Byron Good, *Medicine, Rationality, and Experience: An Anthropological Perspective* (New York: Cambridge University Press, 1994).

12. This is especially good advice in relation to what has been said about Mao Zedong by one of his longtime doctors. In 1994, Dr. Li Zhisui published a scandalous tell-all book about Mao's life in the Chinese Communist Party compound of Zhongnanhai, but much of it is hard to take at face value. See *The Private Life of Chairman Mao* (New York: Random House, 1994).

13. The first chapter of the writings of Zhuangzi is often translated as "Free and Easy Wandering." Zhang Gengguang (ed.), *The Complete Translated Zhuangzi* (*Zhuangzi quanyi* 庄子全译) (Guiyang: Guizhou People's Press 1991).

14. In official police parlance, crime is referred to as "social contradictions," and crime control is often thought of as the management of social contradictions. See Michael Dutton, *Policing Chinese Politics: A History* (Durham: Duke University Press, 2005).

15. How fascinating that Zhao Xinyi is reading this little-known book! The *Guiguzi* is a book of tactics (now included in the Daoist canon) that compiles the activities of Gui Gu, who lived in the Spring and Autumn Annals / Warring States period. He was a colorful legendary figure who studied astronomy and geomancy, observed the movements of sun and stars, calculated fate with the trigrams of the *Book of Changes*, and prognosticated events, all with great penetration. He was especially expert in military strategy, understanding the many forces and constant change—even the dispositions of the gods—affecting the deployment of troops. He was a teacher of several important later philosophers, the most famous being Sun Bin, the author of *The Art of War*.

16. Zhu Hong, one of the exemplary yangsheng practitioners who opens this chapter, once described at great length an acquaintance of hers as having "low *suzhi*." These comments suggest that the concept of social "quality" is not simply

connected to wealth or educational level, since Zhu Hong's sense of her own qualitative superiority could not have come from either.

17. François Jullien, *The Propensity of Things: Toward a History of Efficacy in China* (New York: Zone Books, 1995).

18. Judith Farquhar, "The Park Pass: Peopling and Civilizing a New Old Beijing," *Public Culture* 21.3 (Fall 2009), pp. 551–76.

CHAPTER FOUR: THE MEANING OF LIFE

1. Zhang Qicheng has published a great many books and articles on the cultural history of medicine, the *Book of Changes*, and the *yangsheng* tradition. His process of writing the essay that forms the basis of this chapter partly involved assembling explications of the relevant terms and literatures from writing he had already done for publication.

2. See Introduction, n. 1, for references to theorists of "life itself."

3. Christopher L. Connery, *The Empire of the Text: Writing and Authority in Early Imperial China* (New York: Rowman and Littlefield, 1998); Haun Saussy, *Great Walls of Discourse and Other Adventures in Cultural China* (Cambridge, MA: Harvard University Asia Center, 2001); Michel Strickmann, *Chinese Poetry and Prophecy: The Written Oracle in East Asia* (Stanford: Stanford University Press, 2005).

4. Yanhua Zhang is one of the more recent anthropologists to argue that there is no true analogue to the body of the Cartesian tradition in Sinophone worlds: *Transforming Emotions with Chinese Medicine: An Ethnographic Account from Contemporary China* (Albany: State University of New York Press, 2007). See also Judith Farquhar, "Multiplicity, Point of View, and Responsibility in Traditional Chinese Healing," in Angela Zito and Tani E. Barlow (eds.), *Body, Subject, and Power in China* (Chicago: University of Chicago Press, 1994), pp. 78–99.

5. "Nature" is only one conventional translation for *ziran*. It has also commonly been translated as "the spontaneous" or the "self-so." Modern Chinese language commonly uses the longer term *da ziran*, the great spontaneity, to refer to a modern cosmopolitan idea of the nature that forms "our environment" and to which, when we go camping for example, we go "back."

6. Walter Benjamin, "The Task of the Translator," trans. Harry Zohn, in Marcus Bullock and Michael W. Jennings (eds.), *Walter Benjamin: Selected Writings, Volume 1, 1931–1926* (Cambridge, MA: Harvard University Press, 1996), pp. 253–63.

7. The *Shuowen jiezi* 说文结字 (Explaining characters) is an early Chinese

etymological dictionary, dating from approximately the second Century C.E.

8. Shigehisa Kuriyama's extended consideration of the character of the *mo* (脉), or pulse, in classical Chinese medicine offers an analogue to the noun-verb duality of words such as *sheng*. See *The Expressiveness of the Body and the Divergence of Greek and Chinese Medicine* (New York: Zone Books, 1999), ch. 1 and 2.

9. Definitions of *ming* to be found in etymological dictionaries (such as the *Cihai* or the *Ciyuan*) list the following equivalents: "appointment"; "command or instruction"; "destiny, fate, or lot"; "life span" (*shengming*); "the Way"; and kingly honors, awards, or bestowals. One common modern use of *ming* is in the term for divination or fortunetelling, which is referred to as "calculating one's fate or one's lot in life," *suanming* 算命. Modern uses of cosmological divination are individualizing technologies; most rely on very detailed information about a client's time and place of birth.

10. Shen Nong is the mythic sage-king who invented agriculture and discovered the medicinal uses of "the thousand herbs." An early materia medica text is named the *Shen Nong bencao*.

11. See chapter 18 of the *Zhuangzi* quoted at the end of this chapter for a famous passage in which everything changes into everything—bugs of all kinds, plants, rocks, leopards, horses, and humans are all intertransformative. And rapidly, too.

12. Nathan Sivin, *Traditional Medicine in Contemporary China: A Partial Translation of Revised Outline of Chinese Medicine* (Ann Arbor: Center for Chinese Studies, 1987).

13. Manfred Porkert, *The Theoretical Foundations of Chinese Medicine: Systems of Correspondence* (Cambridge, MA: MIT East Asian Science Series, 1974), especially pp. 9–13.

14. Sivin, *Traditional Medicine in Contemporary China*, p. 47.

15. Ren yi tiandi zhi qi sheng, sishi zhi fa cheng; Fu ren sheng yu di, xuan mingy u tian, tiandi he qi, ming zhi yue ren 人以天地之气生，四时之法成. 夫人生于地，悬命于天，天地合气，命之曰人.

16. See Zhang's comments on seasonality in Chapter 2.

17. Hence Zhang's comment elsewhere in the essay: "Because this is relevant to the treatment of disease and to the waxing and waning of *yin* and *yang* and the transformations of the five phases, we need to manage things in a way that is fitting to the times, 'the sages when they treated disease had to know the *yin* and *yang* of heaven and earth and the circuits and patterns of the four seasons' (*Plain*

Questions [*juan* 23:77]). 'Thus, he who would cure disease must illuminate the Way of heaven and the patterns of earth, the rising and falling [*gengsheng* 更胜] of *yin* and *yang*, the beginnings and endings of *qi*, the life span of humans and the threats to human life, the periods of generation and transformation [*shenghua* 生化]—then he will be able to truly know the *xing*-form 形 and *qi* of Man.' (*Plain Questions* [*juan* 20:70]). These texts more or less reflect the thinking that humans and nature have synchronous patterns."

18. Judith Farquhar, "Objects, Processes, and Female Infertility in Chinese Medicine," *Medical Anthropology Quarterly* (n.s.) 5.4 (December 1991), pp. 370–99; Barry M. Saunders, *CT Suite: The Work of Diagnosis in the Age of Noninvasive Cutting* (Durham: Duke University Press, 2008).

19. Later developments in Chinese medicine, known as the Warm Factor Illnesses School and especially associated with South China culture in the seventeenth century and after, spatialized the body even more clearly with "defensive, *qi*, constructive, and blood" sectors (Sivin's translations). Though these sectors systematized the localizing up-down and in-out motion mentioned in Zhang Qicheng's essay, they also had a clear temporal dimension: they are used in part to classify the stages and sites of an exogenous illness.

20. Note that when *qi* is the agent, in and out makes sense both as breathing, and as lateral motility (inward and outward) of *qi* within the body.

21. Sivin, *Traditional Medicine in Contemporary China*, p. 47.

22. The *hun* (魂) and *po* (魄) "souls" are thought of in medicine as elusive substances correlated respectively with liver/blood and lung/seminal essence. They are glossed in Wiseman and Ye's dictionary as the "ethereal soul" and the "corporeal soul," and a distinction between them is maintained in popular religion (for example, in relation to funerary ritual), as well as in medicine. See Nigel Wiseman and Feng Ye, *A Practical Dictionary of Chinese Medicine* (Brookline: Paradigm Publications, 1998).

23. For this point, see Hall and Ames, *Thinking Through Confucius*, especially pp. 17–21.

24. Porkert, *The Theoretical Foundations of Chinese Medicine*.

25. There is no space here to discuss the technical elaborations enabled by five-phases (*wuxing* 五行) analysis in Chinese medicine. The topic has been much developed by Joseph Needham and Gwei-djen Lu (who translate the term as "five elements"). See *Celestial Lancets: A History and Rationale of Acupuncture*

and Moxibustion (Cambridge: Cambridge University Press, 1980); Porkert, *The Theoretical Foundations of Chinese Medicine*; Sivin, *Traditional Medicine*; and Judith Farquhar, *Knowing Practice: The Clinical Encounter of Chinese Medicine* (Boulder: Westview Press, 1994), among others.

26. Hence, this model, despite its careful discriminations, is unlike anatomy.

27. In volume 2 of *Science and Civilization in China*, Joseph Needham developed the classic discussion of resonance in early Chinese scientific thought. See also his essay, "Human Law and the Laws of Nature," in *Human Law and the Laws of Nature in China and the West* (London: Oxford University Press, 1951). On "resonance," see also Major, *Heaven and Earth in Early Han Thought*.

28. *Lunheng* is a philosophical and scientific work attributed to Wang Chong, who lived in the first century C.E.

29. Jullien is only the latest in a long string of interpretive readers of Zhuangzi; see his *Vital Nourishment*. A. C. Graham's large corpus of works on Zhuangzi and Daoism is another important source.

30. Apparently Dylan Thomas didn't think human life was so different from that of plants. His poem "The Force That Through the Green Fuse Drives the Flower" combines botanical and cosmological processes in ways very similar to the literatures we discuss in this chapter. Also see Kuriyama, *Expressiveness*, ch. 4, on the botanic metaphor in Chinese medicine.

31. See Gilles Deleuze and Félix Guattari, *A Thousand Plateaus: Capitalism and Schizophrenia*, trans. Brian Massumi (Minneapolis: University of Minnesota Press, 1987).

32. The centrality of "questions of life and death" to the concerns of philosophy (which he here understands as a modern scholar) is noted by Zhang Qicheng in his 2004 survey *Philosophical Foundations of Chinese Medicine* (*Zhongyi zhexue jichu* 中医哲学基础) (Beijing: China Chinese Medicine Press), pp. 278–80.

33. See Roger Ames, *The Art of Rulership: A Study in Ancient Chinese Political Thought* (Honolulu: University of Hawai'i Press, 1983).

34. Charles Dickens, *Our Mutual Friend* (New York: Hurd and Houghton, 1867), book 3, chapter 2, finds a moment as the rascal Rogue Riderhood is hovering between living and dying to describe a great interest in the "spark of life" that is there to be saved in him regardless of the general dislike of Riderhood the person. Once the patient is quite alive again, everyone loses interest in his life and goes back to wishing he were dead.

35. According to the early Confucian editors of the *Book of Changes*, the trigrams and hexagrams and the relations between them were born directly of the Dao, not invented by humans. These signs are often thought of as existing at the origin of writing; they embody what Marcel Granet called the "cosmo-magical effect" of the Chinese written character in *The Religion of the Chinese People*, trans. Maurice Freedman (Oxford: Blackwell, 1975). Examples of the natural-cultural unity that is the Chinese cosmos abound: one could note that astronomy, *tian-wenxue* 天文学, is knowledge of the writings in the heavens or rehearse arguments cited above that refuse any basic body-mind split in human experience. For the concept of "nature-culture," see Bruno Latour, *We Have Never Been Modern*, trans. Catherine Porter (Cambridge, MA: Harvard University Press, 1993).

36. Zhuangzi 18: "Happiness Attained" (*zhile* 至乐), our translation. The original text is available at http://ctext.org/zhuangzi/perfect-enjoyment at passage 7. See also Zhang Gengguang, *The Complete Translated Zhuangzi* (*Zhuangzi quanyi* 庄子全译) (Guiyang: Guizhou People's Press 1991).

CONCLUSION

1. We were accompanied by Zhang Fan, then a graduate student in anthropology at Beijing University. She was very helpful at certain points in our talk in providing translations into Chinese of some names and anthropological concepts that Judith Farquhar was only able to express in English. She had earlier translated a chapter draft for Zhang Qicheng's perusal, for which assistance we thank her. The dialogue as we present it here not only edits out her assistance, it is also a bit amplified with relevant background, mostly derived from earlier conversations.

2. We are both aware that philology has been subject to many discrediting critiques in Anglophone scholarship and that it has been especially questioned for its (sometime) commitment to finding pure origins and sorting civilizational genealogies into insiders and outsiders. See Geoffrey Harpham, "Roots, Races, and the Return to Philology," *Representations* 106.1 (Spring 2009), pp. 34–62. The Chinese term that Zhang Qicheng and Judith Farquhar use for philology, however, when speaking in Chinese, is *wenxianxue* 文献学, which refers to little more than documentary studies; Judith Farquhar would be inclined to translate it as "archive studies," rather than as "philology." Though Chinese *wenxianxue* has certainly had its periods of obsession with origins and purifications, the term does not need to connote such scholarship.

3. See Chaohua Wang (ed.), *One China, Many Paths* (London: Verso, 2003). A number of the authors translated in this collection mention the emergence of National Studies as an intellectual movement especially associated with the journal *Xueren* beginning in 1993–94. None were yet in a position to notice the popular fad that National Studies has now become.

4. Zhang Qicheng refers here to Samuel P. Huntington's *The Clash of Civilizations and the Remaking of World Order* (New York: Simon and Schuster, 1996). Huntington uses "civilization" much of the time for his reified notion of particular cultures, but he also much abuses the notion of culture. In Chinese and for Zhang Qicheng, *wenhua* 文化 refers to both the notion of culture and that of civilization; we somewhat unpack this topic below.

5. Eric Karchmer, "Orientalizing the Body: Postcolonial Transformations in Chinese Medicine," Ph.D. dissertation, University of North Carolina Department of Anthropology. Zhang Qicheng and Judith Farquhar had discussed Eric's research and the problem of Orientalist essentialisms before.

6. Bruno Latour, *We Have Never Been Modern* (Cambridge, MA: Harvard University Press, 1993).

7. Though Zhang Qicheng at times claims a place among National Studies scholars, as was seen in Chapter 2, he does not simply focus his historical attention on Warring States and Han texts. His list of "five canons" that "every schoolchild should read," for example, includes a later Buddhist work, *The Canon of the Sixth Patriarch (Liuzu tanjing* 六祖坛经) (see his lectures, *The Great Way of Yangsheng: Zhang Qicheng Lectures on the Yellow Emperor's Inner Classic [Zhang Qicheng jiangdu Huangdi neijing yangsheng da dao* 张其成讲读黄帝内经养生大道] [Nanning: Guangxi Science and Technology Press, 2008]), and as a historian of Chinese medicine and the *Book of Changes*, he has extensively historicized knowledge that emerges through a long tradition of commentary and innovation right up into the twentieth century.

8. "Postmodern" thought has had a particular career in Chinese letters, importantly inflected by a vast national preoccupation with "modernization" since the late 1970s. See Wang Min'an, *Modernity (Xiandaixing* 现代性) (Guilin: Guangxi Normal University Press, 2005); and *The Body, Space, and Postodernity (Shenti, kongjian yu houxiandaixing* 身体，空间与后现代性) (Nanjing: Jiangsu Peoples Press, 2006). Judith Farquhar was using the term in this particular Chinese sense, not likely to be seen as a negative criticism by Zhang Qicheng.

9. Zhang Qicheng is also an authority on the *Book of Changes* and its historical development at the center of a vast East Asian discourse on fate and causality in life.

10. Matthew Arnold, *Culture and Anarchy: An Essay in Political and Social Criticism* (London: Smith, Elder & Co., 1869), p. viii.

11. Perhaps the most common use of *wenhua* is in the phrase "cultural level," *wenhua shuiping di* 文化水平底: "[his/her] cultural level is low," meaning (most often) educational level.

12. Edward Burnett Tylor, *Anthropology: An Introduction to the Study of Man and Civilization* (New York: D. Appleton & Co., 1898).

13. Richard Kraus, *Pianos and Politics in China: Middle-Class Ambitions and the Struggle over Western Music* (New York: Oxford University Press, 1989).

14. Zhang Qicheng here adopts imagery from the model opera and revolutionary play *The White-Haired Girl*. See my discussion in *Appetites: Food and Sex in Postsocialist China* (Durham: Duke University Press, 2004) p. 85–89.

15. Jason Ingersoll, "Depression, Subjectivity, and the Embodiment of Suffering in Urban Reform China," Ph.D. dissertation, University of Chicago, June 2010.

Bibliography

Agamben, Giorgio. *Homo Sacer: Sovereign Power and Bare Life*. Stanford: Stanford University Press, 1998.

American Herbal Pharmacology Delegation. *Herbal Pharmacology in the People's Republic of China*. Washington, D.C.: National Academy of Sciences, 1975.

Ames, Roger. *The Art of Rulership: A Study in Ancient Chinese Political Thought*. Honolulu: University of Hawai'i Press, 1983.

Anagnost, Ann. *National Past-Times: Narrative, Representation, and Power in Modern China*. Durham: Duke University Press, 1997.

Arnold, Matthew. *Culture and Anarchy: An Essay in Political and Social Criticism*. London: Smith. Elder & Co., 1869.

Augé, Marc. *Non-Places: Introduction to an Anthropology of Super-Modernity*. New York: Verso, 1995.

Barmé, Geremie. *Shades of Mao: The Posthumous Cult of the Great Leader*. Armonk: M. E. Sharpe, 1996.

DeBary, William Theodore, and Irene Bloom (eds.). *Sources of Chinese Tradition*, vol. 1. New York: Columbia University Press, 1999.

Baudrillard, Jean. *Simulacra and Simulation*. Translated by Sheila Faria Glaser. Ann Arbor: University of Michigan Press, 1995.

Benjamin, Walter. "Paris, the Capital of the Nineteenth Century (Exposé of 1935)." In *The Arcades Project*, pp. 3–13. Translated by Howard Eiland and Kevin McLaughlin. Cambridge, MA: The Belknap Press of Harvard University Press, 1999.

———. "The Task of the Translator." Translated by Harrry Zohn. In Marcus Bullock and Michael W. Jennings (eds.), *Walter Benjamin: Selected Writings, Volume 1, 1931–1926*, pp. 253–63. Cambridge, MA: Harvard University Press, 1996.

Biehl, João. *Vita: Life in a Zone of Social Abandonment.* Berkeley: University of California Press, 2005.

DeBord, Guy. *Society of the Spectacle.* Detroit: Black and Red, 1977.

Broudehoux, Anne-Marie. *The Making and Selling of Post-Mao Beijing.* New York: Routledge, 2004.

Buck-Morss, Susan. *Dreamworld and Catastrophe: The Passing of Mass Utopia in East and West.* Cambridge, MA: MIT Press, 2000.

不生病的智慧 *Bushengbingde zhihui* [The wisdom of not getting sick]. 3 vols. Nanjing: Jiangsu Literature and Art Publishing House, 2007–2008.

Canguilhem, Georges. *The Normal and the Pathological.* New York: Zone Books, 1989.

de Certeau, Michel. "Walking in the City." In *The Practice of Everyday Life*, pp. 99–110. Translated by Steven F. Rendall. Berkeley: University of California Press, 1984.

———. *The Writing of History.* New York: Columbia University Press, 1988.

Chakrabarty, Dipesh. "Afterword: Revisiting the Tradition/Modernity Binary." In Stephen Vlastos (ed.), *Mirror of Modernity: Invented Traditions of Modern Japan*, pp. 285–96. Berkeley: University of California Press, 1998.

Chen, Nancy. *Breathing Spaces: Qigong, Psychiatry, and Healing in China.* New York: Columbia University Press, 2003.

———. Constance D. Clark, Suzanne Z. Gottschang and Lyn Jeffery (eds.). *China Urban: Ethnographies of Contemporary Culture.* Durham: Duke University Press, 2001.

Chu, Julie Y. "The Attraction of Numbers: Accounting for Ritual Expenditures in Fuzhou, China." *Anthropological Theory* 10.1–2 (March 2010), pp. 132–42.

———. "To Be 'Emplaced': Fuzhounese Migration and the Politics of Destination." *Identities: Global Studies in Culture and Power* 13.3 (July–September 2006), pp. 395–425.

Clarke, John, Janet Norman, and Louise Westmarland. "Creating Citizen-Consumers?: Public Service Reform and (Un)Willing Selves." In Sabine Maasen and Barbara Sutter (eds.), *On Willing Selves: Neoliberal Politics vis-à-vis the Neuroscientific Challenge*, pp. 125–45. New York: Palgrave Macmillan, 2007.

Cohen, Lawrence. *No Aging in India: Alzheimer's, The Bad Family, and Other Modern Things.* Berkeley: University of California Press, 1998.

中西医结合浅论 *Zhongxiyi jiehe qianlun* [Comments on the integration of Chinese

and Western medicine]. Available at http://journal.shouxi.net/qikan/article.
php?id=406696.

Connery, Christopher L. *The Empire of the Text: Writing and Authority in Early Impe-rial China*. New York: Rowman and Littlefield, 1998.

Davis, Deborah S., Richard Kraus, Barry Naughton, and Elizabeth J. Perry (eds.). *Urban Spaces in Contemporary China: The Potential for Autonomy and Community in Post-Mao China*. Cambridge: Cambridge University Press and Woodrow Wilson Center Press, 1995.

Dean, Mitchell. "Risk, Calculable and Incalculable." In Deborah Lupton (ed.), *Risk and Sociocultural Theory: New Directions and Perspectives*, pp. 131–59. Cam-bridge: Cambridge University Press, 1999.

Deleuze, Gilles, and Félix Guattari. *A Thousand Plateaus: Capitalism and Schizo-phrenia*. Translated by Brian Massumi. Minneapolis: University of Minnesota Press, 1987.

Deng Tietao 邓铁涛 and Cheng Zhifan 程之范 (eds.). 中国医学通史*Zhongguo yixue tongshi* [A general history of Chinese medicine]. 4 vols. Beijing: Peoples Medi-cal Press, 2000.

Dewey, John. "Self-Realization as the Moral Ideal." In *The Early Works of John Dewey, 1882–1898*, vol. 4, pp. 44–53. Carbondale: Southern Illinois University Press, 1971.

Dickens, Charles. *Our Mutual Friend*. New York: Hurd and Houghton, 1867.

Dong, Jinxia. "Women, Nationalism, and the Beijing Olympics: Preparing for Glory." *The International Journal of the History of Sport* 22.4 (2005), pp. 530–44.

Dun An 安顿. 绝对隐私:当代中国人情感口述实录 *Juedui yinsi: Dangdai Zhongguo ren qinggan koushu shilu* [Absolute privacy: The emotional stories of contem-porary Chinese people]. Shanghai: New World Press 1998.

Dutton, Michael. *Policing Chinese Politics: A History*. Durham: Duke University Press, 2005.

———. *Streetlife China*. New York: Columbia University Press, 1998.

Esposito, Roberto. *Bios: Biopolitics and Philosophy*. Minneapolis: University of Min-nesota Press, 2008.

Fabian, Johannes. *Time and the Other: How Anthropology Makes Its Object*. New York: Columbia University Press, 1983.

Farquhar, Judith. *Appetites: Food and Sex in Postocialist China*. Durham: Duke Uni-versity Press, 2002.

——. "Eating Chinese Medicine." *Cultural Anthropology* 9.4 (November 1994), pp. 471–97. Translated by Lili Lai as "吃中药" *Chi zhongyao. Chayi* [Differences], no. 1 (2005).

——. "For Your Reading Pleasure: Popular Health Advice and the Anthropology of Everyday Life in 1990s Beijing." *Positions* 9.1 (Spring 2001), pp. 105–30.

——. "How to Live: Reading China's Popular Health Media." In Kai Khiun Liew (ed.), *Liberalizing, Feminizing, and Popularizing Health Communications in Asia*, pp. 197–216. Surrey, UK: Ashgate, 2010.

——. *Knowing Practice: The Clinical Encounter of Chinese Medicine.* Boulder: Westview Press, 1994.

——. "Multiplicity, Point of View, and Responsibility in Traditional Chinese Medicine." In Angela Zito and Tani Barlow (eds.), *Body, Subjectivity and Power in China*, pp. 78–99. Chicago: University of Chicago Press, 2004.

——. "Objects, Processes, and Female Infertility in Chinese Medicine." *Medical Anthropology Quarterly* (n.s.) 5.4 (December 1991), pp. 370–99.

——. "The Park Pass: Peopling and Civilizing a New Old Beijing." *Public Culture* 21.3 (Fall 2009), pp. 551–76.

——. "Sketching the Dao: Chinese Medicine in Modern Cartoons." In Vivienne Lo (ed.), *Globalising Chinese Medicine: A Visual History* (Beijing: Renmin Weisheng Chubanshe, forthcoming).

——. and Margaret Lock. "Introduction." In Judith Farquhar and Margaret Lock (eds.), *Beyond the Body Proper: Reading the Anthropology of Material Life*, pp. 1–16. Durham: Duke University Press, 2007.

——. and Zhang Qicheng. "Biopolitical Beijing: Pleasure, Sovereignty, and Self-Cultivation in China's Capital." *Cultural Anthropology* 20.3 (August 2005), pp. 303–27.

Festa, Paul E. "Mahjong Politics in Contemporary China: Civility, Chineseness, and Mass Culture." *Positions: East Asia Cultures Critique* 14.1 (Spring 2006), pp. 7–35.

Feuchtwang, Stephan (ed.). *Making Place: State Projects, Globalisation, and Local Responses.* London: University College London Press, 2004.

Fischer, Michael. *Emergent Forms of Life and the Anthropological Voice.* Durham: Duke University Press, 2003.

Franklin, Sarah. S.v. "Life." In *The Encyclopedia of Bioethics*, 3rd ed., vol. 3. New York: Macmillan Reference, 2004.

——, and Margaret Lock (eds.), *Remaking Life and Death: Toward an Anthropology of the Biosciences*. Santa Fe: School of American Research Press, 2003.

Foucault, Michel. *The Birth of Biopolitics: Lectures at the Collège de France, 1978–79.* Edited by Michel Senellart. Translated by Graham Burchell. New York: Palgrave Macmillan 2008.

——. *The Birth of the Clinic: An Archaeology of Medical Perception.* Translated by A. M. Sheridan Smith. New York: Random House 1973.

——. *Discipline and Punish: The Birth of the Prison.* Translated by Alan Sheridan. New York: Pantheon Books, 1977.

——. *The History of Sexuality, Volume 1: An Introduction.* Translated by Robert Hurley. New York: Pantheon Books, 1978.

——. *The History of Sexuality, Volume 2: The Use of Pleasure.* Translated by Robert Hurley. New York: Pantheon Books, 1985.

——. *The History of Sexuality, Volume 3: The Care of the Self.* Translated by Robert Hurley. New York: Pantheon Books, 1986.

——. *Security, Territory, Population.* Edited by Michel Senellart. Translated by Graham Burchell. New York: Palgrave Macmillan, 2007.

——. *"Society Must Be Defended": Lectures at the Collège de France, 1975–76.* Edited by Mauro Bertani and Alessandro Fontana. Translated by David Macey. New York: Picador 2003.

Freud, Sigmund. *Moses and Monotheism.* Translated by Katherine Jones. New York: Vintage Books, 1967.

Furth, Charlotte, Judith T. Zeitlin, and Ping-chen Hsiung (eds.). *Thinking With Cases: Specialist Knowledge in Chinese Cultural History.* Honolulu: University of Hawai'i Press, 2007.

Gardiner, Michael E., and Gregory J. Seigworth (eds.). *Rethinking Everyday Life: And Then Nothing Turns Itself Inside Out.* Special issue of *Cultural Studies* 18.2/3 (2004).

Geertz, Clifford. "Common Sense as a Cultural System." In *Local Knowledge: Further Essays in Interpretive Anthropology*, pp. 73–93. New York: Basic Books, 1983.

Goldschmidt, Asaf. *The Evolution of Chinese Medicine, Song Dynasty 960–1200.* London: Routledge, 2009.

Good, Byron. *Medicine, Rationality, and Experience: An Anthropological Perspective.* New York: Cambridge University Press, 1994.

Graezer, Florence. "Breathing New Life into Beijing Culture: New 'Traditional' Public Spaces and the Chaoyang Neighborhood *Yangge* Associations." In Stephan Feuchtwang (ed.), *Making Place: State Projects, Globalisation, and Local Responses*, pp. 61–78. London: University College London Press, 2004.

Gramsci, Antonio. *Selections from the Prison Notebooks of Antonio Gramsci*. Edited and translated by Quintin Hoare and Geoffrey N. Smith. New York: International Publishers, 1971.

Granet, Marcel. *The Religion of the Chinese People*. Edited and translated by Maurice Freedman. Oxford: Blackwell, 1975.

Greenhalgh, Susan. *Just One Child: Science and Policy in Deng's China*. Berkeley: University of California Press, 2008.

Hall, Donald, and Roger Ames. *Thinking Through Confucius*. Albany: State University of New York Press, 1987.

Hansen, Thomas Blom, and Finn Stepputat. "Introduction." In Thomas Blom Hansen and Finn Stepputat (eds.), *Sovereign Bodies: Citizens, Migrants, and States in the Postcolonial World*, pp. 1–36. Princeton: Princeton University Press, 2005.

———. and Oskar Verkaaik. "Urban Charisma: On Everyday Mythologies in the City." *Critique of Anthropology* 29.1 (March 2009), pp. 5–26.

Haraway, Donna. *Modest_Witness@Second_Millennium.FemaleMan©_Meets_ Oncomouse*™. New York: Routledge, 1997.

Hardt, Michael, and Antonio Negri. *Empire*. Cambridge, MA: Harvard University Press, 2000.

Harpham, Geoffrey. "Roots, Races, and the Return to Philology." *Representations* 106.1 (Spring 2009), pp. 34–62.

Henderson, Gail, and Myron S. Cohen. *The Chinese Hospital: A Socialist Work Unit*. New Haven: Yale University Press, 1984.

Hevia, James. *English Lessons: The Pedagogy of Imperialism in Nineteenth Century China*. Durham: Duke University Press, 2003.

Highmore, Ben. "Introduction: Questioning Everyday Life." In Ben Highmore (ed.), *The Everyday Life Reader*, pp. 1–34. New York: Routledge, 2002.

Hobsbawm, Eric, and Terence Ranger (eds.). *The Invention of Tradition*. Cambridge: Cambridge University Press, 1983.

Huntington, Samuel P. *The Clash of Civilizations and the Remaking of World Order*. New York: Simon and Schuster, 1996.

Huang Jitang, 黄吉堂 et al. (eds.). 中医学导论 *Zhongyixue daolun* [Introduction to

Chinese medicine]. Guangzhou: Guangdong Higher Education Press, 1988.

Huang Ping 黃平. 健康，发展不能突破的底线—迪庆藏区医疗考察报告 "Jiankang, fazhan buneng tupode dixian—Diqing Zangqu yiliao kaocha baogao" [The baseline that health and development can't surmount: A report of a health survey in Diqing and Tibet]. In Huang Ping (ed.), 西部经验：对西部农村的调查与思索 *Xibu jingyan: Dui xibu nongcun de diaocha yu sisuo* [Experience of the West: Investigation and critical thought on the rural West]. Beijing: Social Science Literatures Press, 2006.

Ingersoll, Jason. "Depression, Subjectivity, and the Embodiment of Suffering in Urban Reform China." Ph.D. dissertation, University of Chicago, June 2010.

"Inside China." *Life* 70.15 (April 30, 1971), pp. 22–52.

Jin Dapeng 金大鹏 and Guan Chunfang 关春芳 (eds.). 登上健康快车 *Dengshang jiankang kuaiche* [Get on the Health Express]. Beijing: Beijing Publishers, 2003.

Jullien, François. *The Propensity of Things: Toward a History of Efficacy in China.* New York: Zone Books, 1995.

——. *Vital Nourishment: Departing from Happiness.* New York: Zone Books, 2007.

Kang, Liu. *Globalization and Cultural Trends in China.* Honolulu: University of Hawai'i Press, 2004.

Kaplan, Alice, and Kristin Ross (eds.). "*Everyday Life.*" *Yale French Studies* 73 (Fall 1987).

Karchmer, Eric. "Orientalizing the Body: Postcolonial Transformations in Chinese Medicine." Ph.D. dissertation, University of North Carolina Department of Anthropology, 2004.

Kaufman, Sharon. *And a Time to Die: How American Hospitals Shape the End of Life.* New York: Scribners, 2005.

Kim, Won Bae, Mike Douglass, Sang-Chuel Choe. and Kong Chong Ho (eds.). *Culture and the City in East Asia.* Oxford: Clarendon Press, 1997.

Kraus, Richard. *Pianos and Politics in China: Middle-Class Ambitions and the Struggle over Western Music.* New York: Oxford University Press, 1989.

Kuriyama, Shigehisa. *The Expressiveness of the Body and the Divergence of Greek and Chinese Medicine.* New York: Zone Books, 1999.

Lamb, Sarah. *Aging, Gender, and Body in North India.* Berkeley: University of California Press, 2000.

Latour, Bruno. *We Have Never Been Modern.* Translated by Catherine Porter. Cambridge, MA: Harvard University Press, 1993.

Layton, Kelly. "Qianmen, Gateway to a Beijing Heritage." *China Heritage Quarterly* no. 12 (December 2007), available at http://www.chinaheritagequarterly.org/articles.php?searchterm=012_qianmen.inc&issue=012 (subscription required).

Lefebvre, Henri. *Critique of Everyday Life, Volume 1: Introduction.* Translated by John Moore. London: Verso, 1991.

——. *Writings on Cities.* Translated by Eleonore Kofman and Elizabeth Lebas. Cambridge, MA: Blackwell, 1996.

Lei, Hsiang-lin (Sean). "When Chinese Medicine Encountered the State: 1910–1949." Ph.D. dissertation, University of Chicago, 1999.

Li, Hsiao-t'i. "Making a Name and a Culture for the Masses in Modern China." *Positions* 9.1 (Spring 2001), pp. 29–68.

Li, Jingwei 李经纬 and Liang Yan. 梁延. 西学东建与中国近代医学思潮 *Xi xue dong jian yu Zhongguo jindai yixue sichao* [The Eastern spread of Western learning and China's early modern history of medical thought]. Wuhan: Hubei Science and Technology Press, 1990.

Li Qiang 李强. 转型时期的中国社会分层结构 *Zhuanxing shiqide Zhongguo shehui fenceng jiegou* [China's class divide in the transitional era]. Harbin: Heilongjiang People's Press, 2002.

Li, Zhisui. *The Private Life of Chairman Mao.* New York: Random House, 1994.

Litzinger, Ralph. *Other Chinas: The Yao and the Politics of National Belonging.* Durham: Duke University Press, 2000.

Liu Youliang 刘友. 红旗 *Hong qi* [Red flag] no. 2 (1970).

Lloyd, Geoffrey, and Nathan Sivin, *The Way and the Word: Science and Medicine in Early China and Greece.* New Haven: Yale University Press, 2002.

Lock, Margaret. *Encounters with Aging: Mythologies of Menopause in Japan and North America.* Berkeley: University of California Press, 1993.

Lu, Duanfang. *Remaking Chinese Urban Form: Modernity, Scarcity, and Space, 1949–2005.* New York: Routledge, 2006.

Lu Xueyi 陆学艺. 三农论: 当代中国农业、农村、农民研究 *San nong lun: Dangdai Zhongguo nongye, nongcun, nongmin yanjiu* [On the three rural problems: Research on contemporary China's agriculture, villages, and peasants]. Beijing: Social Sciences Literature Press, 2002.

Lü, Xiaobo, and Elizabeth Perry (eds.). *Danwei: The Changing Chinese Workplace in Comparative Perspective.* Armonk: M. E. Sharpe, 1997.

Maasen, Sabine, Barbara Sutter, and Stephanie Duttweiler. "Self-Help: The Making of Neosocial Selves in Neoliberal Society." In Sabine Maasen and Barbara Sutter (eds.), *On Willing Selves: Neoliberal Politics vis-à-vis the Neuroscientific Challenge*, pp. 26–49. New York: Palgrave Macmillan, 2007.

Major, John S. *Heaven and Earth in Early Han Thought: Chapters Three, Four, and Five of the Huainanzi*. Albany: State University of New York Press, 1993.

Marcus, George, and Michael M. J. Fischer. *Anthropology as Cultural Critique: An Experimental Moment in the Human Sciences*. Chicago: University of Chicago Press, 1986.

Markell, Patchen. "The Potential and the Actual: Mead, Honneth, and the 'I.'" In Bert van den Brink and David Owen (eds.), *Recognition and Power: Axel Honneth and the Traditional of Critical Social Theory*, pp. 100–32. New York: Cambridge University Press, 2007.

Marx, Karl. "The German Ideology." Excerpted in *The Marx Engels Reader*, 2nd ed. Edited by Robert C. Tucker. New York: W. W. Norton, 1978.

Massumi, Brian (ed.). *The Politics of Everyday Fear*. Minneapolis: University of Minnesota Press, 1993.

Meisner, Maurice. *Mao's China and After: A History of the People's Republic*. New York: Free Press, 1999.

Meng, Yue. *Shanghai and the Edges of Empire*. Minneapolis: University of Minnesota Press, 2006.

Mumford, Lewis. *The City in History: Its Origins, Its Transformations, and Its Prospects*. New York: Harcourt Brace Jovanovich, 1961.

Munn, Nancy. *The Fame of Gawa: A Symbolic Study of Value Transformation in a Massim (Papua New Guinea) Society*. 2nd ed. Durham: Duke University Press, 1992.

Myerhoff, Barbara. *Number Our Days*. New York: Dutton, 1978.

Needham, Joseph. *Human Law and the Laws of Nature in China and the West*. London: Oxford University Press, 1951.

———. *Science and Civilisation in China, Volume II: History of Scientific Thought*. Cambridge: Cambridge University Press, 1954.

———. and Gwei-djen Lu. *Celestial Lancets: A History and Rationale of Acupuncture and Moxibustion*. Cambridge: Cambridge University Press, 1980.

Ning Ying 宁瀛. 找乐 *Zhao le* [(Looking) for fun]. 1993.

———. 民警的故事 *Minjingde gushi* [Police story]. 1995.

———. 夏日暖洋洋 *Xiari nuan yangyang* [I love Beijing]. 2001.

Osborne, Thomas, and Nikolas Rose. "Governing Cities." Working Paper No. 19, Toronto Urban Studies Programme, York University, 1998.

———. "Governing Cities: Notes on the Spatialization of Virtue." *Environment and Planning D: Society and Space* 17.6 (1999), pp. 737–60.

Osburg, John. "Engendering Wealth: China's New Rich and the Rise of an Elite Masculinity." Ph.D. dissertation, University of Chicago, 2008.

Palmer, David. *Qigong Fever: Body, Science and Utopia in China*. New York: Columbia University Press, 2007.

Parker, Andrew (ed.). *Nationalisms and Sexualities*. New York: Routledge, 1992.

Porkert, Manfred. *The Theoretical Foundations of Chinese Medicine: Systems of Correspondence*. Cambridge, MA: MIT East Asian Science Series, 1974.

Qu Limin 曲黎敏. 皇帝内径养生智慧*Huangdi neijing yangsheng zhihui* [The *yangsheng* wisdom of the *Yellow Emperor's Inner Canon*]. Xiamen: Lujiang Press, 2007.

Rabinow, Paul. *Marking Time: On the Anthropology of the Contemporary*. Princeton: Princeton University Press, 2008.

Rogaski, Ruth. *Hygienic Modernity: Meanings of Health and Modernity in Treaty-Port China*. Berkeley: University of California Press, 2004.

Rose, Nikolas S. *The Politics of Life Itself: Biomedicine, Power, and Subjectivity in the Twenty-First Century*. Princeton: Princeton University Press, 2007.

———. *Powers of Freedom: Reframing Political Thought*. New York: Cambridge University Press, 1999.

Rosen, Tracey. "Coming of Age on the World Stage: Beijing's Candidature for the 2008 Olympic Games." M.A. Thesis, University of Chicago Department of Anthropology, 2004.

Rural Health Systems Delegation. *Rural Health in the People's Republic of China*. Washington, D.C.: U.S. Department of Health and Human Services, 1980.

Sagan, Carl. S.v. "Life." In *Encyclopedia Brittanica*, 15th ed., vols. 10 and 22. Chicago: Encyclopedia Brittanica, 1992.

Saunders, Barry F. *CT Suite: The Work of Diagnosis in the Age of Noninvasive Cutting*. Durham: Duke University Press, 2008.

Saussy, Haun. *Great Walls of Discourse and Other Adventures in Cultural China*. Cambridge, MA: Harvard University Asia Center, 2001.

Scheid, Volker. *Currents of Tradition in Chinese Medicine 1626–2006*. Seattle: Eastland Press, 2007.

Schein, Louisa. "The Consumption of Color and the Politics of White Skin in Post-Mao China." *Social Text* 41 (Winter 1994), pp. 141–64.

Scott, James. *Seeing Like a State: How Certain Schemes to Improve the Human Condition Have Failed*. New Haven: Yale University Press, 1998.

"Senior Momentum." *National Geographic*, special issue on China (May 2008), n.p.

Sidel, Victor W., and Ruth Sidel. *Serve the People: Observations on Medicine in the People's Republic of China*. Boston: Beacon Press, 1973.

Sivin, Nathan. *Chinese Alchemy, Preliminary Studies*. Cambridge, MA: Harvard University Press, 1968.

——. *Traditional Medicine in Contemporary China: A Partial Translation of Revised Outline of Chinese Medicine*. Ann Arbor: Center for Chinese Studies, 1987.

Sleigh, Adrian C. "Health-System Reforms to Control Tuberculosis in China." *The Lancet* 369. 9562 (February 24, 2007), pp. 627–27.

Smith, Terry. "Contemporary Art and Contemporaneity." *Critical Inquiry* 32.4 (Summer 2006), pp. 681–707.

——. "Introduction: The Contemporaneity Question." In Terry Smith, Okwui Enwezor, and Nancy Condee (eds.), *Antinomies of Art and Culture: Modernity, Postmodernity, Contemporaneity*, pp. 1–19. Durham: Duke University Press, 2008

——. "The State of Art History: Contemporary Art." *Art Bulletin* 92.4 (December 2010), pp. 266–83.

The Sociocultural Unit of the Ministry of Culture and the Chinese Mass Culture Society 文化部社会文化局和中国群众会. 论城市群众文化 *Lun chengshi qunzhong wenhua* [On urban mass ulture] Beijing: Zhongguo Wuzi Chubanshe, 1998.

Strickmann, Michel. *Chinese Poetry and Prophecy: The Written Oracle in East Asia*. Stanford: Stanford University Press, 2005.

Su Xiaokang 苏晓康 and Luxiang Wang 王鲁湘 (eds.). 河殇 *He shang*. Introduced, translated, and annotated as *Deathsong of the River: A Reader's Guide to the Chinese TV Series Heshang* by Richard W. Bodmann and Pin P. Wan. Ithaca: East Asia Program, Cornell University, 1991.

Sunder Rajan, Kaushik. *Biocapital: The Constitution of Postgenomic Life*. Durham: Duke University Press, 2006.

Tang, Shenglan, Qingyue Meng, Lincoln Chen, Henk Bekedam, Tim Evans, and Margaret Whitehead. "Tackling the Challenges to Health Equity in China." *The Lancet* 372.9648 (October 25, 2008), pp. 1493–1501.

Tsing, Anna L. *Friction: An Ethnography of Global Connection*. Princeton: Princeton University Press, 2005.

Tylor, Edward Burnett. *Anthropology: An Introduction to the Study of Man and Civilization*. New York: D. Appleton, 1898.

Visser, Robin. *Cities Surround the Countryside: Urban Aesthetics in Postsocialist China*. Durham: Duke University Press, 2010.

Waley, Arthur. *The Way and Its Power*. New York: Macmillan, 1934.

Wang, Chaohua (ed.). *One China, Many Paths*. London: Verso, 2003.

Wang, Hong. "China's Fragmented Health System." *The Lancet* 366.9493 (October 8, 2005), pp. 1257–58.

Wang, Jing. *High Culture Fever: Politics, Aesthetics, and Ideology in Deng's China*. Berkeley: University of California Press, 1996.

Wang Min'an 汪民安. 身体，空间与后现代性*Shenti, kongjian yu houxiandaixing* [The body, space, and postmodernity]. Nanjing: Jiangsu People's Press, 2006.

——. 双重物质 *Shuangzhong wuzhi* [A double materiality]. In 形象工厂,如何去看一幅画 *Xingxiang gongchang, ruhe qu kan yifu hua* [The factory of images: How to look at a painting]. Nanjing: Nanjing University Press, 2009.

——. 现代性*Xiandaixing* [Modernity]. Guilin: Guangxi Normal University Press, 2005.

Wang, Shaoguang. "The Politics of Private Time: Changing Leisure Patterns in Urban China." In Deborah S. Davis, Richard Kraus, Barry Naughton, and Elizabeth J. Perry (eds.), *Urban Spaces in Contemporary China: The Potential for Autonomy and Community in Post-Mao China*, pp. 149–72. Cambridge: Cambridge University Press and Woodrow Wilson Center Press, 1995.

Wen, Tiejun 温铁军. 三农问题与世纪反思 *San nong wenti yu shiji fansi* [The three rural problems and the millennial shift]. Beijing: Sanlian Press, 2005.

Wiseman, Nigel, and Feng Ye, *A Practical Dictionary of Chinese Medicine*. Brookline: Paradigm Publications, 1998.

Wu, Fulong (ed.). *Globalization and the Chinese City*. New York: Routledge, 2006.

Wu, Yi-ching. "The Other Cultural Revolution: The Politics and Practice of Class in the Chinese Cultural Revolution." Ph.D. dissertation, University of Chicago, 2007.

Yan, Yunxiang. "McDonald's in Beijing: The Localization of Americana." In James L. Watson (ed.), *Golden Arches East: McDonald's in East Asia*, pp. 39–76. Stanford: Stanford University Press, 1997.

Yang Nianqun 杨念群. 再造病人 *Zai zao bingren* [Remaking patients]. Beijing: Renmin University Press, 2005.

Yates, Robin D. S. *Five Lost Classics: Tao, Huang-Lao, and Yin-yang in Han China*. New York: Ballantine Books, 1997.

Yue, Gang. *The Mouth that Begs: Hunger, Cannibalism, and the Politics of Eating in Modern China*. Durham: Duke University Press, 1999.

Zhan, Mei. *Other-Worldly: Making Chinese Medicine through Transnational Frames*. Durham: Duke University Press, 2009.

Zhang Gengguang 张耿光 (ed.). 庄子全译 *Zhuangzi quanyi* [The complete translated Zhuangzi]. Guiyang: Guizhou People's Press 1991.

Zhang Hude 张湖德 et al. (eds.). 皇帝内径 养生全书 *Huangdi neijing yangsheng quanshu* [The complete book of *The Yellow Emperor's Inner Canon yangsheng*: The *yangsheng* of the four time periods]. 10 vols. Beijing: Light Industry Press, 2001.

Zhang, Li. *Strangers in the City: Reconfigurations of Space, Power, and Social Networks within China's Floating Population*. Stanford: Stanford University Press, 2001.

Zhang Qicheng 张其成. 易学与中医 *Yixue yu Zhongyi* [Changes Studies and Chinese medicine]. Beijing: China Bookstore Press, 1999.

——. 张其成讲读黄帝内经养生大道 *Zhang Qicheng jiangdu Huangdi neijing yangsheng da dao* [The great Way of *yangsheng*: Zhang Qicheng lectures on the *Yellow Emperor's Inner Canon*]. Nanning: Guangxi Science and Technology Press, 2008.

——. 易经养生大道 *Yijing yangsheng dadao* [The life-nurturing great Way of the *Book of Changes*]. Nanning: Guangxi Science and Technology Press, 2009.

——. 易道主干 *Yidao zhugan* [The main stem of the way of the changes]. Beijing: China Bookstore Press, 1999.

——. 中医哲学基础 *Zhongyi zhexue jichu* [Philosophical foundations of Chinese medicine]. Beijing: China Chinese Medicine Press, 2004.

—— and Limin Qu 曲黎敏. 中华养生智慧 *Zhonghua yangsheng zhihui* [The wisdom of Chinese life nurturance]. Beijing: Huaxia Press, 2005.

Zhang, Yanhua. *Transforming Emotions with Chinese Medicine: An Ethnographic Account from Contemporary China*. Albany: State University of New York Press, 2007.

Zhao Hongjun 赵洪钧. 内径时代 *Neijing shidai* [The era of the *Inner Canon*]. Hebei: China Integrated Research Association, 1985.

Index

343

Typesetting by Meighan Gale
Image placement and production by Julie Fry
Printed and bound by Thompson-Shore